THE BRIDGE BETRAYED

Comparative Studies in Religion and Society

MARK JUERGENSMEYER, editor

THE BRIDGE BETRAYED

Religion and Genocide in Bosnia

Michael A. Sells

With a New Preface

UNIVERSITY OF CALIFORNIA PRESS

Berkeley   Los Angeles   London

University of California Press
Berkeley and Los Angeles, California

University of California Press, Ltd.
London, England

First Paperback Printing 1998

© 1996 by
The Regents of the University of California

New Preface © 1998 by The Regents of the University of California

Library of Congress Cataloging-in-Publication Data

Sells, Michael Anthony.
    The bridge betrayed : religion and genocide in Bosnia /
Michael A. Sells.
        p.   cm. — (Comparative studies in religion and
society ; 11)
    Includes bibliographical references (p.   ) and index.
    ISBN 978-0-520-21662-4
        1. Yugoslav War, 1991- —Atrocities.   2. Yugoslav
War, 1991- —Bosnia and Herzegovina.   3. Yugoslav
War, 1991- —Destruction and pillage—Bosnia and
Herzegovina.   4. Muslims—Bosnia and Herzegovina—
History—20th century.   5. Genocide—Bosnia and
Herzegovina—History—20th century.   6. Persecution—
Bosnia and Herzegovina—History—20th century.
    7. Bosnia and Herzegovina—History—1992-   I. Title.
    II. Series.
    DR1313.7.A85S45   1996
    949.702'4—dc20   96-4854
                                                            CIP

Printed in the United States of America

16   15   14   13   12   11   10

12   11   10   9   8

This book is dedicated to the tens of thousands of Bosnian civilians who are now missing; and to the effort to find them if they are alive, to account for their fate if they are not, to bring to justice those who harmed them; and to the possibility of a genuine peace.

In memory of my mother, Simona Sally Trbovich (1926–1961).

CONTENTS

GUIDE TO PRONUNCIATION

j = English "y"
The names Lejla and Jasmina are pronounced LAY-la and yas-MEEN-a.

ć = English "ch"
Jović, a last name, is pronounced YO-vich. Some Slavs in the West add an "h" to make the pronunciation clear, while others keep the original spelling.
Mihajlovic (Michaelson) is pronounced Mi-HAY-lo-vich.

č = a slightly different form of English "ch"
The town of Foča is pronounced FO-cha.

š = English "sh"
Pašić and Bašić (common last names derived from the Ottoman honorific title "Pasha") are pronounced PAH-shich and BAH-shich. Mušanović (Moses-son) is pronounced Mu-SHA-no-vich.

ž = French "j" or "z" as in "azure"
The southeast Bosnian town of Žepa is pronounced ZHEH-pa.

k = English "k"

c = English "tz"
Stolac, a town in Herzegovina, is pronounced STO-latz.

Map 1. Yugoslavia, 1945–1991

PREFACE TO THE PAPERBACK EDITION

Whoever is a Serb of Serbian blood
Whoever shares with me this heritage,
And he comes not to fight at Kosovo,
May he never have the progeny
His heart desires, neither son nor daughter;
Beneath his hand let nothing decent grow
Neither purple grapes nor wholesome wheat;
Let him rust away like dripping iron
Until his name be extinguished.[1]

The Balkan tragedy began in the Serbian province of Kosovo as the mythology embodied in this famous "curse of Kosovo" was, in the words of one Serbian nationalist, "resurrected" on Lazar's day (Vidovdan), June 28, 1989, which commemorated the 600th anniversary of the death of the Serb prince Lazar at the battle of Kosovo in 1389. Religious nationalists manipulated the vision of Lazar as a Christ figure to portray all Yugoslav Muslims, not just the Ottoman Turks who fought Lazar, as responsible for the death of the Christ-prince Lazar at the "Serbian Golgotha." Serbian President Slobodan Milošević stood before the crowd of more than a million people and used the battle of Kosovo to threaten a new crusade against the Islam and other enemies, both in Kosovo province and throughout Yugoslavia. The passion play brought about a classic collapse of time in which the audience felt themselves to be participants in the primordial passion and death of the Christ-prince. In Bosnia they acted as if they were living in 1389 and carrying out revenge against the Christ-killers. The same violence now threatens to explode at the epicenter of the conflict—Kosovo.

In Sarajevo the guns are silent. Bosnia rebuilds. Forensic teams excavate mass graves near the concentration camps and killing centers. NATO forces have arrested some indicted war criminals. In a moment of hope and pathos, the stones of the Old Bridge at Mostar have been retrieved from the bottom of the Neretva River under a plan to rebuild the bridge and the old city.

Yet those war criminals still at large continue to resist the key element of the Dayton Accords: the return of refugees to their homes. The two men most responsible for the destruction of Yugoslavia, Serbia's Milošević and Croatia's Franjo Tudjman, remain in power. Croat religious nationalists and gangsters control West Mostar and its surroundings. Survivors of the Srebrenica massacre desperately seek information on loved ones last seen being selected in front of UN troops and led away for extermination. And in Kosovo, Serb nationalist forces are testing the same tactics of "ethnic cleansing" they used with impunity in Bosnia.

Newly publicized statements of Bosnian Serb President Biljana Plavšić demonstrate the relationship between Kosovo religious mythology, extreme nationalism, and racialist theory that this book explores. At the height of the "ethnic cleansing" against Bosnian Muslims, Plavšić announced that "it was genetically deformed material that embraced Islam. And now, of course, with each successive generation this gene simply becomes concentrated. It gets worse and worse. It simply expresses itself and dictates their style of thinking and behaving, which is rooted in their genes."[2]

Plavšić, former dean of the Faculty of Natural Science and Mathematics in Sarajevo, transformed herself from a secularist and a professional biologist into an ethnoreligious theorist of religious conversion as genetic deformation. Her sudden conversion exemplifies the power and function of the Kosovo-based ideology of Christoslavism examined in this book. Christoslavism maintains that Slavs are Christian by nature, that conversion to another religion entails or presupposes a transformation or deformation of the Slavic race, and that all Muslims in Yugoslavia (whether ethnic Slavs or Albanians) have transformed themselves into Turks and are personally responsible for the death of the Christ-prince Lazar at the Serbian Golgotha (the battle of Kosovo) and for the pollution of the Slavic race. At moments of crisis, the Kosovo ideology helps efface the boundaries between notions of religion and race and turns religious nationalism into the most virulent form of racialist ideology. It must be emphasized that the power of this racio-religious mythology is unaffected by the personal piety or lack of personal piety of those who accept it or exploit it. As the cases of Plavšić and many of her former secularist and communist colleagues show, the abuse of religious symbolism is not dependent upon self-conscious beliefs or personal sincerity; rather it operates on the levels of the subconscious and mass psychology.

Despite the efforts of religious leaders like Ibrahim Halilović, the Mufti of Banja Luka (a center of systematic atrocities against Muslims and Muslim clerics), and Vinko Cardinal Puljić of Sarajevo to work for peace, other religious leaders continue to incite religious war.[3] The highest leader of the Serbian Orthodox Church allied himself with the most extreme element of Serbian religious nationalism.[4] At the Catholic pilgrimage site of Medjugorje in Herzegovina, the Virgin's announced appeals for peace clash with the open support for indicted Croat war criminals and their militias by those who control the lucrative pilgrimage site.[5]

Bosnian Muslim religious leaders have largely refrained from religious militancy, but some foreign missionary groups, including those from Saudi Arabia and Kuwait, have manipulated humanitarian aid to pressure Bosnian Muslims toward another view of society and of Islam—an effort that so far has failed.[6] The ultimate success of such efforts depends upon whether NATO carries out its obligations under the Dayton Accords to support a multireligious and culturally pluralistic Bosnia or instead heeds those who call for the partition of Bosnia into three zones of "ethnically pure" religious apartheid, with Bosnian Muslims consigned to an Islamic ghetto vulnerable to attack by Croatia and Serbia.[7] Whether Bosnians of all religions, whose spirit remained unbroken in the face of the most brutal assault and betrayal, can rebuild their splendid multireligious civilization also depends upon the world's response to the deepening crisis in the nearby Serbian province of Kosovo.

In Kosovo, where seeds of the Bosnian genocide were planted, the Albanian-Serb conflict is on the verge of mass violence. After ten years of repression, some Albanians have abandoned the nonviolent resistance and joined an armed rebellion. Special Serbian police have carried out retaliatory atrocities, which have increased support by Albanians for armed resistance.[8] Slobodan Milošević's governing partner, Vojislav Šešelj, the organizer of atrocities in Bosnia, has called for violent repression against Albanians. Arkan, the militia leader who draped himself and his militiamen in Kosovo mythology before sending them to commit atrocities in Bosnia, openly champions the violent expulsion of Albanians from Kosovo. The Milošević regime has rejected international mediation, which remains the only plausible framework for finding a compromise between Albanians' wish for autonomy and the desire of many Serbs to keep the cultural heritage of the "Serb Jerusalem" as part of Serbia.

This book explores the vital role of the manipulation of Kosovo symbols in motivating and justifying atrocities in Bosnia. It also should raise an urgent question about what will happen if the world allows the same Serbian leaders who led the assault on Bosnia to return full circle. If they are able to act with impunity in Kosovo—the epicenter of the symbols of sacred time and sacred space, and a place they exploited in their rise to power—it would mean the final desecration of Serb traditions and culture by Serbia's religious, intellectual, and political elite.

The Albanian Muslim and Catholic clergy in Kosovo and Father Sava Janjić, Orthodox Prior of Visoki Dečani, warn that war will bring misery to all sides. Father Sava offers a lonely and profound contrast to the Serbian Orthodox hierarchy and to Serbian police who praise Serbia's crusade to protect Europe from Islam. The international community seems as indecisive over Kosovo in 1998 as it was over Bosnia in 1992.[9] If Father Sava's warnings are ignored, the conflict may engulf not only Kosovo, Serbia, Montenegro, Bosnia, Albania, and Macedonia, but also Greece and Turkey. The consequences to the security of Europe and the relations between the Western and Islamic world would be inestimable. Should this come to pass, the bridging of religions, civilizations, and cultures symbolized by the great Old Bridge at Mostar, now in the process of a courageous and tenuous reconstruction, will once again be threatened. The Western world, which recently celebrated the fiftieth anniversary of the liberation of Nazi death camps, will find itself once more degraded by its appeasement of organized persecution in Europe and confronted with the tragic triumph of Slobodan Milošević's 1989 call, made in Kosovo, for a new spirit of religious war and crusade.

Michael Sells
Vidovdan, June 28, 1998
Haverford, Pennsylvania

NOTES TO PREFACE OF THE 1998 PAPERBACK EDITION

1. Translated by Milorad Ekmečić, "The Emergence of St. Vitus Day," in Wayne Vucinich and Thomas Emmert, eds., *Kosovo: Legacy of a Medieval Battle* (Minneapolis: University of Minnesota Press, 1991), p. 335. For more on this curse, see below, page 39.

2. Biljana Plavšić, *Svet*, Novi Sad, September 1993, cited and translated by Slobodan Inić, "Biljana Plavšić: Geneticist in the Service of a Great Crime," *Bosnia Report: Newsletter of the Alliance to Defend Bosnia-Herzegovina* 19 (June–August 1997), translated from *Helsinška povelja* (Helsinki Charter), Belgrade, November 1996.

3. For the courage and compassion of Mufti Halilović, see Dan De Luce's Reuters report, "Tribute to Serbs Who Tried to Help Muslims,"

The Herald (Glasgow), 31 January 1996, and Robert Fisk, "One Candle in the Heart of Darkness: The Mufti of Banja Luka Lives on Among Those Who Killed His People," *The Independent* (London), 27 October 1996.

Under threats from Catholic militants in Herzegovina, Archbishop Puljić showed a rare willingness to resist militant members of his own tradition during a moment of crisis—a willingness that is essential to the moral credibility of any religious leader. See Vinko Cardinal Puljić, *Suffering with Hope: Appeals, Addresses, Interviews* (Zagreb: HKD Napredak, 1995) and "Statement of Vinko Cardinal Puljić," Carnegie Endowment for International Peace, Washington, D.C., 21 February 1997, which is available on-line at http://www.haverford.edu/relg/sells/heroes.html.

4. On the Feast of the Holy Cross 1997, Serbian Orthodox Patriarch Pavle endorsed the Declaration of The Association of Writers of Serbia. See Srpska Republika News Agency (SRNA), 16 October 1997; Agence France Presse, 16 October 1997. The account by SRNA states that His Holiness, Patriarch of the Serbs, Pavle, gave his blessing for the Declaration, which was signed by sixty intellectuals, including fourteen members of the Serb Academy of Science and Art (SANU) (cf. *Naša Borba*, 18 October 1997). The Declaration states that the Hague Tribunal has "acted solely as an instrument for persecution of Serbs." This was inflammatory and grotesque, given that the main trial at The Hague when the Declaration was issued was the Čelebići trial against Bosnian Croats and Muslims accused of crimes against Serb civilians. See the reports from Tribunal Update (London: Institute for War and Peace Reporting) for September 1997 to March 1998, which are available on-line at http://www.demon.co.uk/iwpr.

5. See the Medjugorje Press Bulletin 88 (8 April 1998), which praises a "Wall of Love" ritual at Medjugorje with prayers for suspected Croat war criminals facing trial in The Hague and the other "Croat defenders." For diversion of funds collected abroad for humanitarian relief to Croat militias for the purchase of military equipment, see Madeleine Bunting, "'Charity' supplied militia," *The Guardian*, 27

November 1997. Reporters attempting to investigate the links between Medjugorje-based fund appeals and nationalist militias were kidnapped in Medjugorje and beaten. See Agence-France, "British Journalists Assaulted Before Escaping," 1 March 1998. For the central role of militant Franciscan friars in the exaltation of the Croat architect of "ethnic cleansing" in Herzegovina, Mate Boban, see the 9 July 1997 Reuters report on the funeral of Boban in Mostar.

6. See the Barbara Demick, *Philadelphia Inquirer*, 22 June 1996, report that a Saudi backed relief organization, *al-Nur* (The Light), preached that the assault on Bosnian Muslims was deserved punishment for their "cavalier attitude about their faith," while a Kuwaiti missionary group preached that Allah demands women stay in the home. Such messages have so far sparked a strong backlash by Bosnian Muslims.

7. For proposals for such a partition see John R. Mearsheimer, "The Only Exit from Bosnia," *New York Times*, 7 October 1997, and J. Mearsheimer and Stephen Van Evera, "Partition Is The Inevitable Solution For Bosnia," *International Herald Tribune*, 25 September 1996. For a discussion and critique of Senator Kay Bailey Hutchinson's and former Secretary of State Henry Kissinger's demands for U.S. withdrawal and an imposed religious apartheid for Bosnia, see Marshall Freeman Harris, "U.S. Withdrawal Would Reignite Bosnian War," *Dallas Morning News*, 26 September 1997, and Robert Kagan and Morton Abramowitz, "Bosnia: In for the Long Haul," *Wall Street Journal*, 1 October 1997.

8. Chris Hedges, "Albanians Bury 24 Villagers Slain by Serbs," *New York Times*, 4 March 1998.

9. Tom Walker, "Marooned Serb Monk Calls for Kosovo Ceasefire," *Times* (London), 29 April 1998; Philip Smucker, "Seething Hatred Bred in Faith," *Toronto Star*, 25 April 1998; Tom Walker, "Serbs Pouring into Kosovo as Albanian Rebels Prepare for War," *Times* (London), 28 April 1998.

PREFACE TO THE
1996 EDITION

The story told here is not one I wish to believe or to tell. My mother's family is Serbian American, and I know personally that Serbs have suffered in the Bosnian war—some of my Serb relatives in Bosnia and Krajina (the Serb-inhabited area of Croatia) have been killed, some are missing, and others are living in refugee camps. However, the evidence in Bosnia leads to conclusions that are as unavoidable as they are unpalatable. Genocide has occurred. It has occurred with the acquiescence of Western governments, in violation of the United Nations Charter and the Convention on Genocide of 1948. It has been motivated and justified in large part by religious nationalism, fueled financially and militarily from Serbia and Croatia, and grounded in religious symbols. And the primary victims have been Bosnian Muslims, selected for destruction because of their religion.

In situations of genocide a disengaged, purely objective stance would be inhuman. Yet precisely to the extent that genocide demands a response, it also demands a continual willingness to examine and reexamine the evidence. For over three years the atrocities were documented by refugee workers, human rights groups, and war crimes investigators (see the Note on Sources). That evidence shows a religious violence far more systematic than the media accounts of the shellings in Sarajevo have suggested.

A particular abuse of history, "Balkanism," has been used to justify the genocide in Bosnia by suggesting that people in the Balkans are fated, by history or genetics, to kill one another. It is true that, like the rest of Europe, Bosnia was caught up in the violence of World War I, World War II, and earlier conflicts. But just as Germans, Dutch, French, and British today live together peacefully, only a few years ago Bosnians had every reason to believe the peace they had enjoyed for fifty years would continue.* That their friends and neighbors would one day seek to destroy them, that their family members would be sent to concentration camps, that their cultural heritage would be methodically burned and dynamited—such possibilities seemed remote to most of the people of Bosnia-Herzegovina.

A resurgence in religious violence has caught the post–cold war world off guard. From the subways of Tokyo to the ruins of a mosque in India, from the World Trade Center and the federal building in Oklahoma City to a Jerusalem rally for the Israeli prime minister, religious militants have transgressed the boundaries of civil society in pursuit of their aims. Bosnians have faced the most brutal religious violence unleashed in the aftermath of the cold war, but the forces that assaulted Bosnia are not due to "age-old antagonisms" peculiar to Balkan peoples, as the cliché would have it. They are forces with us all.

The story told here has clear historical parallels with earlier periods of European history. At the heart of the religious nationalism used to motivate and justify the assault on Bosnia, and

*Bosnians are defined in this book as all residents of the internationally recognized sovereign nation of Bosnia-Herzegovina, regardless of their religious affiliation, who consider themselves Bosnian, that is, who remain loyal to a Bosnian state built on the principles of civic society and religious pluralism.

on Bosnian Muslims in particular, is the same myth of the Christ killer that was exploited in the past to instigate attacks on Jews. How Muslims, a people whose religion began six centuries after Jesus, could have been singled out for genocide as Christ killers and race traitors is a tale this book seeks to tell.

The ancient bridge at Mostar, destroyed by Croat religious nationalists on November 9, 1993, has come to symbolize the multireligious character of Bosnia. But it symbolizes something larger as well: the ability of a culturally pluralistic society to flourish for almost five centuries, despite the very real tensions among the different religious groups. For those who choose a pluralistic society where different religions coexist—whether in Banja Luka, London, or Los Angeles—the struggle to rebuild that bridge is not something occurring over there and far away, but something frighteningly close to home.

I wish to thank Mark Auslander, Amila Buturovic, Carin Companick, Deborah Cooper, Vanja and Mirza Filipović, Bridget Gillich, Laurie Kain Hart, Nader Hashemi, Richard Hecht, Mark Juergensmeyer, Walter Lee, Kathleen MacDougall, Janet Marcus, Aida Premilovac, Emran Qureshi, András Riedlmayer, Ellen Schattsneider, and the Haverford College community for support in writing this book, and the Greek Studies Yearbook for permission to reprint the lithograph of Adam Stefanović's *The Feast of the Prince*. Special thanks to Douglas Abrams Arava, Reed Malcolm, and Marilyn Schwartz of the University of California Press for their encouragement, judgment, and care during the preparation of this book.

CHAPTER ONE

FIRE IN THE PAGES

RAIN OF ASH

"It was the most apocalyptic thing I'd ever seen," said Aida Mu-šanović, an artist from Sarajevo, describing the burning of the National Library in Sarajevo.[1] For days, a thick black cloud of ash hung over the city and residents would find pieces of charred paper or ashes of burned books and manuscripts in their hair and on their clothes.

On August 25, 1992, the Serb army began shelling the National Library of Bosnia-Herzegovina in Sarajevo from positions on the mountainside directly in front of it. In the next few days, in the largest book-burning in modern human history, over a million books, more than a hundred thousand manuscripts and rare books, and centuries of historical records of Bosnia-Herzegovina went up in flames. Volunteers formed a human chain to rescue what they could. One of them, a graduate student at the University of Sarajevo, never made it home.

What was in the pages of those manuscripts and rare books, survivors of centuries of peace and war, that the Serb army was determined to destroy? What was there in those burning pages that many Sarajevans—Croats, Serbs, Muslims, and Jews—were willing to risk their lives to save?

The destruction of the National Library was one component of a systematic campaign of cultural eradication. Three months earlier, on May 17, 1992, the Serb army had targeted the Oriental Institute in Sarajevo, which housed the largest collection of Islamic and Jewish manuscripts in the Balkans. More than five thousand manuscripts in Persian, Arabic, Ottoman Turkish, and Adžamijski (Slavic in Arabic script) were incinerated.

The Serb army then turned its fire on the National Museum, hitting it repeatedly and destroying much of its contents. One special item was saved: an ancient Jewish prayer book used for celebration of the *seder* or Passover feast. The *Sarajevo Haggadah*, with its exquisite Hebrew calligraphy and colored illustration, had been created in fourteenth-century Spain. Jewish refugees from the Inquisition in Spain had brought it to Bosnia. During World War II the *Sarajevo Haggadah* had been preserved by a Muslim curator who hid it from Nazi soldiers. In 1992, it was saved at great personal risk by a team of Bosnian museum workers that included a Muslim, an Orthodox Serb, and a Catholic. The *Haggadah* has thus survived three historic persecutions: the expulsion of the Jews from Spain in 1492, the Holocaust, and what has been called "ethnic cleansing" in Bosnia.[2]

The shelling of these cultural institutions was purposeful. They were chosen for destruction and shelled in a precise manner. Areas around them were left untouched. During one particular shelling of the National Museum, the Serb gunners missed and struck the Holiday Inn directly in front of it. Kate Adie, a BBC reporter, interviewed the Serb officer afterward. When she asked him why he had been shelling the Holiday Inn, the major hotel for journalists in Sarajevo, the officer apologized, explaining that he had been aiming at the museum and had struck the Holiday Inn by mistake.[3]

Since April 1992 the Serb army has targeted for destruction the major libraries, manuscript collections, museums, and other cultural institutions in Sarajevo, Mostar, and other besieged cities. What the Serb artillery missed, the Croat nationalist militia known as the "Croatian Defense Council" (HVO) took care of.

Where the Serb and Croat armies have been able to get closer than shelling range, the destruction has been even greater. The Croatian Defense Council dynamited mosques and Orthodox churches throughout the regions controlled by the Croat military. Serb militias have dynamited all the mosques (over six hundred) in areas they have occupied, some of them masterworks of European architecture such as the sixteenth-century Ferhadija Mosque in Banja Luka and the Colored Mosque in Foča built in 1551. Between them, the Croat and Serb nationalists have destroyed an estimated fourteen hundred mosques. In many cases the mosques have been ploughed over and turned into parking lots or parks; every evidence of their existence has been effaced. Graveyards, birth records, work records, and other traces of the Bosnian Muslim people have been eradicated.[4]

Western political leaders have spoken of "ancient animosities," portraying Bosnians as a group of Balkan tribal killers who have hated one another for centuries and who are incapable of living in peace. In the fires of the National Library, the irony of that portrayal becomes apparent. What the Serb and Croat armies were destroying, there and elsewhere, was the graphic and palpable evidence of over five hundred years of interreligious life in Bosnia. Despite the wars and strife of the past, religious monuments and houses of worship in Mostar and Sarajevo had been built next to one another and shared the same skyline. It is this architectural, literary, and human evidence—the monuments, the books, and the people who treasured them—of a flourishing multiconfessional culture that ethnoreligious militants have sought to efface.[5]

The northeast Bosnian town of Zvornik was known for its heritage of Bosnian Muslim poets, saints, rebels, and mystics. From April through July of 1992 the Serb military killed or expelled the entire Muslim population. After all the mosques in the primarily Muslim town were dynamited and ploughed over, the new Serb nationalist mayor declared: "There never were any mosques in Zvornik." Destroyed with those mosques was the evidence not only of the Muslim heritage of Zvornik but also of five hundred years of shared living between Christians and Muslims. History could now be rewritten according to the desires of those who wished to claim that this land was always and purely Christian Serb. In May 1993 to celebrate Zvornik's new status as 100 percent "pure" and cleansed of all Muslims, the mayor dedicated a new church, renamed a local, formerly Muslim village "Saint Stephen," and kissed a crucifix.[6]

Aida Mušanović, the artist who described the burning of the National Library, had visited the hospital in Sarajevo and seen the carnage brought by the war. Yet the burning of the library struck her with a special horror. In the fire of the National Library, she realized that what she was experiencing was not only war but also something else. The centuries of culture that fell back in ash onto the besieged city revealed a secret. The gunners on the hills above Sarajevo did not seek to defeat an enemy army; at that time, there was no organized, opposing army. They sought to take territory, but not only territory. They sought political concessions, but also something more. Their goal was the eradication of a people and all evidence of that people's culture and existence.

WHO ARE BOSNIANS?

In 1945, communist guerrilla fighter Josip Broz Tito, better known as Marshal Tito, reestablished the Yugoslav federation, which had existed from 1918 to 1941 and then had been dismembered by Nazi Germany. The constituent nations of the reconstituted Yugoslavian republic were Macedonia, Serbia, Montenegro, Bosnia-Herzegovina, Croatia, and Slovenia (see Map 1).

The word "Yugoslavia" means "land of the South (Yugo) Slavs." The central part of Yugoslavia was populated by three major groups (Serbs, Slavic Muslims, and Croats), all of whom spoke dialects of the South Slavic language until recently called Serbo-Croatian. The vast majority of Croats were Roman Catholic and lived in Croatia, Bosnia-Herzegovina, and some parts of Serbia. The vast majority of Serbs were Orthodox Christians and lived in Serbia, Montenegro, Macedonia, and parts of Croatia and Bosnia known as the Krajina. Slavic Muslims were concentrated in Bosnia-Herzegovina, the adjacent areas in Serbia and Montenegro, and in Macedonia. Croatians used a Latin-based script, while Serbs preferred a Cyrillic script (based on Greek characters), but despite dialectical differences, Serbs,

Croats, and Bosnian Muslims spoke the same language. Many Serbs and Croats were devoted to the ideal of a multireligious and multiethnic Yugoslavia. Religious nationalists, however, desired religiously homogeneous national states, a greater Catholic Croatia and a greater Orthodox Christian Serbia. Slovenes and Macedonians spoke South Slavic languages distinct from but belonging to the same language family as Serbo-Croatian. The non-Slavic Albanians were primarily Muslim and resided in Macedonia and a region in Serbia known as Kosovo, adjacent to the independent nation of Albania. A large Hungarian population lived in another province of Serbia, Vojvodina.

Like the rest of Europe, Yugoslavia had been torn apart in World War II. Slovenia had been made part of the Greater German Reich. Croatia and Bosnia-Herzegovina had been incorporated into a puppet state of Nazi Germany. Italy had occupied parts of the coastline. Germany had occupied and ruled Serbia through a collaborationist Serbian regime. The "independent" Croatian state under German and Italian occupation was controlled by a fascist militia known as the Ustashe, dedicated to an independent "Greater Croatia." In 1941 the Ustashe began to "cleanse" Croatia of Serbs either by forcing them to convert to Roman Catholicism or by killing and expelling them. Various groups of Serb fighters organized themselves as a nationalist guerrilla force, called the "Chetniks," loyal to the Serb royal dynasty. Some Chetniks espoused the idea of a "Greater Serbia" and carried out atrocities against non-Serbs. Tito's army of Partisans, on the other hand, was made up of people from all the major Yugoslav religious and ethnic groups and fought for a unified Yugoslavia under communist rule. At the end of the war, the Partisans carried out mass executions against both their Ustashe and Chetnik enemies.

After the war Tito set out to reestablish Yugoslavia and to balance the various nationalities. "Brotherhood and Unity" was the slogan meant to replace calls for independent and greater Croatia and Serbia. By the 1970s Tito had positioned Yugoslavia as a communist state independent of the Kremlin and a leader of the nonaligned movement—finding a strategic niche between Soviet and Western spheres. Yugoslavia was relatively robust economically. The hatreds and tragedies of World War II began to fade, particularly in the new generations, and intermarriage increased. The 1984 Winter Olympic Games brought thousands of visitors to Sarajevo; many came away enchanted by the culture they found.

After Tito's death in 1980, Yugoslavia was ruled by a rotating presidency; each term would be filled by a representative of a different Yugoslav republic. In the late 1980s Serbs became involved in a bitter struggle with Albanians in the region of Kosovo. As Serb nationalists demanded a Greater Serbia in ways that would never have been tolerated under Tito, the other republics, especially Slovenia and Croatia, became fearful. By 1987 a Serbian communist party official, Slobodan Milošević, used the Serb nationalism to dominate Yugoslavia. The Slovenes and Croats declared independence from Yugoslavia in 1991 and Yugoslavia disintegrated.[7]

The Yugoslav army invaded Slovenia but retreated; there were few Serbs in Slovenia and Serbia had no territorial ambitions in it. Croatia was different. The new Croatian president, Franjo Tudjman, countered Milošević's aggressive Serb nationalism with an aggressive Croat nationalism. Tudjman refused to acknowledge the full extent of Ustashe persecution of Serbs during World War II. While moderate Croats and Serbs tried to prevent war, the nationalists associated with Tudjman and Milošević stoked it. The result was a brutal conflict between the Yugoslav army with its allied Serb militias on one side and the new Croat army on the other.

The people of Bosnia, especially the Muslims, were caught in the middle. Croat and Serb nationalism is based upon an identification of nationhood with a particular branch of the Christian religion. In such religious nationalism, a Muslim is treated as a second-class citizen at best. The majority of Bosnian Muslims and many of the other Bosnians—Serb, Croat, Jew, Gypsy, and others—rejected the identification of religion and nationhood. These people considered themselves Bosnian. Many people in Bosnia-Herzegovina sought a nation based not on exclusive religious affiliation but on constitutional rule and respect for differing religions.

If Bosnians refused to fight in the Yugoslav army against Croatia, they were labeled as traitors by Serb militants. If they fought in the Serb-dominated Yugoslav army, they were considered enemies by Croat nationalists. The president of Bosnia-Herzegovina, Alija Izetbegović, had seen this trap and had opposed the independence of Croatia until these explosive issues could be resolved.[8] When war in neighboring Croatia broke out, the Bosnian government was faced with a further trap. If it tried to procure arms, the Yugoslav army and the Serb nationalist militias would interpret the effort as aggression and would attack. If Bosnia refrained from arming itself, Croat nationalists would set up their own militias in Bosnia and any attack by the Serb army would be justified by blaming the Bosnians for not being better prepared. The final trap was the issue of independence. If Bosnia remained in Yugoslavia, Serb nationalists could persecute non-Serbs in Bosnia and say to the world that the persecution was an "internal affair." If Bosnia declared independence, it would face assault by the heavily armed Yugoslav army and the Serb militias.[9] In a chilling speech before the Bosnian Assembly, a Serb religious nationalist by the name of Radovan Karadžić pointed out the vulnerability of the Muslim population and what lay in store for them if they opposed him: "Do not think that you will not lead Bosnia-Herzegovina into hell, and do not think that you will not perhaps make the Muslim people disappear, because Muslims cannot defend themselves if there is war."[10]

On April 6–7, 1992, after Bosnians had voted for independence in a referendum, the European Community and the United States recognized Bosnia-Herzegovina as a sovereign state. Meanwhile, Bosnian Serb nationalists had declared their own independent "Republika Srpska" (Serbian Republic) and set up their headquarters in the town of Pale, not far from Sarajevo, with Karadžić as their president and backed by Serbia. The Yugoslav army and the Serb militias invaded the new nation from all sides: from the Serb-controlled areas of Croatia known as Krajina, from Serbia, and from Montenegro. Units of the Yugoslav army stationed in Bosnia had ringed the hills around Sarajevo with massive artillery, ostensibly as a "training exercise." And local Bosnian Serb extremists had been armed in advance by agents of Serbian militias and the Yugoslav army. By the fall of 1992, the Serb military had occupied 70 percent of Bosnia-Herzegovina, after rolling over towns and villages that were lacking in basic defense capability. Bosnians had expected an attack by the Serb military; what occurred after Serb nationalists gained military control over most of the country was not expected, however, and to many, inconceivable.

WHAT CANNOT BE SAID

The careful use of the term "genocide" represents a fragile yet critical strand in the fabric of internationally shared and legally recognized values. Genocide is a term that can be manipulated and misused. It is also a name for something that seems to elude naming. It is embodied in the Geneva Convention of 1948 outlawing genocide. That convention also requires signatories not only to prevent genocide when it occurs but to punish it, a provision that can provide a disincentive to speak out and name genocide when it does occur.

The problem of language is illustrated by the case of the invisible mass killings. On October 18, 1995, a front-page headline in the *New York Times* indicated that there had been new "mass killings" of civilians in the Banja Luka region of northern Bosnia. The story described the last phase of the four-year "cleansing" of the Banja Luka region, during which some 500,000 non-Serbs were killed or expelled. The final phase involved the last 20,000 non-Serbs, mostly Bosnian Muslims. They had survived over three years of atrocities and use as slave laborers by Serb nationalists.

As the Bosnian and Croat armies closed in to within a few miles of the Banja Luka area, the final killings were launched. In late October 1995, women and children were brutally expelled. Serb militias selected out men and boys (twelve years and older) and led them away. Refugee workers on the scene warned of a mass killing similar to that carried out earlier by Serb army forces at the UN "safe area" of Srebrenica.

Despite its placement on the front page of a leading American newspaper, the story did not register. In the aftermath of the NATO air strikes of September 1995, which broke the siege of Sarajevo, a statement by NATO that mass atrocities were a cause for resumption of air strikes would have been enough to forestall any killings and probably secure release of the captives. No such statement was given.[11] The last surviving non-Serb population of the Banja Luka region was being taken away, before the eyes of the world, yet unnoticed. For three years the phrases "civil war," "age-old antagonisms," "blame on all sides," and a coded set of stereotypes about Muslims had helped make the killing of Bosnian Muslims appear natural and helped naturalize the refusal to stop it.

What has been called "ethnic cleansing" is not only invisible but also unspeakable. To describe it is to be forced to use a language from which any compassionate human being recoils. Herein lies the irony: the more obscene the crime, the less visible it is. The human capacity for acknowledging religiously based evil is particularly tenuous. The crime is committed by those who appeal to religiously sanctioned absolutes to justify their behavior. Then it is condoned by those who base their response, in part, on religious stereotypes.

For a moment what was being committed in Bosnia became visible. On August 6, 1992, the camps of Omarska and Trnopolje, near Banja Luka, appeared on television screens around the world. We saw those skeletal figures, eyes riveted to the ground, too terrorized to lift their gaze. We knew what had happened there. And when the television crew persisted in demand-

ing access to the camp and the manager of the camp patiently insisted that it was not a camp, but a center, we knew of what kind
of realm Omarska was the center. Subsequent reports indicated
that those who perished at Omarska would have been saved if
the United Nations and the NATO nations, which had had information on the camps for months, had revealed them. We
knew what the repression of the reports entailed.[12]

That moment of visibility at Omarska was made possible, in
part, by recent meditations on the Holocaust, the extermination
of six million Jews by Nazis and their collaborators in World
War II. It was not in a house of worship, then, that the truth
was most effectively spoken. It was during the dedication to the
Holocaust Museum on April 22, 1993, that Holocaust survivor
Elie Wiesel could turn to President Clinton and demand that
the killing be stopped. What was happening in Bosnia was not
the Holocaust or Shoah. Yet much of the response to the atrocities exemplified by Omarska has appealed to categories of value
shaped in response to that event, which entered its final phase
fifty years earlier. To be faithful both to those who perished in
the Holocaust and to those who perished in Bosnia, however, we
need to deepen our understanding of all acts of genocide. Then
the phrase "Never again" might be retrieved as meaningful.

THE EUPHEMISM

What do we call Omarska and the network of other such places
throughout Serb army–occupied (and, for a time, Croat army–
occupied) Bosnia-Herzegovina? The evidence gathered by human rights reports and war crimes investigators shows that most
of those taken to Omarska were not expected to emerge alive.

Detention was not the object of such places.[13] The existence of Omarska came to light as a result of a series of articles for *New York Newsday* written by the reporter Roy Gutman. It was both the use of the term "death camp" and the content of the articles that finally forced Bosnian Serb leaders to allow a television crew into Omarska, but not until after they had spent time cleaning up and disposing of the most mutilated prisoners.[14]

Unlike Auschwitz, Treblinka, Sobibor, Chelmno, or Belzec, Omarska had no gas chambers and lacked the mechanized mass-killing and disposal methods associated with Nazi death camps. The killings at Omarska were personalized, entailing prolonged beating and torture, frequently by former associates of the victim. How can we grasp the meaning of Omarska and the realm of which it is the center?

The word "ethnic" in "ethnic cleansing" is a euphemism. Bosnian Serbs, Croats, and Muslims all speak the same language, despite the fact that for political reasons they each call it now by a different name.[15] They all trace their descent to tribes that migrated to the area around the sixth century and were Slavic in language and culture by the time they settled in the area.[16] Those who have been singled out for persecution have fallen on the wrong side of a dividing line based solely on religious identity.

As in most wars, innocent civilians from all sides have suffered in the war, the quest for territory, and population expulsions. But Bosnian Muslims—and those who would share a body-politic with them—have been the victims of a consistently more brutal and more methodical violence. Even in the context of the conflict between Croatian and Serb nationalists, who engage in expulsions and atrocities against each other's population as a continuation of the conflict of World War II, the Muslim population has been separated out and treated (by both Croat and Serb nationalists) with particular cruelty. Most victims were Bosnian Muslim noncombatants in areas taken by Serb and Croat militias without significant combat.[17]

In such cases, Muslim religious identity was determined by strictly extrinsic criteria. A Bosnian Muslim in a Serb or Croat camp was there not because of any particular act, expression, or thought. Some in the targeted population defined themselves as Muslims according to the Islamic testimony of belief in one deity and in Muhammad as the messenger of the one deity. Some were observant, for example, keeping the required fast during the Islamic holy month of Ramadan or the prohibition against pork and alcohol. Some were unobservant. Many Bosnian Muslims were atheists. Many were observant of some of the Islamic practices such as the Ramadan fast but considered themselves religious skeptics and their observances cultural. Some supported the political leaders of the Bosnian government; some did not. Some were indifferent to politics.[18]

In the 1971 census a new national category of "Muslims" in Bosnia was recognized by the Yugoslav government. This nationality label led to numerous contradictions within Yugoslavia: an Albanian Muslim was not considered to be a "Muslim" in the Yugoslav census of nationalities, but many Bosnians of Muslim background who considered themselves atheists or skeptics declared themselves "Muslim" in the census to avoid the categories of "Serb" and "Croat," both of which had religious implications. For those who wanted a Bosnian nationality to be affirmed, alongside those of Croat, Slovene, Macedonian, Serbian, and Albanian, this classification of "Muslim" was problematic; it finally gave Bosnian Muslims a political voice alongside Catholics and Orthodox Serbs, but it did so at the cost of further reinforcing the identity between religion and nationality.[19]

In the world of Omarska, if an inhabitant of Bosnia had a name identifiable as Muslim or parents with names identifiable as Muslim, that was considered guilt enough, whatever the beliefs or practices of that individual and whether or not that person was categorized as "Muslim" in the nationalities census. Those organizing the persecution, on the other hand, identified themselves and their cause through explicit religious symbols. The symbols appeared in the three-fingered hand gestures representing the Christian trinity, in the images of sacred figures of Serbian religious mythology on their uniform insignia, in the songs they memorized and forced their victims to sing, on the priest's ring they kissed before and after their acts of persecution, and in the formal religious ceremonies that marked the purification of a town of its Muslim population. The term "ethnic" in the expression "ethnic cleansing," then, is a euphemism for "religious." It entails a purely extrinsic yet deadly definition of the victim in terms of religious identity; the intrinsic aspect— in the form of religious mythology—becomes the motivation and justification for atrocities on the part of the perpetrator.

THE REALM OF OMARSKA

Vladimir Srebrov was one of the founders, along with Radovan Karadžić, of the Serbian Democratic Party (SDS) in Bosnia. In early 1992 Srebrov became aware of a plan within the Yugoslav army, supported by his colleagues in the party, to destroy the Muslim population of Bosnia as part of a partition of the country between Serbia and Croatia. When he attempted to leave Sarajevo to plead with Serb nationalists to abandon the planned killings, he was arrested by Serb militiamen, placed in the Kula prison, and tortured.[20] Srebrov is one of many Serbs who have refused the nationalist program of the Serb governments. He is also one of a number of Serbs who have risked their lives and the lives of their families to protect non-Serbs, to denounce the "ethnic cleansing," and to call for a civil society that is not confined to one particular religious group.

Osman and Sabiha Botonjić were a middle-class Muslim couple in the town of Sanski Most, not far from Banja Luka. In the spring of 1992 the Serb army had occupied their town with little military resistance. Osman was met at work by a former colleague and told to come to the police station for a few questions. He was first held in a small cell jammed with prisoners, without food or water. Beatings were continual. After several days the prisoners were taken out and thrown onto a truck to be driven to a concentration camp at Manjača. Of the sixty-five prisoners in the truck, forty-seven survived the journey. Others, weakened by beatings, died of suffocation, thirst, trauma, or blood loss. Osman was held at Manjača, where prisoners slept on bare ground coated with sheep dung washed in by each new rain. Osman said that many survivors of Manjača had lost feeling in parts of their body because of prolonged exposure to the cold. A special room in Manjača was used for torture.

For most of this period, Sabiha and her daughters had no idea where Osman was and whether or not he was alive. As the terror increased, Sabiha was more and more reluctant to leave the house. Yet she had to go out to find food for her children. Sabiha was further burdened with the knowledge of what happened to Muslim girls if they were picked up by Serb militias. Muslims were required to display identification marks: white armbands or white marks on their homes. When standing in line for food, Muslims were required to give up their place to Serbs. Sabiha spent one whole morning in line as one after another of her Serb neighbors took places in front of her, until all the stocks were gone.

In 1993 Osman, Sabiha, and their daughters started a new life in the United States as refugees. In the fall of 1995 they heard that the last surviving Muslims in Sanski Most had been expelled or killed just before the town was retaken in the final Bosnian army offensive. The Botonjić family's experience illustrates what has been endured by a great many Bosnian Muslims except that they were fortunate enough to have survived intact as a family.[21]

What happened to Vladimir Srebrov and the Botonjić family exemplifies twin policies of religious-based violence in Bosnia-Herzegovina: elimination of all dissent within a particular religious group and destruction of the people outside of it. While the media focused global attention upon the shelling of Sarajevo, major events were occurring in the countryside, away from television cameras. Evidence and testimonies collected by the UN Special Rapporteur for Human Rights in the Former Yugoslavia, the UN Commission of Experts on War Crimes in the Former Yugoslavia, human rights groups such as Helsinki Watch, Doctors without Borders, and Amnesty International, and the International Criminal Tribunal on War Crimes in the Former Yugoslavia indicate systematic, widespread, and methodical persecution beyond anything the popular media has shown.[22]

These sources report that in each area occupied by the Serb army, killing camps and killing centers were established

Map 2.   Genocide in Bosnia-Herzegovina, 1992–1995

and individual massacres were carried out.[23] The term "killing camps" indicates those camps (such as Omarska, Brčko-Luka, Sušica, and the industrial site of the Keraterm company in Prijedor) where the primary object of detention was killing. Many of the prisoners appear to have been beaten to death over a period of hours or days. The killing went on daily and nightly. The term "killing camp" is meant to avoid false identification with the death camps of the Holocaust, while at the same time avoiding falsifications and euphemisms such as "detention camp." Manjača (the camp in which Osman was held), Trnopolje, Batković, and other smaller areas were concentration camps; killings and torture were common, but the majority of detainees did survive.[24]

"Killing centers" were places where the victims were brought for immediate or nearly immediate execution. Thus the famous Drina River bridge in the eastern Bosnian town of Višegrad was used for nightly executions and "sport atrocities" against Bosnian Muslims by Serb militiamen; the victims would be tortured and then thrown off the bridge and shot as they fell down into the Drina River.[25] Similar centers were found in Zvornik, Foča, and most other centers of Bosnian Muslim population occupied by the Serb army.[26]

Massacres, one-time acts of mass killing at discreet locales, occurred in every area occupied by the Serb army. There were various basic forms of massacre: those that took place as Serb militias entered a village or town; those that took place against unarmed civilians behind Serb lines during the time an area was already occupied and fully under the control of Serb forces; those committed against Bosnian villagers in deportation transit; and those committed against Bosnian prisoners of war. Even when

captives thought they were being released, they were often dis-
abused of their hope. In the Vlašić mountain massacre, busloads
of Bosnians who had been released from the Trnopolje camp
were stopped by Serb soldiers and killed.[27]

In late 1992, after the Serb army had consolidated the 70 percent of Bosnian territory it controlled, the mass killings changed
into steady, individualized killings and rapes. In the fall of 1994,
the International Committee of the Red Cross (ICRC) made an
extraordinary appeal to world leaders to stop the atrocities. The
appeal was ignored.[28]

When a town fell to the Serb army, the first inhabitants to be
targeted were intellectual and cultural leaders: religious authorities, teachers, lawyers, doctors, business people, artists, poets,
and musicians. The object of such "elite-cide" was to destroy
the cultural memory of the Bosnian Muslims and Bosnians who
would live with them. Gradually, acts of cruelty and massacre
took on an interior momentum and logic of their own. In many
cases, the Serb population was alerted to leave a village before
the killing began.

Because the Serb governments have refused UN war crimes
investigators access to alleged killing sites and have tampered
with mass graves, it is impossible to calculate the number of
dead. Whatever the final number, given the small size and
population of Bosnia (only four million total population), the
primitive methods used for the killings, and the interference by
reporters and refugee workers, the killing was methodical, systematic, and of a tragic enormity.

In 1993, when Croat religious nationalists saw that Serb army
aggression and atrocities were not being punished but were be-

ing rewarded by international peace negotiators with territorial concessions, they began their own persecution of Bosnian Muslims, modeled on the actions of the Serb militias.

GYNOCIDE

The following testimony was offered by a survivor of the Sušica camp in eastern Bosnia, whose commandant, Dragan Nikolić, has been charged by the International Criminal Tribunal with crimes against humanity. The witness was testifying about several young women who had been "selected" from other refugees: "They started selecting young women. The first was only 14, the second could have been 16 or 17. . . . I knew them all, they were from Vlasenica. . . . Then they started yelling: 'We want the Muslims to see what our seed is.' The women were never seen again. . . . We know that Dragan Nikolić knows about it very well. That's what he did. . . . He told us himself: 'I'm the commander of the camp. I'm your God and you have no other God but me.'"[29]

In one sense, the rapes in Bosnia are a manifestation of the toleration for and condoning of rape throughout history. Rape is also a feature of warfare, and some have argued that it is a rationale for war—that a purpose of war is the free rein it gives to rape.[30] But the use of rape against Muslim women in Bosnia has been overwhelming even by the bleak standards of war. In one town, Foča, a rape center was set up in the former Partizan Sports Hall in May 1992. Muslim girls and women were held there, underwent continual rape and other physical violence, and also were sent out to apartments where they were held for several days and then returned to the Partizan Hall.[31] The organized rape of Muslim women took place throughout the portions of Bosnia occupied by the Serb military, as well as in areas controlled by Croat nationalist forces.[32] Militiamen boasted about their gang rapes of Muslim women.[33] Human rights reports also show rapes of Christian women, but to a lesser extent and apparently without organization and planning.

The organized rape of Bosnian women was gynocidal—a deliberate attack on women as childbearers. In this connection, Serb and Croat nationalists were aware of two facts. The first fact was that the birthrate for Muslims in Yugoslavia was higher than that of Christians, and in some rural places, such as Kosovo province, this birthrate differential was dramatic. Birthrate became so heated an issue that Serb nationalists charged Muslims with a premeditated plot to use their higher birthrates to overwhelm and ultimately destroy the Christian Serbs.[34]

The second fact was that in traditional, Mediterranean societies women who have been raped are often unable to find a husband and have a family. Patriarchal traditions of shame and honor make it difficult—and in some cases, impossible—for women who have been raped to be accepted as wives and mothers. The organized rapes were meant to destroy the potential of the women as mothers. The statements attributed to many rapists—that the victim would bear "Serb seed"—are the flip side of this ideology: forced impregnation of Serb nationhood, a bizarre mixture of religion and biology that can only be understood against the underlying religious mythology.

The rapes were a form of desecration, closely related to the desecration of the sacred spaces symbolized by mosques. The term for sacred space in Islam is *ḥaram*, originally an Arabic term that Serb nationalists associate with one small aspect of Islamic sacred spaces, the women's quarters. Fantasies of "the harem" were commonplace among Serb nationalist clergy, academics, and soldiers. The commander of the Manjača camp, for example, justified the attack on Muslims on the grounds that the Bosnian Muslims had a plan to seize Serb women and put them in harems.[35] Serb religious nationalists used radio broadcasts to spread the charge that Bosnian Muslims were plotting to put Serb women in harems. Many Bosnian Serbs believed, or claimed to believe, these charges despite their being wildly, even ludicrously, inconsistent with the marriage practices of their Bosnian Muslim neighbors.[36] The harem fantasy involves a particularly cruel version of the use of women's bodies as a battlefield. The phrase allegedly used by Dragan Nikolić, "I am your God and you have no other God but me," appears to be a play upon the Islamic declaration of faith, "There is no god but God."[37]

A final dispossession awaited Bosnian Muslim women. Buses of refugees expelled from Serb army territory were stopped by militias and army units. From these refugees, who had already lost their communities, homes, and household possessions, everything else of possible value was now taken, from hard currency to jewelry of little value and sometimes even shoes. Stolen wedding rings—of little monetary value in relation to the enormous booty taken by the militias—represented the last symbol of group identity as well as a symbol of a future procreative possibility. The symbolism of a procreative future seems to be behind the curious obsession of some Serb religious nationalists with stealing wedding rings from Muslim women and giving them to their own girlfriends.[38]

GENOCIDE

The term "genocide" was coined by the jurist Rafael Lemkin as part of an effort to learn from the experience of the Holocaust and to develop an international legal consensus about certain kinds of systematic atrocities.[39] In 1948 the term was formally adopted in the Geneva conventions, and the act of genocide was prohibited. All contracting parties, which included the NATO nations, agreed that "it is a crime under international law which they undertake to prevent and to punish." Genocide was specifically defined as acts committed to "destroy, in whole or in part, a national, ethnic, racial or religious group, as such." Such acts include killing, torture, and efforts to prevent the procreation and regeneration of the targeted people.

Lemkin emphasizes that the term does not necessarily mean the immediate destruction of an entire nation. Rather, it entails "a coordinated plan of different actions aiming at the destruction of essential foundations of the life of national groups." Among the targets for destruction in such a plan, Lemkin lists institutions of culture, language, and national feelings, and the security of property, liberty, health, dignity, and human life. The key criterion for genocide, according to Lemkin, is that it be "directed against the national group as an entity"; violence against individuals is directed against them "not in their individual capacity, but as members of the national group."[40]

The organized persecution in Bosnia from 1992 to 1995 was

an effort to destroy both Bosnian Muslim culture and Bosnian multireligious culture and to destroy the Bosnian Muslims as a people. The campaign was made up of interlocking elements: cultural annihilation, mass killings, organized rape, and a code of euphemisms. Although Bosnian Muslims may have survived as individuals within refugee camps, they would be destroyed as a people and culture, and Bosnia could be partitioned between the religiously purified Christian states of Serbia and Croatia.

For the NATO powers to acknowledge genocide in Bosnia would have been to acknowledge that not only were they breaking the Genocide Convention of 1948 by refusing to prevent and punish genocide, but also that they were rewarding genocide by ceding territory to forces that carried it out. The UN-imposed arms embargo had locked into place the vast Serb-army advantage in heavy weapons, violating Article 51 of the UN Charter, which guarantees every recognized nation the right to defend itself; the embargo reinforced the power imbalance that allowed genocide to be carried out with impunity.

Many have denied, without reference to the history and definition of the term, that genocide has occurred in Bosnia.[41] These denials have done harm. No one wants to believe that a people are being exterminated because of race, religion, or ethnic identity and that governments who have the power to stop it refuse to do so. If an entire people are being killed, then on some level we may wish to believe, as we are constantly being told about Bosnia, that "there are no innocents in this war," that the people suffering deserve what they get. To acknowledge even the possibility of genocide, the mass killing of people simply because of who they are, calls into question fundamental beliefs about the possibility of a just foundation to our existence. Denial, however thinly argued, can be effective in lessening public appetite for the difficult process of enforcing the Geneva Genocide Convention.

At the time of this writing, eight major nationalist Serb and Croat military and civil leaders and numerous lower-level soldiers and civilians have been indicted by the International Criminal Tribunal on multiple charges of crimes against humanity. Five have been indicted on the charge of genocide by the tribunal, made up of distinguished jurists from around the world. In all the indictments for genocide, the vast majority of victims were Muslims. The indictments are based upon meticulous investigations. Much of the vast collections of evidence and testimony have been available to the public since the summer of 1992.[42] In this sense, the genocide was committed in full view of the world.

Srebrenica has become the symbol of the failure to enforce the Geneva Convention on Genocide. Srebrenica, a Muslim-majority town on the Drina River, was an ancient center of civilization in Bosnia. In 1992, as the Serb army burned its way through eastern Bosnia, thousands of refugees fled to the Srebrenica area. On April 16, 1993, as the Serb army entered the Srebrenica enclave, the United Nations declared Srebrenica a "safe area" and empowered the United Nations Protection Force in Bosnia (UNPROFOR) to supply humanitarian aid and to use the power of NATO to protect it. Less than a month later, five other besieged cities were declared safe areas.[43]

For more than a year, the Muslims in Srebrenica lived in hunger and fear as the Serb army blocked most UN convoys into the besieged enclave, and the UN commanders refused to use their authorized "necessary means" to break the blockade. A UN report suggesting the enclaves should be abandoned—despite the solemn UN resolutions—served as a green light to Serb army commanders. In the summer of 1995, the Serb army entered Srebrenica and another safe area, Žepa, as UN officials turned down requests for NATO air support. After the safe areas were overrun, Serb general Ratko Mladić drank a toast with the Dutch commander of the Srebrenica UN contingent, at the same time that Mladić's men were selecting out thousands of boys as young as twelve years of age, men, and some young women for torture, rape, and mass killings. Mass graves have been identified, but Serb nationalist authorities have refused war crimes investigators access to the graves. An estimated 8,000 people are missing, but after serious grave tampering, it is impossible to determine how many were killed.[44]

RELIGION AND THE IDEOLOGY OF GENOCIDE

Many deny a religious motive in the assault on Bosnia and upon Bosnian Muslims in particular and in the three-year refusal by the major powers of the Christian world (Britain, France, the U.S., Canada, Germany, and Russia) to authorize NATO power to stop it or allow Bosnians to defend themselves. This book explores religious dimensions of the genocide. The focal point is a national mythology that portrays Slavic Muslims as Christ killers and race traitors. When that national mythology was appropriated by political leaders, backed with massive military power, and protected by NATO nations, it became an ideology of genocide.

CHAPTER TWO

CHRIST KILLERS

THE CHRIST-PRINCE LAZAR

The Good Friday story of the crucifixion of Jesus has been a central, enduring, and powerful symbol within Christianity. The story of the sufferings and death of Jesus Christ, the divine Son in the belief of many Christians, is ritually performed and re-enacted in masses and services, in sermons, in literature, and particularly during the Good Friday commemorations in Easter week in the practice of meditating on the Stations of the Cross and in solemn Good Friday mass. In the Middle Ages, the story was formally performed, with actors on a stage, in passion plays.

The word "passion" refers to what a person suffers or undergoes, what happens to a person. Yet the word also has a much more active meaning, referring to the most powerful drives and emotions, the passions of life. In the performance of the passion play, the sufferings of Jesus Christ, the Son of God, become universal. As the Son of God carries the cross, he carries the sins and sorrows of the entire cosmos. At the moment of his death, those who participate in the passion play die with him and are reborn three days later with his resurrection.

As the innocent victim is sacrificed, there is a moment of intense catharsis. All the fears, sorrows, and sins of the audience are evoked, called out, and purged. This is one of the most emotive moments in human experience. In performance of the Passion, time is collapsed; the event long ago and far away is made present and immediate. The boundary between audience and actors is also effaced. Those who act the evil characters in passion plays know that a quick exit from the stage may be necessary to prevent a pummeling at the hands of an audience for whom temporal boundaries and differences between event and representation have broken down. The power evoked in the passion play can be and has been used for both good and evil.

In the Good Friday mass, in the sermons that relate the Good Friday story from the Christian gospels, and in the narratives of the medieval passion plays, Jews play a central role in the death of Jesus. For those who wish to harness the emotion of the Passion for their own purposes, the charge that the Jews were the killers of Christ, the killers of the Son of God, has been easy to fabricate and manipulate. Words from the New Testament account of the condemnation of Jesus, such as "Let his blood be on us, and on our children" (Mt. 27:26) could be taken out of context and applied to all Jews, with devastating implications. From the time of the first Crusade in 1096, the charge that Jews were Christ killers was used to foment attacks on Jewish communities, attacks that frequently reached genocidal proportions. As formal Good Friday celebrations of the passion play developed in Europe, attacks on Jews became a standard feature of

Easter week, and up until World War II, Jews in Europe would stay inside during Easter week to avoid being attacked.[1] In the Nazi-organized destruction of Jewish communities, the Christ-killer charge was also evoked; it was particularly effective in inflaming European churches and individual Christians to collaborate with the persecutions.

At the heart of the agitation by Serb radicals against the Muslims of Yugoslavia there has been a mythology which presents Slavic Muslims as Christ killers. How could members of a religion which began six centuries after the death of Jesus be responsible for his death?

The answer lies in the central event of Serb national mythology, the martyrdom of Prince Lazar. In 1389, the forces of the Ottoman Turkish Sultan Murat clashed at Kosovo with the Serb army led by Prince Lazar. Both Lazar and Murat were killed. In the view of Serb tradition, the death of Lazar marked the end of Serb independence and the beginning of five centuries of rule by the Ottoman Empire.[2]

During the nineteenth century, Serbian nationalist writers transformed Lazar into an explicit Christ figure, surrounded by a group of disciples, partaking of a Last Supper, and betrayed by a Judas. Lazar's death represents the death of the Serb nation, which will not be resurrected until Lazar is raised from the dead and the descendants of Lazar's killers are purged from the Serbian people. In this story, the Ottoman Turks play the role of the Christ killers. Vuk Branković, the Serb who betrays the battle plans to the Ottoman army, becomes the Christ killer within. In the nationalist myth, Vuk Branković represents the Slavs who converted to Islam under the Ottomans and any Serb who would live with them or tolerate them.[3]

BOSNIA IN MYTH AND HISTORY

The ancestors of the South Slavs arrived in the Balkans in the sixth and seventh centuries.[4] By the ninth century, the South Slavs were converting in large numbers to Christianity. Credit for the conversion is given to two Christian saints, Methodius and Cyril. The Bible and liturgy were translated into a South Slavic language (Slavonic). Followers of Cyril are credited with the invention of the Cyrillic script, based upon Greek characters, used in Serbia and Russia today.

The South Slavs were divided by the split or Great Schism in Christianity between the Catholic Church of the West, which recognized the authority of the Pope in Rome and used Latin, and the Orthodox Churches of the East, which refused the priority of the Bishop of Rome and used Greek or other languages in religious texts and practices. The South Slavs inhabiting the northern areas, the Slovenes and Croats, became Catholic and those in the southern and eastern areas, the Serbs, became Orthodox. In 1159 a Serbian dynasty was founded. In 1346, under the Emperor Stefan Dušan, a Serbian Orthodox Church Patriarchate was established, with its seat in the Kosovo region of present-day Serbia. Serbia's rise as a powerful state is expressed in the art and architecture of its many monasteries.

Adjacent to the Serbian kingdom was Bosnia. The early period of Bosnian history is an enigma. What remains as witness to this period are *stećaks*, large funerary monuments decorated with enigmatic, sculpted symbols. Bosnia grew powerful as a crossroads for trade between the flourishing city-state Ragusa (present-day Dubrovnik) and Constantinople, the capital of the eastern Roman Empire and the Orthodox Christian world. Bos-

nia also had mineral wealth in gold and silver. The city of Srebrenica (the name comes from the South Slavic word for silver)
was particularly famous for its mines. The Bosnian state reached
a high point under the rule of King Tvrtko (crowned in 1377),
who ruled at the same time as Prince Lazar of Serbia and who
sent troops to fight at Lazar's side at the battle of Kosovo in June
of 1389.

In medieval Bosnia there were three churches: the Catholic
Church, the Orthodox Church, and a third Christian Church,
called the Bosnian Church, which was independent from both the
Catholic and the Orthodox worlds. The Bosnian Church was accused of heresy and associated by its enemies with heretics from
Bulgaria called Bogomils. Bogomils were accused of being Mani-
chean dualists, that is, believing in two equal principles of good
and evil and rejecting the world as being of the evil principle.

The Catholic rulers of Hungary persuaded the papacy to sanction attacks on Bosnia in order to extirpate the heresy. The papacy also authorized the Franciscan order of friars to establish
monasteries in Bosnia and bring the adherents of the Bosnian
Church back to Catholicism. The Orthodox Church was also involved in persecuting adherents to the Bosnian Church.

The world of the South Slavs was soon to be transformed by
a new force. Ever since the tenth and eleventh centuries, Turkic
tribes from Central Asia had been gaining power in the Islamic
Middle East. By the fourteenth century, one of those Turkic
tribes, the Ottomans, gained ascendancy in Anatolia and began
constructing a major world empire. After the battle of Kosovo,
the Ottomans pursued their advance and in the year 1453 they
captured Constantinople, the capital of the eastern Roman Empire and Orthodox Church. By 1483 they had captured Bosnia.

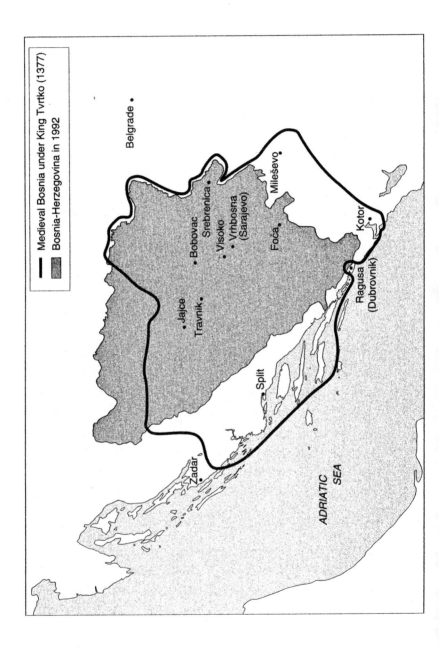

Medieval Bosnia under King Tvrtko (1377)

Bosnia-Herzegovina in 1992

Belgrade •

Bobovac •
Srebrenica •
Visoko •
Vrhbosna
(Sarajevo) •
Foča •
Mileševo •

Jajce •
Travnik •

Kotor •

Ragusa
(Dubrovnik) •

Split •

Zadar •

ADRIATIC
SEA

In the reign of Sultan Suleiman the Magnificent (1520–1566), they were at the gates of Vienna. The Ottomans transformed small villages into the new Ottoman-style cities of Sarajevo, Mostar, and Travnik. Roads, bridges, marketplaces, and inns were constructed throughout the region. As Bosnia grew and prospered, Bosnians converted to Islam in a higher proportion than Serbs or other South Slavic groups.

The conversion of such a large number of Bosnians to Islam has been a major issue in Croatian and Serbian national mythologies. For Croat and Serb nationalists, only the weak and the cowardly converted to Islam; conversions to Islam must have been the product of force or opportunism. Such a mythology is just as distorted as its implied counterpart mythology, that the Slavs who converted to Christianity in the ninth century did so without any economic or political pressures or enticements. Conversion is a complex process, involving intricate interconnections (and sometimes contradictions) between individuals and wider forces in society. Most Bosnians believe that the largest number of converts to Islam were from the Bosnian Church, who were persecuted as Christians and whose beliefs were supposedly more compatible with those of Islam. Historians have challenged this theory, however, showing that there is no evidence that the Bosnian Church in fact was Bogomil and that the patterns of conversion were far more complex than the supposed mass conversion of Bosnian Bogomils to Islam.

Also exposed as historically untenable are the national myths that ethnic groups are or ever were stable entities that remain fixed down through the centuries, or that the Orthodox Serbs, Catholic Croats, and Muslims of Bosnia today are direct descendants through stable ethnoreligious communities of ancient Or-

thodox, Catholic, and Muslim ancestors. The various loyalties in
Bosnia were complex and shifting, and conversions followed
many patterns. Orthodox Christians converted to Catholicism,
Catholics converted to Orthodox Christianity, Orthodox Christians and Catholics converted to Islam. Some Muslims converted to different forms of Christianity.

The final mythic figure of Croatian and Serbian religious nationalism is the evil Ottoman. No occupied nation thinks kindly
of its colonizer and the Ottomans were no doubt capable of cruelty and oppression. Yet the stories of Ottoman depravity at the
heart of nationalist mythology cannot match the evidence. If, as
Croatian and Serbian religious leaders and academics claim, the
Ottomans were constantly massacring Christians, how is it that
such large groups of Catholics and Orthodox Christians not only
survived, but in some cases grew and flourished under Ottoman
rule? If, as today's national myths would maintain, the Ottomans
spent five hundred years busily eradicating all traces of Christianity, how is it that such a magnificent ancient heritage of
Catholic and Orthodox Christianity—manuscripts, art, and architecture—survived Ottoman rule so well? If Islam is an inherently persecuting religion based on forced conversion, how is it
that the Catholic and Orthodox populations not only maintained
themselves for five centuries under Ottoman rule, but grew?

In the nineteenth century, the three myths—conversion to Islam based only upon cowardice and greed, stable ethnoreligious
groups down through the centuries, and complete depravity of
Ottoman rule—became the foundation for a new religious ideology, Christoslavism, the belief that Slavs are Christian by nature and that any conversion from Christianity is a betrayal of
the Slavic race.

THE CURSE OF KOSOVO

Western policy makers maintain that the conflict in the Balkans is "age old." Yet contiguous ethnic and religious groups throughout the world have old antagonisms. Armed conflict between Serbs and Croats is confined largely to this century. The conflict between Serbs and Slavic Muslims dates back to the Ottoman conquest of the Balkans in the fourteenth and fifteenth centuries. However, the development of the Kosovo story in which Slavic Muslims and Serbs are ancient and fated enemies is more recent; it was constructed by nationalist Serbs in the nineteenth century and projected back to the battle of Kosovo in 1389, and then back further, even to the very creation of the universe. It is this rather recent national mythology which was revived in the late 1980s in Yugoslavia.

Until the nineteenth century, the battle of Kosovo was not the central theme of Serbian epic. Rather than Prince Lazar, the main Serbian epic hero was Marko Kraljević, a Serb vassal of the Ottomans. Because he fought both for and against his masters in Istanbul, Prince Marko has served as a figure of mediation between the Serbian Orthodox and Ottoman worlds. In the epic literature, Marko stands in contrast to the polarizing figures identified with the battle of Kosovo as it was configured by nineteenth-century Serbian nationalists.

The reconstruction of Serbian mythology took place during the Serb revolt against Ottoman occupation and under the influence of the German romantic nationalism of Johann Gottfried Herder. The key figure in the Serb romantic literary movement was Vuk Karadžić (1787–1864), viewed by many Serbs as the founder of modern Serbian literary consciousness. Karadžić set

out to produce a Serb collection of folk literature that would ri-
val collections such as Herder's *Stimmen der Völker* (*Folk Voices*).[5]
He collected popular songs and epics and published them in a
four-volume set that became, for Serb nationalists, the canonical
source and voice of the "national spirit."[6] Karadžić succeeded
in forming a linguistic canon based upon certain dialects, which
he deemed linguistically and ethnically pure of foreign contamination. In his view, all speakers of the South Slavic dialects,
whether Catholic, Muslim, or Orthodox, were considered Serbs;
Serb nationality was a function of the language. For Vuk Karadžić and many of his admirers down to the present day, Serbia ex-
ists wherever the Serbian language (what was later called Serbo-
Croatian) is spoken.[7]

As Vuk Karadžić carried out the canonization of the folk epic,
selecting those poems that were to be identified with the Serb
nation as a whole, Serb revolutionaries were moving Serbia toward political independence. The revolt of Karadjordje against
the Ottomans began in 1804, and in 1806 Karadjordje took Belgrade. In 1829, Serbia was granted autonomy from Ottoman
rule in the Treaty of Adrianople and in 1830 Miloš Obrenović
founded the first modern Serb dynasty. The Kosovo legends became part of the Serbian revolutionary movement and those
parts of the tradition especially meaningful for such a movement
were preserved and emphasized.

As early as 1814, Vuk Karadžić had begun to emphasize the
importance of the story of Lazar and Kosovo when he published
a first version of the famous curse of Kosovo: "Whoever will not
fight at Kosovo / may nothing grow that his hand sows, / neither
the white wheat in the field / nor the vine of grapes on his moun-

tains."[8] In 1845, Vuk Karadžić published another version of the curse:

> Whoever is a Serb of Serbian blood
> Whoever shares with me this heritage,
> And he comes not to fight at Kosovo,
> May he never have the progeny
> His heart desires, neither son nor daughter;
> Beneath his hand let nothing decent grow
> Neither purple grapes nor wholesome wheat;
> Let him rust away like dripping iron
> Until his name be extinguished.[9]

Karadžić also emphasized the importance of Miloš Obilić, the assassin of Murat, comparing him to Achilles.[10]

Despite Karadžić's public pronouncements on its importance, Kosovo plays a relatively minor role in the poems he collected. The portrayal of Lazar as a Christ figure, Kosovo as a Serb Golgotha, and Muslims as the evil brood of "cursed Hagar" was to be found in sermons and chronicles.[11] However, the Kosovo legend, as a story that would fix Slavic Muslims as Christ killers and race traitors, was still not fully realized.

The Christological imagery solidified after the middle of the nineteenth century. In the art and literature of late nineteenth-century Serb romanticism, Lazar is depicted at a Last Supper, surrounded by knight disciples, one of whom (Vuk Branković) will betray the Christ-Prince. Lazar mistakenly accuses another disciple, Miloš Obilić, of being the traitor. During the ensuing battle, Miloš avenges Lazar by assassinating the Sultan, only to be cut to pieces in turn by the Sultan's guard.[12] Miloš Obilić, who killed the Sultan to avenge Lazar, became the role model for all Serbs.

EXTERMINATION OF THE TURKIFIERS

Montenegro is the small mountainous nation adjacent to Serbia, with a coastline on the Adriatic Sea. While the area of present-day Serbia was occupied by the Ottomans until the revolutions of the nineteenth century, Serbs in the area of Montenegro were able to use the rugged terrain to carve out more independence from the Ottoman Empire. The leader of the Montenegrin Serbs

Fig. 1.   Prince Lazar as Christ at the Last Supper: *The Feast of the Prince* by Adam Stefanović, lithograph, 1870s. From Wayne S. Vucinich and Thomas A. Emmert, *Kosovo: Legacy of a Medieval Battle* (Minneapolis: University of Minnesota Press, 1991).

had the title of *vladika*, which indicated a combination of the roles of prince and bishop.

The key figure in the reconstruction of the Lazar story was *vladika* Petar II Petrović (1813–1851), better known under the name of Njegoš. Njegoš's key work is *The Mountain Wreath* (*Gorski vijenac*), published in 1847 and considered by many Serb nationalists to be the central work of all Serbian literature.[13] The work, a historical drama in verse, portrays and glorifies the Christmas Eve extermination of Slavic Muslims at the hands of Serb warriors. It is based upon the legend of a campaign said to have been carried out against Slavic Muslims in early eighteenth-century Montenegro.

Njegoš's drama opens with Bishop Danilo, the play's protagonist, brooding on the evil of Islam, the tragedy of Kosovo, and the treason of Vuk Branković. Danilo's warriors suggest celebrating the holy day (Pentecost) by "cleansing" (*čistiti*) the land of non-Christians. The chorus chants: "The high mountains reek with the stench of non-Christians." One of Danilo's men proclaims that struggle will not end until "we or the Turks [Slavic Muslims] are exterminated."[14] The references to the Slavic Muslims as "Turkifiers" (*Poturice*) or as "Turks" crystallizes the view that by converting to Islam from Christianity, the Muslims had changed their racial identity and joined the race of Turks who killed the Christ-Prince Lazar. Throughout the Bosnian genocide of 1992–1995, the Serb nationalists and Serb clerics referred to Bosnian Slavic Muslims as Turks, even though all political ties with Turkey ended with the demise of the Ottoman Empire after World War I.

Western military and political leaders often maintain that the killing in Bosnia is a continuation of an ancient blood feud.[15] In *The Mountain Wreath*, however, the "extermination of the Turkified" is placed explicitly *outside* the category of the blood feud. In tribal societies of Montenegro and Serbia, a blood feud, however ruthless and fatal, could end in reconciliation. The godfather (*kum*) ceremony was the vehicle through which clans who had fallen into blood feud could reconcile with one another.[16] In *The Mountain Wreath*, when the Muslims suggest a *kum* ceremony, Danilo's men object that the ceremony requires baptism. The Muslims offer an ecumenical alternative, suggesting that the Muslim hair-cutting ceremony is a parallel to the tradition of baptism. Danilo's men respond with scatological insults against Islam, its prophet, and Muslims. With each set of insults, the chorus chants *"Tako, već nikako"* ("This way; there is no other") to indicate the act that must be done. The Muslims have two choices: be baptized in water or in blood.

Njegoš's story moves the conflict from the realm of blood feud into a cosmic duality of good and evil; Slavic Muslims become the "other." The sympathetic qualities of the Muslims are Danilo's last temptation. However sympathetic in person, Muslims are Christ killers, "blasphemers," "spitters on the cross." In quieter scenes, *The Mountain Wreath* offers a brooding lyricism in which a cosmic duality of good (Serb) versus evil (Muslim) is reinforced through metaphor, historical analogy, and explicit assertion. The antagonism in this representation is not just "old"; it is eternal.

The necessity to purify the Serb nation of the pollution of non-Christians is stated in powerful terms by the anonymous chorus that accompanies the dance (*kolo*), a choir portrayed as the voice of the people. The last hesitation of Bishop Danilo has been overcome by Abbot Stefan, who urges Miloš Obilić as a model and who rejoices openly in killing. *The Mountain Wreath* ends with the Christmas Eve extermination of the Slavic Muslims—men, women, and children. On return from the slaughter, Serb warriors take communion, without going to confession, which was mandatory after acts of blood vengeance.

Acts of blood vengeance were believed to cause religious defilement that rendered the actor ineligible to receive the Eucharist. By offering the Serb warriors communion without requiring their confession, the Serb Orthodox clergy take the "extermination of the Turkifiers" out of the category of blood vengeance. Instead, they present it as an act sacred in itself, with the implication of baptism by blood. Here, however, there is a twist. In the Christian doctrine of baptism by blood, it is the martyr whose sins are washed away by the baptism. In the extermination of the Turkifiers the killers who are baptizing the Turkifiers in blood are rendered worthy of communion and receive a full forgiveness for all their sins. Killing Turks or Turkified ones becomes not only worthy, but sacred, raised to the same level of sacrality as baptism or confession.

As *The Mountain Wreath* and the national mythology it expressed became more popular, Slavic Muslims were placed in a particularly impossible situation. By the linguistic standards of Vuk Karadžić, since the Slavic Muslims spoke South Slavic dialects Vuk Karadžić labeled Serb, they were considered Serbs. But by the standards of *The Mountain Wreath*, all Serbs had to be Christian, and any conversion to Islam was a betrayal of Serb blood and entailed a transformation from Slavic to Turkish blood. Slavic Muslims could not escape being considered Serb because of the Vuk Karadžić linguistic criteria, but as Serbs they had to be considered traitors according to the Njegoš mythology. They were delegitimized as a group and dehumanized as individuals. Finally, in the words of an influential Orthodox bishop, Njegoš portrays Miloš Obilić, the symbol of revenge, as "some kind of divinity; this is why we speak of Obilić's altar."[17]

Shortly after the appearance of Njegoš's *Mountain Wreath*, the feast day of St. Lazar, which had never before been recognized in Church calendars as a holy day, began to take on increased importance. In the 1860s the feast day of Prince Lazar was combined with the feast day of Vid (or Vitus), a pre-Christian Slavic god. In 1889, the 500th anniversary of Kosovo increased the interest in Vid's Day (*Vidovdan*). In 1892 Vid's Day appeared for the first time as an official holiday in the Church calendar as "Prophet Amos and Prince Lazar (Vid's Day)."[18]

The political and religious significance of the day increased in the twentieth century. It was on Vid's Day in 1914 that Gavrilo Princip, who had memorized Njegoš's *Mountain Wreath*, assassinated Archduke Ferdinand and set off World War I.[19] The 1921 constitution of Yugoslavia was called the Vidovdan constitution because it was proclaimed on June 28, Vid's Day. Vid's Day also became the day on which the school year ended throughout Yugoslavia, marking the death of Lazar in a conspicuous manner for all people in Yugoslavia, not just for Serbs. The more militant aspects of the Lazar story continued to grow in importance.

Although the day is Vid's Day, it is the death of the Christ-Prince Lazar that is at the center of the observance.[20] On the occasion of the 600th anniversary of Lazar's martyrdom, the resurgent Serb nationalists began to harness the excitement in order to heighten the symbolism of the event. At the same time there was a revival of interest in Njegoš. Pictures of Njegoš and posters with his verses were in wide circulation. A Serb writer exclaimed in 1989, "Is there anything more beautiful, more sincere and more profound than those pictures and verses [of Njegoš] written out from memory, not dictated by learned people or copied out of collected words. . . . Njegoš was resurrected in the memory of the people."[21] Njegoš, the poet of the death and resurrection of the Serb nation, was himself resurrected.

CHRISTOSLAVISM

"Race betrayal" is a key theme of *The Mountain Wreath* and the strand of Serbian literature it represents. By converting to Islam, Njegoš had insisted, Slavic Muslims "turkified." To "turkify" was not simply to adopt the religion and mores of a Turk, but to transform oneself into a Turk. To convert to a religion other than Christianity was simultaneously to convert from the Slav race to an alien race.

This ideology, originally set forth in the nineteenth century, found a new and powerful form in the work of Ivo Andrić (1892–1975), Yugoslavia's Nobel laureate in literature. Even more explicitly than Njegoš, Andrić presents religious conversion to Islam as conversion to the Turkic race. In his doctoral dissertation of 1924, Andrić makes the following statement about Njegoš and "the people": "Njegoš, who can always be counted on for the truest expression of the people's mode of thinking and apprehending . . . [described] the process of conversion thus: 'The lions [those who remained Christians] turned into tillers of the soil, the cowardly and covetous turned into Turks (*isturčiti*).'"[22] Andrić ascribes to "the people" Njegoš's judgment that Slavic Muslims who converted to Islam were the "cowardly and covetous" who "turned into Turks." Bosnian Slavic Muslims are thus doubly excluded from "the people": first, they became an alien race by converting to Islam; and second, it is the judgment of "the people"—not of one nationalist writer—that they have changed race along with religion.

The verse quoted by Andric´ ("the cowardly and covetous turned into Turks") is followed immediately in Njegoš's *Mountain Wreath* by the curse: "May their Serb milk be tainted with the plague." Few Serb readers of Andrić would be unfamiliar with the famous line about "Serb milk." Njegoš had applied the curse of Kosovo, leveled against those who refused to fight at the battle of Kosovo in 1389, to all Slavic Muslims. Andrić revived this curse and reinstated Njegoš's chorus as the "voice of the people." This voice of the people excludes all Slavic Muslims from the people, and curses them to disappear through a lack of progeneration.

Andrić finds a historical rationale for such exclusion in the belief that the Slavs who converted to Islam were primarily Bogomil heretics from the Bosnian Church. For Andrić, the ancient Bosnian Church showed a "young Slavic race" still torn between "heathen concepts with dualistic coloring and unclear Christian dogmas."[23] Andrić portrays the Bosnian Slavs who converted to Islam not only as cowardly and covetous and the "heathen element of a young race," but finally as the corrupted "Orient" that cut off the Slavic race from the "civilizing currents" of the West.[24]

The notion that the Bosnian Slavs who embraced Islam in the fifteenth and sixteenth centuries did so out of cowardly and covetous reasons is based upon a particular ideology of conversion held by Christian nationalists in the Balkans. As explained earlier, a Slav who converted from Christianity to Islam must have done so out of greed or cowardice. Yet such terms are never applied to the conversion of the Slavs to Christianity, believed to have occurred around the eighth century. It is a premise so basic that its authors do not even bother to argue that conversion to Christianity is based upon genuine religious sentiments.[25] Slavs are racially Christian. The conflation of Slavic race and Christian religion is illustrated in Andrić's popular historical novels.

Andrić's most famous novel centers on the bridge constructed over the Drina River at the eastern Bosnian town of Višegrad.[26] The bridge was commissioned by Mehmed Pasha Sokolović, the Bosnian who had become a vizier or minister to the Ottoman Sultan in Istanbul. According to popular legend, as related by the narrator of the novel, the fairies (*vile*) thwart the bridge's construction, causing all kinds of disasters and accidents. It is learned that for reasons unexplained the fairies will only be mollified if two Christian babies are walled up inside the bridge. Later generations of folk interpret the two holes in the bridge as the place where the infants' mothers would suckle their infants. The essentially Christian race of Slavs is trapped within the monumental structures of an alien religion.[27]

For Andrić, the evil is represented by the practice known as *devşirme*. In this practice, the Ottomans would select young boys from all over the empire to be taken to Istanbul, brought up in the court, and serve as soldiers, bureaucrats, and sometimes high officials. Although in Bosnia both Muslims and Christians were taken, and although the reaction of the boy's family could range from horror at the loss of a son to joy at the possibility of future high position, the Serbian nationalists portrayed the system as a "child tribute" or "blood tribute" by which the Ottomans

6th–7th centuries	Ancestors of South Slavs enter the Balkans
869	Death of St. Cyril, symbol of the Christianizing of the South Slavs
1159	Stefan Nemanja founds the Serbian dynasty
1219	St. Sava becomes the first Archbishop of the Serbian Orthodox Church
1346	Founding of the Patriarchate of Serbian Orthodoxy
1377	Tvrtko is crowned King of Bosnia
1389	Death of Lazar at the battle of Kosovo
1453	Ottomans take Constantinople and change its name to Istanbul
1459	Last Serb stronghold at Smederevo falls to the Ottomans
1483	Ottomans take control of all of Bosnia and Herzegovina
1531	Gazi Husrev Beg Mosque constructed in Sarajevo, the major mosque in Bosnia
1551	Colored Mosque of Foča is constructed
1556	Construction of the great Mostar bridge
1557	Construction of the Drina River bridge at Višegrad
1804	Karadjordje's revolt against Ottoman rule
1818	Assassination of Karadjordje by rival Miloš Obrenović, founder of the first modern Serbian dynasty
1829	Treaty of Adrianople: Serbia gains autonomy under Miloš Obrenović
1847	Njegoš publishes *The Mountain Wreath*
1864	Death of Vuk Karadžić, collector of Serb poetry and lore
1878	Treaty of San Stefano: Ottomans cede Bosnia to Austro-Hungarian control
1903	Descendants of Karadjordje establish a new dynasty in Serbia
1917	Union of South Slavs is declared
1918	Kingdom of Serbs, Croats, and Slovenes (later to be called Yugoslavia) is established under the authority of King Peter I of Serbia

would sap the blood of Christians by stealing their children. The novel's hero represents this image of blood tribute. In history, Sokolović led a fabled life. From the humble town of Višegrad, he rose to become the grand vizier (prime minister) to the greatest empire of the time and married Sultan Suleiman's granddaughter, Princess Esmahan. He endowed his town with great monuments, such as the bridge. According to some accounts, he placed a relative, Makarije, in the position of patriarch of the Serb Church, and thus his family remained thoroughly interreligious. In the novel, however, Mehmed Pasha, despite personal and family success, can never escape the sadness inside; the Christian boy is entombed within the Islamicized man.

The key event in *The Bridge on the Drina* is the impaling of a Serb rebel who tried to destroy the bridge by the Turks and their helpers, Bosnian Muslims and Gypsies. The scene contains a long, anatomically detailed account of the death of the heroic Serb, with explicit evocations of the crucifixion. The scene fits into that genre of Christian literature that details the sufferings and torments of Jesus. It is a scene that is constantly evoked by readers of Andrić as one of the most memorable, if not the most memorable, passage in all of Andrić's writings.[28]

Serb and Croat nationalists have turned the practice of impalement to punish those who defied their authority into a symbol of Turkish and Muslim depravity, despite the fact that the punishment of impalement was also practiced in Christian Austria and elsewhere in Europe at that time. Followers of Serb nationalist leaders in Bosnia have evoked the Ottoman use of impalement in justifying the attacks on Bosnian Muslims who are alleged to be Turks because of the conversion of their ancestors to Islam. Ironically, the most famous impaler of all time was the fifteenth-century Prince Vlad of Wallachiá (transformed by later legend into Count Dracula), whose victims were dissidents and Turks.[29]

Andrić's works are characterized by a command of local setting, a sense of the power of myth and folklore, and skill in historical fictive narration.[30] Indeed, it is their literary quality that has given Andrić's views on race betrayal such a key place within the Serb nationalist tradition.[31] The one Ottoman monument that remains intact in areas occupied by Serb nationalists today is the sixteenth-century Višegrad bridge on the Drina that Andrić made famous. Serb nationalists chose that same bridge as a killing center for Muslims in the spring of 1992.

TIME AND THE PASSION PLAY

Radovan Karadžić, President of the Republika Srpska, likes to appear in public with a *gusle*, the stick-fiddle used by bards to recite epic poetry. He makes a point of visiting the countryside frequently, where, he believes, the true Serb folk spirit can be found, unpolluted by the ethnic and religious mixing of the cities. His soldiers are accompanied by *gusle* players. As the *gusle* player sings, the Serb soldiers pass around an alcoholic drink and make the sign of the cross before drinking. They sing: "Serb brothers, wherever you are, with the help of Almighty God / For the sake of the Cross and the Christian Faith and our imperial fatherland / I call you to join the battle of Kosovo."

Karadžić explains that his favorite epic is "The Last Supper": "It has something to do with Jesus Christ, symbolizing Serbian faith after that last supper—so we lost our empire." Radovan Karadžić proudly claims as his ancestor the linguist and collector of folk epic, Vuk Karadžić. Vuk, he says, "reawakened the spirit of the Serbian culture that had been buried in the memory of the Serb people during long centuries of Turkish occupation." He speaks of the *gusle* epics as being songs of "our people" (that is, Serbs as opposed to Bosnian Muslims) thus using them to divide Serb from Slavic Muslim. Such a definition of "our people" ignores the fact that the *gusle* epics were a major aspect of folk culture for both Muslim Slavs and Orthodox Serbs, who shared the same epic traditions, conventions, and sensibility.[32]

Christoslavism—the premise that Slavs are by essence Christian and that conversion to another religion is a betrayal of the people or race—was critical to the genocidal ideology being developed in 1989. Christoslavism places Slavic Muslims and any Christian who would tolerate them in the position of the Judas figure of Kosovo, Vuk Branković. It sets the Slavic Muslims outside the boundaries of nation, race, and people. As portrayed in *The Mountain Wreath*, it demonstrates what can be done to those defined as nonpeople and what is, under certain circumstances, a religious duty and a sacred, cleansing act. It transfers the generalized curse of Kosovo onto Slavic Muslims in particular, a curse against the natal milk that will allow them to progenerate. In their acts of genocide from 1992 through 1995, Radovan Karadžić and his followers integrated the Kosovo tradition, as it was handed down through Vuk Karadžić and transformed by Njegoš and Andrić, into the daily rituals of ethnoreligious purification.

Milovan Djilas, Tito's colleague in the Partisans, a chronicler of the events of World War II in Yugoslavia, and a famous critic of the later Tito regime, was an admirer of *The Mountain Wreath*. In his book on Njegoš, he argued that the historical extermination of Montenegrin Muslims, the *istraga Poturica*, was a "pro-

CHAPTER THREE

PERFORMING THE PASSION

SERB JERUSALEM

In 1989, the "Kosovo question" did not refer directly to the ancient battle of 1389 or to the feast day of Lazar and Vid. It referred to a political crisis in the Serbian province of Kosovo, a crisis that enraged Serb nationalists and tore apart the Yugoslav federation. Kosovo is more than the site of the archetypal founding event in Serb romantic mythology. It is also the center of many of Serbia's greatest works of religious art and architecture and the ancient seat of the Serb Orthodox leadership. Some call it the "Serb Jerusalem."[1]

The Serb Patriarchate (the institutional heart of Serb Orthodox Christianity) was established at Peć in the Kosovo region in 1346. It was abolished after the Ottoman conquests in the fifteenth century. The Patriarchate was reestablished in 1557 by Mehmed Pasha Sokolović, the famous Bosnian who became the grand vizier at the court of the Ottoman Sultan Suleiman the

Magnificent. The first occupant of the newly reestablished position of Patriarch is believed to have been a relative of Mehmed
Pasha. The restored Patriarchate lasted until 1766 when Ottoman authorities abolished it on the grounds that it offered support to anti-Ottoman revolutionary activity.

During most of the past three hundred years, the province of
Kosovo has been inhabited primarily by Albanians. Albanians are
not a Slavic people; they speak a completely different language
from the other inhabitants of Yugoslavia. Most Albanians traditionally profess Islam, but during the cold war Albania was ruled
by an antireligious Stalinist regime; Albanians in Kosovo were
less brutally but still effectively secularized under Tito's moderate communism.[2]

After the Balkan wars at the beginning of the twentieth century, Kosovo was recaptured by Serbian patriots and made part
of the modern Serb state. During the period between the two
world wars, Serbia colonized Kosovo, pushing Albanians out and
bringing in Serb settlers. When Tito reestablished Yugoslavia,
he was concerned to avoid ethnic and religious conflict and so
abandoned the Serb colonization of Kosovo. Serb nationalists
complained that Serb settlers who had fled Kosovo during World
War II were not allowed to return. In 1974 Tito promulgated a
constitution that offered Kosovo and Vojvodina the status of autonomous provinces within Serbia. These two provinces were
administratively still part of Serbia, but they were given a vote in
the Yugoslav presidency equal to the constituent nations of Yugoslavia (Slovenia, Serbia, Bosnia-Herzegovina, Croatia, Macedonia, and Montenegro). The logic behind this arrangement
was that both provinces had large populations of non-Serbs and
deserved a measure of autonomy.

The new constitution enraged Serb nationalists. After World War II, the Albanian population in Kosovo had increased in proportion to the Serbian population. Kosovo was the poorest region of Yugoslavia; some Serbs migrated to better employment and living opportunities available for them elsewhere, while Albanians tended to remain in an area where their language was spoken. Impoverished Kosovo Albanians also had one of the highest birthrates in Europe, and the Serbs, already a minority in Kosovo, began to look at the large Albanian families with demographic fear.

In 1981 Albanian students demonstrated over conditions at the University of Priština, the major university in Kosovo province. Serbs in Kosovo complained of harassment by young Albanian men and of pressure to leave the province. After Serb nationalists revoked Kosovo's autonomy in 1987, Albanians in Kosovo protested the harsh rule of the Serb-dominated Yugoslav police. Albanian protestors began to demand the status of a republic for Kosovo within the Yugoslav federation. Republic status would seal Kosovo's constitutional separation from Serbia, and Albanians were an increasing majority in the province; for many Serbs a Kosovo republic was just a step toward independence, a merger with the neighboring nation of Albania, and the formation of a "Greater Albania."

In 1986 Serb clerics and nationalists orchestrated the charge that Albanians were engaged in genocide against Serbs. Serb nationalists alleged that the high Albanian birthrate was part of the genocide, a "*dirty demographic war for an ethnically pure Kosovo* [italics in original]."[3] Serb women and girls, Serb nationalists contended, were targeted for rape as part of the genocidal Albanian policy. Continuous references to the birthrate differ-

ences between Albanians and Serbs contributed to a gynecologi-
cal hatred against Albanians within portions of the Serb population. Serb nationalists alleged that Albanian women were "breed-
ing machines" that would destroy Serbs, while Serb women were
supposedly exposed to an ethnically based genocidal assault. Albanians were accused of a plot to eradicate Serb cultural heritage
in Kosovo by destroying monasteries. The Muslim identity of
most Albanians led Serb nationalists to conflate anti-Albanian
and anti-Muslim stereotypes.

As the conflict intensified, Serbian intellectuals and clergy
claimed an Albanian plot to "ethnically cleanse" Kosovo, unite
it with Albania proper, and create a "Greater Albania" and an
"ethnically pure Kosovo."[4] In January 1986, two hundred Belgrade intellectuals signed a petition to the Yugoslav and Serbian
national assemblies known as the "Serbian Memorandum."[5] The
guiding force behind this movement was the novelist Dobrica
Ćosić, a former communist who had become an ethnoreligious
zealot. The Memorandum demanded a restructuring of the relationship of the autonomous province of Kosovo to Serbia. It
condemned the autonomy and majority rule in Kosovo, established in the constitution of 1974, as national treason. It argued
that the treason was part of an anti-Serb plot to keep Serbs dis-
united and separate.[6] It made reference—as if to a known fact
that needed no elaboration—to the "genocide" in Kosovo. On a
like note, a Serb intellectual complained of an atrocities rate in
Kosovo "unprecedented in the twentieth century."[7]

What was the truth of the charges that galvanized Serbian nationalism within Yugoslavia and led to movements of secession
in Slovenia and Croatia? According to police records, the inci-
dence of rape in the Albanian region of Kosovo was at a rate *be-*

low that of Serbia proper. According to the same records, there was only one recorded instance of the rape of a Serb by an Albanian.[8] When proponents of the genocide charge in Kosovo were confronted with these facts, they had no answer. Instead they claimed, without evidence, a plot by the Albanian leadership to create an "ethnically clean" Kosovo.[9] Serb nationalists also charged, without evidence, that not only did Albanians side with Italy and Germany during World War II, but that a pro-Nazi organization, the Balli Kombetër, was still playing a key role in Albanian politics. The allegation contained two elements central to the ideology of genocide. First, Serb nationalists attached generic blame to entire peoples (Albanians, Croats, Slavic Muslims) for the acts of some during World War II. Second, Serb nationalists charged, without evidence, that pro-Nazi organizations were still operating within generically defined ethnic groups.

The gap between actual incidents of vandalism and the language used to depict them is vividly illustrated in one essay, in which the undemonstrated tales of ethnically based rape and genocide are placed next to a year-by-year ledger from 1969 to 1982 of the supposed systematic effort by Albanians to annihilate Serb cultural heritage. The list shows several incidents of vandalism per year: cutting of trees on monastery property, writing of graffiti, breaking of windows—hardly the kind of systematic cultural annihilation that was to occur in Bosnia in 1992.[10] As for charges that Albanians were being given lenient treatment, Amnesty International reported that Albanians, 8 percent of the population of Yugoslavia, accounted for 75 percent of prisoners of conscience.[11]

The escalation of charges to false accusations of genocide is especially clear in the language of the Christian Orthodox clergy. In 1969, the Holy Council of Serbian Orthodox Bishops wrote to Yugoslav President Tito to express concern about the neglect of Serb religious property by the state, the vandalism of Serb property by Albanians, and intimidation of Serbs in Kosovo. The language was specific and the concerns were grounded in factual incidents that were described without ethnic or religious vilification or generic blame against all Albanians.[12] By 1982, in a Good Friday appeal by Serb priests and monks, the language had changed. With repeated allusions to the "crucifixion" of the Serb nation, the battle of 1389, a centuries-long plot by Albanians to exterminate Serb culture, and the depravity of the Ottoman Turks, the appeal culminated in the charge of genocide: "It is no exaggeration to say that planned GENOCIDE [emphasis in original] is being perpetrated against the Serbian people in Kosovo! What otherwise would be the meaning of 'ethnically pure Kosovo' which is being relentlessly put into effect through ceaseless and never-ending migrations?"[13] In 1987, 60,000 Serbs signed a petition protesting the "fascist genocide" in Kosovo.[14] In 1988, Serb Orthodox bishops in New Zealand, Europe, and the Americas published a petition entitled "Declaration of the Bishops of the Serbian Orthodox Church Against the Genocide Inflicted by the Albanians on the Indigenous Serbian Population, Together with the Sacrilege of their Cultural Monuments in their Own Country."[15] None of these appeals offered any evidence for the charges that there was an Albanian plot to create an "ethnically pure" state in Kosovo, or that 250,000 Albanians had migrated to Kosovo from Albania.

The charges became more and more extreme. One writer asserted that 300,000 Albanians in Kosovo are refugees from Albania proper and should be forcibly returned. His call for ethnic expulsion was grounded in a quote from Njegoš: "We [Serb and Slavic Muslims] must fight until one of us is exterminated."[16] He went on to ridicule "brotherhood and unity," an ideal that had helped keep the fragile Yugoslav federation together since the end of World War II: "Do not pretend that you [Albanians] love us, because we do not love you. We have long ago eaten up the moldy pretzel of internationalism that falsely joins us in brotherhood and falsely unites us." The writer concludes with an open-ended threat: "We are neither brothers nor are we united, but let us examine how we shall . . . [ellipsis part of original]."[17] Such language was dominating the most prestigious publications of Serbian writers and intellectuals. By 1989, references to the crucifixion of Serbia mixed with threats of revenge. Those who engineered the "Serbian Golgotha," the writer warned, forget that executioners can become victims.[18]

Although the hate was directed at Albanians in Kosovo, the literature and archetypes made Slavic Muslims (rather than specifically Albanian Muslims) particularly vulnerable. It was Slavic Muslims who were associated by Njegoš with the treason of Vuk Branković, an association renewed in the novels of Ivo Andrić. It was the Slavic Muslims who were portrayed as Turkifiers and still called Turks in a national mythology that saw the Turks as the killers of the Christ-Prince. The Serb nation was again being crucified; the archetype of national myth was tied into the actual situation in Kosovo province. The relics of Lazar were paraded around the province of Kosovo as a reminder of the killing of the Christ-Prince and as a territorial claim.

From within such a perspective, there is no safety. Even the peaceful smile is the smile of the traitor. One poem, based upon the art within the Peć monasteries, meditates on the figure of Christ while "In the neighboring nave / Judas threatens him with a knife / the eye's calm smile." The poem appeared in a volume of hate literature published in 1989 by the Serbian writers union as part of the celebration of the 600th anniversary of Kosovo.[19] When through historical circumstance such rage was diverted from the Albanians in Kosovo to Slavic Muslims in Bosnia, there was nothing the Bosnian Muslims could possibly do to convince their attackers of their peaceful intent; even their peaceful smile could be read as the smile of a Judas.

RETURN OF THE USTASHE

The village of Jasenovac stands near the border between Bosnia and Croatia in an area known as Western Slavonia. From 1991 to 1995 this area was held by Serb rebels and formed part of the self-declared "Serbian Republic of Krajina."

During World War II, Jasenovac was the site of the largest death camp in Yugoslavia for Serbs as well as Jews, Gypsies, dissident Croats, and others deemed undesirable by the Croat nationalist forces known as the Ustashe. The Ustashe regime lasted from 1941 to 1944 and was kept in power through its patron, Nazi Germany. The brutality of the Ustashe was such that even some Nazis complained about it.

The role of the Catholic Church in the atrocities of the Ustashe state has been a source of deep bitterness to Serbs. The highest-ranking Catholic at the time, Bishop Stepinac, was a Croat nationalist who celebrated the coming to power of an independent government. When the depravity of the Pavelić regime began to show itself, Stepinac was slow to condemn it and slow to condemn the role of many Catholic priests in instigating the killings and, in numerous cases, actually supervising or carrying them out. After the war, a Croat monastery in the Vatican became the center for the smuggling of Ustashe war criminals to safety. Stepinac (who had been elevated to cardinal) never really came to grips with the open participation of many Croat priests in the religious-based genocide or with his own weak response to the atrocities of the Pavelić regime. Even after the war, he failed to show empathy with the hundreds of thousands of Serbs killed, referring to the killings as "errors." In the early 1980s, Serb Orthodox clergy asked the Catholic clergy of Croatia for dialogue on this issue. The Croatian bishops refused. The Catholic Church generally has refused to fully acknowledge the Ustashe genocide.[20]

Parallel to their construction of an alleged genocide in Kosovo, Serb nationalists began alleging the imminent repetition of the Ustashe genocide of World War II, which was all too real and all too recent. The atrocities of World War II were relived continually in the Belgrade media along with the standard use of generic blame familiar from Kosovo. Just as Kosovo Albanians were, as a group, held responsible for German collaborators in World War II, all Croats came under suspicion for Ustashe activities in World War II. Both sides manipulated numbers. Serb nationalists claimed that anywhere from 700,000 to more than a million Serbs were killed at Jasenovac. Croat nationalist and historian Franjo Tudjman started low (60,000) and kept revising downward. In such an environment, every sign becomes a symbol, every symbol becomes charged. Thus, a provocative ruling by the newly independent Croatian state limiting the official use of the Cyrillic alphabet, used by Serbs in certain areas, inflamed

Serb fears and angers. The adoption by the Croat state of a flag based upon the checkerboard pattern was, for Croat nationalists, an assertion of an ancient Croatian symbol dating back into the medieval times; for many Serbs, the checkerboard was the prime symbol of their Ustashe persecutors of World War II.

Serb clergy and Serb nationalists began to disinter the remains of Serb victims of the Ustashe in World War II. Ignoring the fact that thousands of Croats fought against the Ustashe and Nazis in World War II, Serb nationalists used this grim exercise to re-iterate their charge of generic Croat responsibility for collaboration with the Nazi regime. The Croatian people were genocidal by nature, the Serb nationalists maintained, and would carry out their genocide again; indeed, they were already planning a re-peat of Jasenovac. As late as 1995, Bosnian Serb President Rado-van Karadžić contended that in 1992 Croatians were prepared to repeat the World War II genocide against the Serbs.[21]

The Bosnian Muslims were also targeted with the generic blame of Serb nationalism. During World War II, Bosnian Mus-lims were caught on all sides of the battle lines; some fought with the Ustashe, many with the Partisans, and many others were massacred by both Ustashe and Chetniks. Indeed, the propor-tion of Bosnian Muslims killed in World War II rivaled that of the Bosnian Serbs. The Nazis recruited Bosnian Muslims into two divisions of the SS. Those two divisions have been used as an emblem to identify Bosnian Muslims with Nazi atrocities of World War II, ignoring the major role played by other Bosnian Muslims in the Partisan resistance and in saving the lives of Jew-ish and Serb neighbors.[22] The writings of politician Vuk Draš-ković were especially important in stirring up hatred against all Croats and Muslims. Drašković portrayed Muslims as Serbs who betrayed their race by converting to Islam and, within the context of World War II, as sadistic monsters.[23]

Lazar's bones were paraded around Bosnia, tying the bones of the victims of the Ustashe to the bones of the Christ-Prince. The pain and anger of living memory (most Serbs had family members who perished in World War II) combined with the pain and anger of mythic time; Jasenovac and 1389 were brought into a single moment in the present. Accompanying the procession of Lazar's relics in Bosnia was a proclamation about enemies of "long-suffering Serbs": "We will do our utmost to crush their race and descendants so completely that history will not even remember them."[24]

APPROPRIATING THE PASSION

The genocide charges against Kosovo Albanians, the alleged Ustashe nature of all Croats, and the alleged race betrayal of Slavic Muslims formed a lethal brew.[25]

The work of political cartoonist Milenko Mihajlović offers a taste of this brew. In May 1989, at the height of the Kosovo dispute and Serb anger over the Albanian birthrate, Mihajlović published a cartoon showing throngs of Albanian babies with demented, leering grins swarming out from behind Marshal Tito, who is depicted as a queen bee. In September of the same year, Mihajlović depicted Ustashe members fishing for Serb babies with barbed fishing line. As the Serb media stepped up its accusations that all Croats were genocidal, Mihajlović published a cartoon in January 1990 showing a Roman Catholic prelate with a rosary made out of the eyeballs of Serb children; the Serb infants with their eye sockets empty surround the priest. The deadly

Fig. 2. Religious nationalist cartoon by Milenko Mihajlović: a Catholic cleric and a Muslim cleric fight over a Serbian baby; the Muslim wields a circumcision knife. From *The New Combat*, September 1990.

position of Bosnian Muslims appeared in a Mihajlović cartoon of September 1990. In the cartoon, a Roman Catholic prelate and a fez-topped Muslim leader argue over a Serb baby. The prelate wants to baptize the baby, the Muslim to circumcise him. The second frame shows the prelate gouging out the baby's eyes, while the Muslim stretches out the foreskin under a large knife. It is a measure of the degree to which nationalism had degraded Serb culture and civic values that the cartoons of Mihajlović were published not in some obscure journal but in the *Literary Gazette (Književne novine)* of Belgrade, the official arm of the Association of Serbian Writers.[26]

By 1992, the charges against Albanians, Croats, and Slavic Muslims had been woven together into a claim of both actual and imminent genocide against Serbs by a worldwide Islamic conspiracy aided by Germany and the Vatican. The charges were repeated by Serb Church leaders such as Metropolitan Amfilohije Radović in cosmic terms reminiscent of Njegoš: orthodoxy in the Balkans was "the last island of holiness, of untroubled and unpolluted truth," against which "all the demonic forces are directed."[27] Fears of a demographic plot by Muslims were exploited to spur a higher Serb birthrate. Serb Orthodox Bishop Vasilije, of the Zvornik–Tuzla area in northeast Bosnia, warned of catastrophe from the low Serb birthrate. The Serb Orthodox Church offered medals to Serb mothers for bearing many children. A Serb artist demanded that Serb women give birth every nine months. If a woman refused, "We will hand her over to the *Mujahidin* (Islamic fighters) from the [United Arab Emirates]. Let her have them inseminate her."[28]

By the time the Bosnian conflict began, the national mythology, hatred, and unfounded charges of actual genocide in Kosovo and imminent genocide in Bosnia had been shaped into a code: the charge of genocide became a signal to begin genocide. In 1992, witnesses began to notice a pattern in the atrocities by Serb forces in Bosnia. A massacre would take place in a village immediately after the local news announced that the Croats and Muslims were about to exterminate Serbs.

José Maria Mendiluce, an official of the UN High Commission for Refugees, was witness to the organized killing of unarmed Muslims in the town of Zvornik. He observed that they fit a pattern of atrocities carried out by the militia of Serb religious nationalist Vojislav Šešelj: "For days, the Belgrade media had been writing about how there was a plot to kill all Serbs in Zvornik. The authorities in Zvornik realized that the point in question was a typical maneuver by Šešelj's Radical Volunteers. This maneuver always precedes the killing of Muslims, as had already happened in Bijeljina and many places along the left bank of the Drina River."[29] An overlapping and robust ideology had taken shape. To refute any part or even most of the Serb radical position would only lead to new charges and channel the rage in new directions. In justifying the atrocities in Bosnia, Serb nationalists would point to atrocities by Croatian army forces in World War II or in the 1991 Serb-Croat war. When it was pointed out that the largely Muslim population selected for extermination had nothing to do with the Croat army and indeed had been attacked by the Croat army in 1993, Serb nationalists would shift to blaming all Muslims for the acts of those who fought with the Ustashe in World War II. When it was pointed out that many of the families who suffered worst in the Serb army onslaught in Bosnia were families of World War II Partisans who fought against the Ustashe, Serb nationalists would shift to claims of Ottoman depravity and treat the Muslims as Turks. When it was pointed out that the Slavic Muslims were just as indigenous to the region as Orthodox Christians or Catholics, the discussion would then shift to allegations that the Bosnian Muslims were fundamentalists and that Serbia was defending the West against the fundamentalist threat of radical Islam. When it was pointed out that most Bosnian Muslims were antifundamentalist by tradition and character, the Serb nationalist would move to the final fallback position: that this was a civil war in which all sides were guilty, there were no angels, and the world should allow the people involved to solve their own problems.[30] Hatred of Albanians, hatred of Croats, hatred of Muslims (both Albanian and Bosnian) were combined and reinforced through endless loops of victimization not accountable to evidence or reason. Then the language of eternal victimization was flipped into a code in which charges of genocide against Serbs became a signal to begin genocidal operations against Bosnian Muslims.

In 1987, a Serbian communist party official by the name of Slobodan Milošević was upbraided by Serb nationalists in Kosovo for not attending to Serb concerns in the province. Milošević returned to a tense meeting with Kosovo Serbs. A large Serbian crowd surrounded the building in which the meeting was held. When Milošević emerged, a vulnerable-looking elderly Serb ran up and shouted that the Albanian-dominated Kosovo police were beating people in the crowd.

"These people will not beat you again!" The response by Milošević was shown throughout Serbia on all the major television networks. What the viewers were not shown was how the incident was staged. Serb nationalists, with Milošević's approval, had supplied the crowd with truckloads of heavy stones. At a given moment the crowd threw the stones directly into the face of police who had been standing by. The violence was instigated through crowd manipulation and exploited through media manipulation, tactics Milošević would refine during his rise to absolute power.[31]

On June 28, 1989, the Serb Orthodox Patriarch led a procession of three hundred Serb priests in scarlet robes at the Gračanica monastery in Kosovo. They were marking the 600th anniversary of the death of Lazar at the battle of Kosovo. The Patriarch lit two ten-foot candles in honor of the martyrs of the battle of Kosovo and then stored the candles away until they could be lit in another century on the 700th anniversary. For a week, Serb pilgrims had gathered at the monastery to pray before the relics of Lazar.[32]

Nearby, on the plain of Gazimestan where the battle had taken place, a vast crowd of pilgrims estimated at between one million and two million gathered for the commemoration of the battle of Kosovo.[33] On this occasion, June 28, 1989, Serb President Slobodan Milošević consolidated three years of effort to instigate and appropriate radical nationalist sentiment.

Serbia was accustomed both to a cult of mythic personality (Miloš Obilić, Lazar) and the cult of personality under Tito, whose image adorned homes and businesses throughout Yugoslavia. As he stood on the podium before the massive throng at Kosovo on June 28, 1989, Milošević could see the evidence that he had become the bridge between the Titoist Great Leader and the Serb nationalist icon; in the crowd, next to pictures of Lazar, were pictures of Slobodan Milošević. Before the vast and euphoric throng, Milošević spoke of ancient battles to defend Europe and warned of battles to come.

Three vectors of mythic power came together in the 1989 passion play performance. The fourteenth-century ancestors of Slavic Muslims were characterized as Christ killers and then, through temporal collapse effected by the performance, identified with present-day Slavic Muslims in Bosnia. The hatred of Albanians in Kosovo province in 1989 was fused with the hatred of Slavic Muslims. And the atrocities of World War II were resurrected and attributed to Croats and Muslims as entire peoples.

Three streams of rage—disinterment of remains of Serb victims of genocide in World War II, procession of Lazar's relics through Bosnia and around Kosovo, and pilgrimage of Serbs to visit the relics in Kosovo—were channeled into a single raging torrent. Within three years, those who directed the festivities in 1989 were organizing the unspeakable depravities against Bosnian civilians.[34]

IN THE CROSSHAIRS OF THE SNIPER

In December 1993, a resident of Sarajevo walked out of his home. He was the father of the graduate student who had been killed trying to save books during the burning of the National Library in August 1992. He had fought against the Nazis in World War II as part of the Partisan resistance, alongside Croats, Serbs, Slovenians, and others. After the war, he had been imprisoned by Tito's secret police. In his fedora, he was a handsome man with kind eyes and a thin, hawkish nose.

Some said that of all the tragedies he lived through, the killing of his daughter on the way back from the library was the first thing to shake him. Some thought he was tired of the constant humiliation faced by Sarajevans, having to crawl along walls to

CHAPTER FOUR

MASKS OF OTHERNESS

By 1992, a series of ominous developments had occurred: a language of extremist paranoia had emerged; allegations were made that an ethnoreligious group was plotting and carrying out genocide; militias were arming to battle the federal government, which was allegedly supporting the genocidal plot; a battle was looming to save Christian values and identity; a violent text—read and memorized by militia members—recounted the plot against Christians, the battle to save Christendom, and the punishment in store for race traitors; bombings, shootings, and other terrorist acts carried out by such militias were on the increase . . .

Such was the background to the bombing of the Federal Building in Oklahoma City, on April 19, 1995, carried out by men associated with the militias of the Christian Identity movement. The prime suspect in the bombing, Timothy McVeigh, had studied the "bible" of the Christian Identity movement, William Pierce's *The Turner Diaries*, which contains a fanciful account of an ethnoreligious plot against Aryan Christians, the war by militias to save their Christian identity, the bombing of federal buildings, and the hanging of women who violate the purity of their race by marrying Jews or blacks.[1]

Imagine that such extremists had control over major U.S. media, which for three years broadcast alleged atrocities of non-Christians and non-Aryans against the Aryan Christians. Imagine that such extremists had a high-level supporter in the U.S. military who supplied them not only with assault rifles but with tanks and heavy artillery. Many Americans dismiss the threat of such groups and the possibility of such an ethnoreligious war. In the former Yugoslavia, the extremists were dismissed in the same way. Few imagined that in just a few years neighbors and friends would be shelling them with mortars or tormenting them in killing camps.

CREATING THE PERPETRATOR

Explosive as they were, the symbolic forces marshaled at the Kosovo celebrations of 1989 were not capable alone of producing genocide. The fuse needed to be lit. Serb nationalist forces, protected by Serb President Slobodan Milošević, worked carefully to light it. Milošević and Serbian nationalists had used mob intimidation and media exploitation to overthrow Serbian President Ivan Stambolić and purge the communist party and governments in Serbia's autonomous regions of Vojvodina and Kosovo and in Montenegro. In 1990 Milošević began using purges to transform the Yugoslav Army into a Serb-nationalist controlled implement of the struggle for a "Greater Serbia."[2] In 1991, he used attacks in Belgrade on demonstrators for freedom of the press and the war in Croatia to harden the soldiers. In May

1992, Milošević pretended to withdraw the Yugoslav army from Bosnia but in fact simply transferred all the Bosnian Serb soldiers in the federal army and vast amounts of weapons to the Bosnian Serb army, whose expenses Milošević paid from the Yugoslav federal budget.[3] Milošević gave militia leaders such as Vojislav Šešelj and Arkan access to the media, secret police, military command, and arms depots.[4] These men built private militias and collaborated closely with regular Serb forces to spread terror throughout eastern and northern Bosnia.[5]

Serbs who refused to participate in the persecution of Muslims were killed. In a Serb-army occupied area of Sarajevo, Serb militants killed a Serb officer who objected to atrocities against civilians; they left his body on the street for over a week as an object lesson. During one of the "selections" carried out by Serb militants in Sarajevo, an old Serb named Ljubo objected to being separated out from his Muslim friends and neighbors; they beat him to death on the spot.[6] In Zvornik, Serb militiamen slit the throat of a seventeen-year-old Serb girl who protested the shooting of Muslim civilians. In the Prijedor region, Serb militants put Serbs accused of helping non-Serb neighbors into the camps with those they tried to help. Similar incidents occurred throughout areas controlled by the Bosnian Serb military.[7]

Serb militants tried to provoke revenge attacks by Muslims against Serbs still living in Bosnian-controlled territory. The theory was that such attacks would drive the remaining Serb population out of Bosnian government areas, thus creating two ethnoreligiously pure entities, one Serb, one Muslim. The claim of extreme religious nationalists that Serbs could never live safely with Muslims would be validated.[8] During the "cleansings" of the Bijeljina area in 1994, Muslim survivors of the operation were driven toward the Bosnian-controlled city of Tuzla, which has a large Serb population. Young men were taken to slave labor camps. Their families were told that if they wanted to see those taken to the camps alive again, they should take the houses of Serbs in Tuzla, expel the Serbs into territory held by the Serb army, and then the other captives would be released.[9] Although one attack in Tuzla against Serbs did occur when the first wave of traumatized refugees from the overrun enclave of Srebrenica came into the city in 1993, the Tuzla authorities, against all odds, have maintained a multireligious city.

Serb army officers used alcohol to break down the normal inhibitions of the young men in their commands. Serb soldiers were kept drunk night after night, weeks at a time; military convoys were accompanied by truckloads of plum brandy (*šljivovica*). In Sarajevo, there was an evening *šljivovica* hour during which Serb soldiers would get drunk and broadcast over loudspeakers, in grisly detail, what they were going to do to the Bosnian civilians when they got hold of them. Survivors of mass killings reported that once soldiers began drinking, the atrocities followed.

Commanders of the killing camps made a practice of opening them to local Serb radicals, gangsters, and grudge-holders, who would come each night to beat, torture, and kill the detainees.[10] This practice had the effect of spreading complicity throughout the neighboring area. Distribution of stolen and abandoned goods also spread complicity. Every town "cleansed" meant the availability of automobiles, appliances, stereo and television equipment.[11] Once a family had in their home something that had belonged to a neighbor, they were less likely to object to the "ethnic cleansing."

Militia leaders worked to instill an ethos of brutality. Arkan, the leader of the Tiger militia, used his headquarters in the city of Erdut as a training ground. Serb recruits were taught that in fighting the enemy, they had no right to spare children, women, or the aged.[12] Serb military commanders showed reporters and their own troops how to slit a throat by having pigs killed as demonstrations.

The final dehumanization of the perpetrator occurred in ritualized fashion, when young soldiers were forced to watch torture, gang rape, and killings and forced to participate. To refuse was to risk death. To participate was to learn to believe that the victims were not truly human anyway.

Dehumanization of the victims was achieved through a variety of methods. Captives would be held for months in extremely cramped quarters without toilets or sanitary facilities. Women spoke of the shame of being forced to wear clothes stained with menstrual blood. Weeks of a starvation diet, lack of water, and lack of hygiene would turn captives into filthy, emaciated shadows of the persons they had once been. Cities the Serb army did not capture were blockaded. Few convoys were allowed in, and some safe areas, such as Srebrenica, Žepa, and Bihać, became abodes of misery, what one refugee worker called UN concentration camps.[13]

Dehumanizing labels were also important in motivating genocide. In Serb-occupied areas, Bosnian Croats were invariably called Ustashe, in reference to the fascist units of World War II. Muslims were called Turks (a term of alienation and abuse when used by Serb and Croat militants), Ustashe, and "balije." The origin of the term "balija" (plural "balije") is obscure. Some

Fig. 3. Masks and religious terror: Arkan's Tiger Militia. Ron Haviv, SABA Press Photos, 1990.

believe it is related to the South Slavic term for spit or mucus (*bala*); others suggest different etymologies. Bosnian Muslim survivors of the "ethnic cleansing" reported that nationalist Serbs would "spit" the term out at them.[14] A popular song in Belgrade was based on the rhyme "Alija" (the first name of Bosnian President Alija Izetbegović) and "balija."

In both the Republika Srpska and Serbia proper, militia leaders became patrons in their community through their control over the real estate and moveable properties of the killed or expelled non-Serbs. As the Serb economy faltered under the strain of war expenditures, corruption, and economic sanctions, the person who could get what was needed—extra food, medicine, gasoline, or a new stereo—was the militia leader. No need to ask where the goods came from.

The use of masks symbolized the methods used by the organizers of the genocide. When the fighting broke out in Croatia in 1991, Serb irregular militiamen wore ski-masks or face paint. Survivors of atrocities reported trying to discern the accent of their masked torturers to determine where they came from. Sometimes a victim would recognize the voice of a neighbor.[15] In many cases the man behind the mask was content to allow his identity to be known through his voice, and in some cases even taunted his victim with the fact that they knew one another.

The mask transformed identities. Before he put it on, the militiaman was part of a multireligious community in which Catholic Croats, Orthodox Serbs, Slavic Muslims, Jews, Gypsies, and others had lived together. These were his friends, his work colleagues, his neighbors, his lovers, his spouse's family. Once he put on the mask, he was a Serb hero; those he was abusing were *balije* or Turks, race traitors and killers of the Christ-Prince Lazar.

THE FORGOTTEN SERBS

Despite the effort of Serb religious nationalists to dehumanize both their own population and their target population, many Serbs have resisted and kept their humanity. Serbs in Serbia evaded military service in large numbers. Bosnian Muslim survivors commonly reported that a Serb or (in the case of Croat extremist violence) a Croat helped them escape. A soldier or border guard may have turned a blind eye as a Bosnian slipped away from an atrocity or fled to safe territory. A family might shelter a fugitive in their home, at great risk. A Muslim survivor of the killing camp at Sušica mentioned that a Serb priest tried to help him.[16] Bogdan Bogdanović, the Serb former mayor of Belgrade, has spoken out courageously against the systematic annihilation of mosques and other cultural monuments. Many of the stories of resistance and courage cannot be told at this time, because the resisters or their families are still vulnerable to reprisals.[17]

In 1995, the majority of Bosnian Serbs did not live in Serb-army occupied Bosnia but had fled, many of them to Serbia proper. In 1994, President Milošević allowed agents of Radovan Karadžić and militia leaders like Arkan to sweep through Serbia, rounding up thousands of Serbs from refugee camps, abusing them for refusing to fight, and punishing them by sending them to the front lines with little training.

In Bosnian government areas, the Serb Civic Council was formed to work for a multireligious society and to articulate the concerns of those Serbs loyal to a multireligious Bosnia-Herzegovina. The Civic Council pointed out that the total number of Bosnian Serbs living under the control of the Republika

Srpska was less than 50 percent; over 150,000 lived in Bosnian government–controlled areas and some 500,000 had fled abroad. The council criticized the international community for treating the religious nationalist faction as the sole representative of the Serbian people.[18]

THE SERB CHURCH AND THE STEPINAC SYNDROME

In Bosnia, the Serb Orthodox Church made the same mistake the Catholic Church made in Croatia during World War II; it became a servant of religious nationalist militancy. In many instances, Christian Serb clergy have supported the extremists who carried out the genocide in Bosnia and have given ritual and symbolic support to the programs of ethnic expulsion and destruction of mosques.

In the late 1980s, the Serb Orthodox Church collaborated with academics and literati to highlight the motif of Muslims as Christ killers and race traitors. It was a motif that came to dominate the commemoration of the 600th anniversary of the Kosovo battle. Supporters of the Republika Srpska memorized and quoted Njegoš's *Mountain Wreath* and even more violent religious epics as they planned and carried out their genocide. Verses from these epics glorifying the extermination of Muslim civilians were being posted on the Internet even as various villages and cities in Bosnia-Herzegovina were being "cleansed" of Muslims and all evidence of Muslim civilization was eradicated.[19] Militiamen involved in the atrocities wore patches depicting the battle of Kosovo and received medals with the name of Miloš Obilić, the assassin of Sultan Murat.[20] In an Orthodox monastery near Sarajevo, a Serb priest blessed the followers of the ethno-fascist warlord Vojislav Šešelj, after the names of the towns associated with the worst atrocities against Muslims were read aloud in triumph.[21] The chief of police of Banja Luka—the site of massive atrocities against Muslims carried out with the complicity of the Banja Luka police—received a delegation of Greek Church leaders in honor of Saint Michael the Archangel, the "Patron Saint of the Republika Srpska Ministry of Internal Affairs."[22]

When the city of Foča was purged of its Muslim population and all traces of their existence had been dynamited and bulldozed, the name of the city was changed to Srbinje (Serb Place). More generally, the term *Srbinje* has been shouted at Muslims during killings and expulsions throughout Bosnia ("Serb Place!" "Serb Place!"). The renamed Foča was celebrated with visits by high Church officials. A university professor from Sarajevo, Vojislav Maksimović, explained that "the [Serb] fighters from Foča and the region were worthy defenders of Serbianness and of Orthodoxy."[23] In Trebinje, an Orthodox priest led the way in expelling a Muslim family and seizing their home. Trebinje's 500-year-old mosque and elegant Turkish-style buildings were burned and its Muslim population killed and expelled immediately following celebrations of the feast day of St. Sava, the founder of the Serbian Church. Mirko Jović, leader of the White Eagles terror squad, called for a "Christian, Orthodox Serbia with no Muslims and no unbelievers."[24]

While still an abbot, Serbian Orthodox Bishop Atanasije of Herzegovina characterized the Islamic architectural style of homes with interior courtyards enclosed by walls as a sign of Islamic "primitivism" from "Bihać to Baghdad to Belgrade."[25] The official Serbian Orthodox Church journal promoted the

writings and the cult of personality of militia leader Vuk Drašković, a major instigator of anti-Muslim atrocities; another Serb
Church publication condemned those who would not join the
armed struggle against the "evil forces that are opposed to God
(and by the same token to humanity)."[26] The sustained attacks
on Muslims by Serb Orthodox clergy were based on global stereotypes of Muslims as a people; the complex and variegated nature of Bosnian Islam was ignored. Metropolitan Christopher, a
Serb Church leader in the United States, gave a list of stereotypes about Muslims, implying they were all like the radical followers of Iran's Ayatollah Khomeini. When someone asked him
whether Muslims in Bosnia were Sunnites or Shiites, he said:
"I don't know very much about Muslims in Bosnia, but they
are Muslims."[27] Vasilije, Bishop of the Zvornik–Tuzla area, offered up the bizarre notion that for Muslims in Bosnia, the
more unbelievers they kill, the closer they get to heaven.[28] Religious stereotypes met psychological stereotypes; Jovan Rašković,
a mentor to Radovan Karadžić, claimed that Muslim ablutions
before prayer showed the "anal-analytic" nature of Muslims as a
people.[29]

A worldwide Serb Orthodox campaign was mounted to fi-
nance a massive new cathedral in Belgrade. Serb Orthodox
Church officials promoted the project with constant references
to the fact that this church was to be constructed on the very
spot on which Ottoman Turks had burned the bones of St. Sava,
the founder of the Serbian Church.[30] Serbian religious leaders
lauded those Serbian officials responsible for designing and im-
plementing the policy of "ethnic cleansing." On Orthodox Easter
1993, Metropolitan Nikolaj, the highest-ranking Serb Orthodox
Church official in Bosnia, stood between Radovan Karadžić and

General Ratko Mladić and spoke of the Bosnian Serbs under their leadership as "following the hard road of Christ." Karadžić suggested the problem in Bosnia could be solved if Muslims would just convert to Serb Orthodoxy.[31]

What Serb dissidents have called the clericalist faction of Serb militants is clearly dramatized in the figure of Arkan, who is both a friend and ally of Karadžić and a protégé of Serb President Slobodan Milošević. After the Russian neo-Nazi Vladimir Zhirinovsky had embraced the highest-ranking living Nazi SS officer in Austria, he was given an adoring welcome in Arkan's stronghold of Bijeljina in eastern Bosnia. Arkan led Zhirinovsky on a tour, showing him the parking lot where a mosque once stood.[32]

Serb priests waved incense and offered blessings over a boxing match at a casino owned by Arkan. Serb clergy presided over Arkan's 1995 marriage, staged in public with great fanfare, to a Serb popular music star by the name of Ceca. For the ceremony, attended by Christian Orthodox bishops from Serb-controlled Bosnia and Croatia, Arkan wore an old Montenegrin warrior costume festooned with a huge cross, as his supporters waved paper flags with an Orthodox cross and nationalist slogans. Ceca was dressed as "The Maid of Kosovo" (*Kosovka djevojka*), the Mary Magdalene figure who nurses the Kosovo martyrs as they lie dying on the battlefield. Of the atrocities in Bosnia, Arkan said: "We are fighting for our faith, the Serbian Orthodox Church."[33]

Orthodox Christian clergy sit as elected members of the parliament of the Republika Srpska. When General Ratko Mladić, indicted by the International Criminal Tribunal on multiple counts of genocide, came under criticism, the Serb clergy rallied to his defense. Yet the Orthodox Church has been slow to minister to the Serbs in Bosnian government areas, where churches are intact but priests are lacking. A Serb priest teaches that Croats and Muslims have a genocide plan against Serbs and that "one who forgives is worse than one who did the bad deed in the first place."[34] Orthodox Bishop Atanasije attacked those who criticized expulsions of Muslim civilians and the burning of mosques in the Herzegovinan town of Trebinje.[35]

In 1994, negotiators for the "Contact Group" (Britain, France, the U.S., Russia, and Germany) suggested a peace plan that would give to the 32 percent of Bosnians who were Serb 49 percent of the land, including the areas on which they had carried out the most systematic "ethnic cleansing"; the Serbian Orthodox Church attacked the peace plan as unfair, to Serbs.[36] Both Metropolitan Nikolaj and Radovan Karadžić demanded that Sarajevo be the capital of the Republika Srpska. Karadžić stated that Sarajevo had "always" been a Serb city; since Slavic Muslims were originally Serbs who had converted to Islam, Serbs were "there" first and Slavic Muslims had no rights to Sarajevo. Nikolaj advanced the same specious argument.[37]

Patriarch Pavle, the leader of the worldwide Serbian Orthodox Church, had a different view. Pavle claimed that Serbs were native to Bosnia-Herzegovina, whereas the Muslims had arrived with the Ottoman invasion. Pavle's confusion of religion and ethnic identity was outdone only by the racial theory of Serb religious nationalist Dragoš Kalajić. Kalajić claimed that Slavic Muslims did not belong to Europe, that their culture was an unconscious expression of "semi-Arabic subculture," and that the Slavic Muslims of Bosnia inherited an inferior "special gene" passed on by the Ottomans from North African Arabs.[38]

In fact, the ancestors of both the Bosnian Serbs and the Bosnian Muslims had lived in the area long before the Ottoman conquest. Sarajevo was established by the Ottomans as a major economic, cultural, and political center. But the mythologized history and racial logic of Karadžić and Nikolaj, and their alternate version promulgated by Patriarch Pavle, are based on claims that Slavic Muslims had no right to land in Bosnia because they lacked ethnoreligious priority. People whose ancestors arrived with the ancestors of their Serb neighbors were relegated to a permanent alienness and denied any claim to existence in the region.

After the revelations of the killing camps, organized rape, and systematic destruction of mosques, the Serbian Orthodox Church led the way in denial. The church's government body, the Holy Episcopal Synod, stated: "In the name of God's truth and on the testimony from our brother bishops from Bosnia-Herzegovina and from other trustworthy witnesses, we declare, taking full moral responsibility, that such camps neither have existed nor exist in the Serbian Republic of Bosnia-Herzegovina." The Synod also wrote a protest against the European indifference to genocide in Bosnia—the alleged genocide against Serbs. The document was composed in May 1992 while the Serb armies were rampaging triumphantly through Bosnia and hundreds of thousands of non-Serbs were being killed and driven from their homes, before the eyes of local Serbian Orthodox priests and bishops.[39]

Some have defended the Serb Church leadership by pointing to its criticism of Serb President Slobodan Milošević. Serb Church criticism of Milošević only began, however, when he retreated from the extreme nationalist position he held up until 1994. Bishop Atanasije of Herzegovina urged Serbs not to "ca-

pitulate to the world as Milošević has. The vultures from the
West will not get our signature [on the peace plan]."[40] While
some Orthodox Christian leaders have offered a general condemnation of nationalism as a "sign of apostasy,"[41] they have
refused to condemn specific crimes committed in the name of
Serb Orthodoxy; others have supported Serb extremists. As the
International Criminal Tribunal conducted an investigation that
would lead to the indictment of Radovan Karadžić on multiple
counts of genocide, the Greek Orthodox Church appointed Karadžić to the 900-year-old "Knights' Order of the First Rank of
Saint Dionysius of Xanthe," declaring him "one of the most
prominent sons of our Lord Jesus Christ working for peace."[42]

Some Orthodox Christians have appealed to the Serbian Orthodox Church to take a strong stand against the violence in
Bosnia.[43] Yet, one of the authors of that appeal defended Patriarch Pavle from his harsher critics by pointing to a letter Pavle
wrote condemning the killings of non-Serbs and burning of
Catholic churches in Banja Luka.[44] In it Pavle laid the responsibility for the Banja Luka atrocities on refugees from western
Slavonia who had fled the Croat army offensive in the spring of
1995. These acts were unjustifiable, he argued, but understand-
able as acts of refugees in a state of "vengeful despondency." In
fact, the killings and destruction of mosques and churches in
Banja Luka were organized by Serb civil and military groups
at the very start of the occupation of Banja Luka in April 1992.
By the time Pavle expressed his condemnation, all the mosques
in the Banja Luka region had been dynamited (a fact he did not
mention), and the religious terror had been denounced by international refugee workers for years. The destruction of Catholic
churches and the attacks on some Croats may have been carried

sloga Srbina spašava). The meaning of *sloga* (unity, harmony) was
key to interpreting the slogan. As Milošević began to speak of
the necessity for battles—"not armed battles yet, though it may
come to that"—the unity was being defined as the unity of Serb
against Albanian, and by extension, against all others.[46] It was
natural for a former communist official, raised in the personality
cult surrounding Marshal Tito, to move easily into another kind
of personality cult. As the communist party crumbled, Milošević
had adroitly transformed himself into an ethnoreligious nationalist. At the 600th anniversary of Lazar's death the crowd
chanted "Kosovo is Serb." Other rallies included slogans such as:
"We love you, Slobodan, because you hate the Muslims."[47] During the same period that Milošević stood at Kosovo in front of
the CCCC symbol, that same symbol and other symbols of Serbian religious nationalism such as the Kosovo maiden and the
double-headed eagle were reappearing in Serbian communities
around the world.[48]

Milošević's abandonment of the goal of Greater Serbia in the
negotiations leading up to the Dayton accords of 1995 as well as
the attacks of his wife (Mirjana Marković) upon the clericalist
movement within Serb nationalism suggest that Milošević has
no deep ethnoreligious convictions. Yet, to say that Milošević's
aggression was not motivated by personal religious concerns is
not to say that the forces he unleashed were not deeply, even
fanatically, religious. Many Serb and Croat religious nationalists are not religious in the sense of observing regular religious
practice.

It is important to distinguish between an observant religious
behavior and what is popularly called fundamentalism. The term

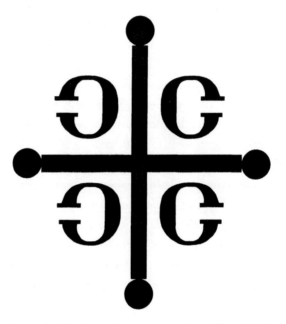

Fig. 4. Symbol of Serbian religious nationalism: The CCCC cross.

"fundamentalism" has been criticized as a cross-cultural category on the grounds that it is rooted in a particular religiosity that has little to do with many of the movements in the world today given that name.[49] Popular usage frequently creates new meanings, and in replying to accusations that Bosnian Muslims were a fundamentalist threat, it is necessary to define the popular meaning. In popular usage, fundamentalism indicates a person's absolute conviction that he knows the truth or at least the way to the truth, an inability to engage in self-criticism, a violent intolerance of those who disagree, and a zeal to use the full power of the state to enforce beliefs and practices deemed proper. In some cases religious fundamentalism is at odds with nationalism and attempts to abolish national states. In other cases, as with Serb and Croat Christoslavism, the fundamentalism and nationalism reinforce one another and merge. In this popular sense, the clericalist wings of both Croat and Serb nationalism are fundamentalist, while personalities like Milošević merely exploit fundamentalism for their own political gain.

Scholars are now studying fundamentalism or religious nationalism as a cross-cultural phenomenon, its distinctive features, and its relationship to modernity and traditionalism.[50] Christoslavic religious nationalism will certainly need to be examined for its similarity and difference from the other contemporary manifestations of religious militancy throughout the world. The goal here is simply to demonstrate what has so repeatedly been denied concerning the genocide in Bosnia: that it was religiously motivated and religiously justified.[51] Religious symbols, mythologies, myths of origin (pure Serb race), symbols of passion (Lazar's death), and eschatological longings (the resurrection of Lazar) were used by religious nationalists to create a reduplicating Miloš Obilić, avenging himself on the Christ killer, the race traitor, the alien, and, ironically, the falsely accused "fundamentalist" next door. The ideology operated not only in speeches and manifestos, but in specific rituals of atrocity. Survivors of concentration camps report that during torture sessions or when they begged for water, they were made to sing Serbian religious nationalist songs, reworded to reflect the contemporary conflict. One of the songs concerned Bosnian President Alija Izetbegović:

> Oh Alija, oh Alija
> If we go to battle
> It's you I'll kill,
> You I'll slaughter,
> Just like Miloš once
> Got rid of Murat. . . .
>
> See the Turk at her Mosque bowing,
> Her love to Serbs only swearing.[52]

The religious ideology of the violence was complex. It was at once part of a modern surge in religious militancy after the cold war, a reappearance of a Serbian nineteenth-century ideology that constructs an "age-old antagonism" between Muslim and Christian in which the Muslim is a race traitor, and a new manifestation in a history of assaults on non-Christian populations in Europe grounded in manipulation of the Christ-killer charge.[53]

Whether such an ideology reflects the Serb Orthodox faith or is instead a perversion of it, is a question that Serb tradition will answer. Serb religion, history, literature, art, and culture have been used to justify a crime the true proportions of which the world has yet to grasp. In a retrieved Serbian Orthodox tradition, the real traitor of Kosovo would not be the non-Christian next door but rather those who used Kosovo and all of Serbian heritage to incite crimes against humanity. In such a retrieval, Serbia might revalidate the more humane aspects of the Lazar tradition, those that present the sorrow of Kosovo not as the property of Serb militancy but as Serbia's distinctive contribution to a shared human understanding.[54]

Christian scholars have been addressing the problem of the Christ-killer theme in the New Testament in light of the Holocaust and its implications for Christian anti-Semitism. The use of a Christ-killer motif in the Bosnian context poses a theological challenge not only to the Serb Orthodox tradition. The silence of self-identified Christian leaders in many parts of the world in the face of the Bosnian genocide makes it clear that the issue demands attention by the wider Christian community as well. If many Serbs have either supported or remained silent in the face of religiously motivated genocide, the same can be said for most nations.

Certainly no one writing from the United States, founded on territory "cleansed" (with religious sanction) of its native inhabitants and built with the labor of another people seized as slaves from their ancestral homeland, could possibly claim a shred of moral superiority. Nor could anyone watching the Christian Identity movement's instigation of racial and religious warfare find any cause for comfort.

To acknowledge the responsibility for genocide within our own traditions is not to abandon the right and the duty to resist new forms of genocide. Indeed, that resistance can be authentic only to the extent that it is rooted in the willingness to confront our own demons. Such resistance is doubly imperative because of the complicity of Western and Christian powers, through the UN Security Council and NATO, in the destruction of Bosnia, a complicity that will be examined in the final chapters of this book.

No account of the fate of Bosnia can be complete without an examination of the role of Croatian Christoslavism in supporting the destruction of the Bosnian people. While the religious element in Croatian nationalism has been more subtle than Serbian religious nationalism, it has been no less effective. It is symbolized in the 1993 destruction of the Old Bridge at Mostar.

CHAPTER FIVE

THE VIRGIN AND THE JEWEL OF HERZEGOVINA

BRIDGE KEEPER

"It is not enough to cleanse Mostar of the Muslims," said a Croat militiaman as his unit worked to destroy the bridge; "the relics must also be destroyed."[1] On November 9, 1993, in a final barrage, the sixteenth-century bridge, which had withstood months of shelling, collapsed into the Neretva River.

Mostar takes its name from its magnificent old bridge. Under Ottoman patronage, Mostar became a major cultural and economic center in the sixteenth century. The Ottomans built bridges, inns, marketplaces, and mosques. By 1987 the old city had been reconstructed and Mostar was an important tourist site. The city was filled with architectural masterworks like the sixteenth-century Karadjoz Beg Mosque.[2] Its skyline was dominated by an Orthodox church, a Catholic bell tower, and a Muslim minaret, testimony to centuries of living among three religious groups.[3]

At the center of Mostar was the "old bridge" (*stari most*), its high-arched, dizzying vault gracefully linking the two sides of the city. The bridge, which dated from 1561, had been designed by Hayruddin, a pupil of the great Ottoman architect Sinan. The construction project was multireligious with engineers and artisans from around the region. The bridge had survived four centuries and thirty earthquakes.

Mostar is the capital of Herzegovina, a term that means "dukedom." Herzegovina occupies the southwest section of Bosnia-Herzegovina, and for some periods in medieval times it had a separate administrative identity from Bosnia proper. The geography, dialect, customs, and cultural personality of the area are distinctive. Particularly striking are the white-bouldered mountains, craggy gorges, pre-Ottoman tombs, and Ottoman fortresses. Other towns in Herzegovina include Stolac and Trebinje (the once-classic city plundered and burned by Serb nationalists in 1992). Of special interest is Počitelj, with its centuries-old mosques, minarets, and Ottoman-style homes perched along a steep hillside like a Herzegovinian Positano or Amalfi.

EUROPEANIZING THE BOSNIANS

Croatian President Franjo Tudjman had fought in World War II with Tito's Partisans. By the time of Croatia's independence in 1991, he had changed from a communist into a religious nationalist. In his 1990 book *Wastelands of Historical Reality*, Tudjman revealed an anti-Semitic tendency. He suggested that Jews are genocidal by nature and that Jews were the major executioners in the Ustashe death camp of Jasenovac where an estimated

300,000 Serbs, Jews, and Gypsies were killed.[4] Earlier Tudjman had claimed that as few as 60,000 people died in all the camps in Croatia during World War II, a number far below the estimates by serious scholars of the Holocaust.[5] The problems of the Jews are of their own making, Tudjman implies; Jews could have avoided them had they heeded what he calls, vaguely, "the traffic signs."

A clue to what Tudjman means by "traffic signs" can be found in his views on Muslims. In 1991, Tudjman stunned U.S. Ambassador to Yugoslavia Warren Zimmerman with his ignorance of and contempt for Bosnian Muslims and with his plan to carve up Bosnia between a "Greater Croatia" and a "Greater Serbia."[6] Tudjman wanted Croatia to be considered part of Europe. He wanted to eradicate what he sees as contamination by the "Orient" (Turkish and Islamic cultures). In September 1995, after his forces had destroyed much of the interreligious culture of Bosnia-Herzegovina, Tudjman asserted that "Croatia accepts the task of Europeanization of Bosnian Muslims." The task, Tudjman claimed, was undertaken at the behest of the Western European powers.[7]

It is now well documented that at a meeting with Serbian President Slobodan Milošević in the town of Karadjordjevo, Tudjman and Milošević decided on a plan to partition Bosnia between Croatia and Serbia and to neutralize any political or social aspirations of Bosnia's Muslim community.[8] Tudjman began his "Europeanization" with the establishment of the Croatian Defense Council (Hrvatsko Vijeće Obrane, or HVO), as the military arm in Bosnia for his political party, the Croatian Democratic Union (Hrvatska Demokratska Zajednica, or HDZ).

The HVO was formed outside of the Bosnian army, on the pretext that it would fight to repel aggression by the Serb army. The underarmed Bosnians had no choice but to accept the arrangement.

The alliance between the HVO and the Bosnian government succeeded in the spring of 1992 in repelling the Serb army's assault on the city of Mostar. In July 1992, however, Croat nationalists declared their own "Union of Herceg-Bosna," a Croat state in Bosnia based upon the same ideals of ethnoreligious purity espoused by the Republika Srpska, only in the name of Catholicism rather than Serb Orthodoxy. Tudjman helped overthrow the moderate Bosnian Croat leader, Stjepan Kljuić, who had been elected Bosnian representative of the HDZ. Kljuić was replaced with nationalist warlord Mate Boban.

In May 1992, Boban had met with Radovan Karadžić in Graz, Austria, to draw up plans for dividing Bosnia between Croat and Serb nationalists. By October 1992, Boban had given up all pretense of alliance with the Bosnian government and ceased all hostilities with the Serb radicals of Radovan Karadžić. In late October 1992, Croat religious nationalists took over much of the town of Novi Travnik. They attacked the town of Prozor, killing, raping, attacking the mosque, and burning Muslim property, in imitation of Serb nationalist actions in eastern Bosnia. Spokesmen for Boban's government of Herceg-Bosna and for Tudjman's government in Croatia claimed that Muslims had attacked Croats and that some Muslim property had been damaged in the fighting. What reporters saw in Prozor contradicted this story: burned-out Muslim homes and businesses sat ruined next to intact Croat structures. When asked why only the

Muslim properties were damaged, a Croat militiaman grinned and said: "The Muslims burned their own homes down with candles."[9] Before Serb nationalist attacks on Muslim populations, Serb inhabitants were told to evacuate; similarly, Croats in Prozor were ordered to leave before the killing began.

For the next eighteen months, Croat and Serb religious nationalists collaborated in "Europeanizing" Bosnia. As the HVO attacked from the west, the Serb army moved in on the last remaining Muslim enclaves in eastern Bosnia: Goražde, Žepa, Cerska, and Srebrenica. Since spring 1992, these towns had held out against the Serb army and had taken in tens of thousands of refugees driven from the surrounding areas. Day by day, mosques were dynamited by the advancing Croat and Serb militias. Tudjman's "Europeanization" was a euphemism, like "ethnic cleansing," for the annihilation of Slavic Muslim people and culture and the creation of pure Christian states on the rubble of the once multireligious Bosnia.

It is too late for the Muslims of Stolac to "heed the traffic signs." Stolac was a magnificent small town, built along a rushing river beneath rugged hills with ancient Ottoman fortifications and ancient pre-Ottoman Bosnian tombstones known as *stećaks*. It was also known for its exquisite, small-scale, seventeenth-century mosques. Stolac was occupied in 1992 by the Serb army; when Serb forces were driven out, they began shelling the town from nearby mountains. Then the HVO, wearing the masks favored by Serb militias during such operations, turned on the people it had helped save from the Serb army only months before. Here is an account from the UN High Commission for Refugees: "On 23 August 1993, four mosques in Stolac were blown up. That night, witnesses said, military trucks carrying [Croatian] soldiers firing their weapons in the air went through the town terrorizing and rounding up all Muslim women, children, and elderly. The cries and screams of women and children could be heard throughout the town as the soldiers looted and destroyed Muslim homes. The soldiers, who wore handkerchiefs, stockings or paint to hide their faces, took the civilians to Blagaj, an area of heavy fighting northwest of Stolac." [10]

THE MADONNA

The Madonna was said to have appeared to six Catholic children, four girls and two boys, at the small village of Medjugorje in Herzegovina on June 24–25, 1981. This village subsequently became one of the world's more popular pilgrimage sites. Millions have made their way to Medjugorje, which means "between the hills." Pilgrims would see the shimmering light, the strange phenomenon around the sun, an intense feeling of both attraction and fear of looking, but only a select group of young visionaries were able to hear the Virgin Mary speak and transmit her message to the rest of the world. Most of the messages were general messages on the need for world peace.

At the time the Virgin was appearing in Medjugorje, the Bishop of Mostar, Monsignor Pavao Žanić, had been attempting to wrest control of some parishes from some local friars of the Franciscan order. Among the first champions of the authenticity of the Virgin's appearances were local Franciscans. When the Virgin was asked by one of her interlocutors about the case of two Franciscans who had been punished by the bishop, she replied that the bishop had made a mistake. The bishop worked tirelessly to have the visions condemned as a fraud.[11]

Various interpretations have been given for the visions, which were declared to be authentic by influential Catholics, including the theologian Hans von Balthasar. Those who interpret the visions psychologically suggest that the vision of the Madonna calling for peace is a return of repressed memories. Herzegovina was the scene of some of the worst atrocities of World War II, with gruesome killings by Catholic Ustashe of Serbs in the very locale of Medjugorje itself. During World War II, the Bishop of Mostar wrote to Archbishop Stepinac of Zagreb, the highest ranking cleric of the Catholic Church in Croatia, describing the slaughter of Serb men, women, and children by the Ustashe, who threw hundreds of women and children over a cliff to their deaths.[12] After the war, Serbs and Croats went back to living side by side; discussion of the atrocities of World War II was forbidden in the Tito era.

Herzegovina is dominated by Croat religious nationalists, who are divided into two political factions. The HVO worked to partition Bosnia with Serbia, destroy Bosnian Muslims, and integrate most of the Croats of Bosnia into a larger Croatian nation. The other faction, the HOS (Croatian Armed Forces), worked to drive Serbs out of Bosnia-Herzegovina and integrate Bosnia into a "Greater Croatia" modeled on the World War II fascist state. Its motto was the Ustashe slogan "ready for the homeland" (*Za dom, spremni*). With the backing of Tudjman's government and the regular Croatian army, the HVO took over Herzegovina and absorbed the HOS.[13] It was out of these elements that Croatian President Franjo Tudjman forged the knife he was to plunge into the back of Croats, Muslims, and Serbs who desired a multireligious Bosnia.

THE CONVOY OF JOY

At the London Conference of 1992, the Western powers condemned ethnoreligious terror, pledged to support Bosnia's territorial integrity, and rejected the use of force to change boundaries. The conference appointed two negotiators to work for peace in Bosnia: Cyrus Vance was to represent the United Nations and David Lord Owen the European Community. The Vance-Owen plan divided Bosnia-Herzegovina into ten cantons with a dominant ethnic group in nine of the cantons. The area designated for Croat control was very generous. The Herceg-Bosna regime used the Vance-Owen map to justify an attack on Muslim communities; where the map said "Croat control," they seized control by disarming Bosnian Muslims and destroying their communities.[14]

While Croats and Bosnians had agreed to the Vance-Owen plan, the Republika Srpska leaders stalled as their army seized more territory. Then in May 1993, they rejected the plan. Owen and Thorwald Stoltenberg, Vance's successor as UN negotiator, then came up with a map that in Owen's phrase, recognized "reality on the ground" and was based on a map drawn by Croatian President Tudjman and Serbian President Milošević. The plan gave Serb nationalists control of almost all the territories they occupied, including the former Muslim-majority cultural centers.[15] The proposed territorial division based upon reality on the ground became a signal that ethnoreligious expulsions would be rewarded by the international peace negotiators. When the

HVO saw that the Serb army would be rewarded for its atrocities, it began copying them, turning its original aggression at places like Prozor into a systematic campaign modeled on the Republika Srpska aggression against the Bosnian Muslims.[16] Bosnia was under enormous pressure to capitulate and accept a plan that would put Bosnian Muslims into religious ghettoes. The pressure was increased when a Muslim businessman, Fikret Abdić, supported by both Croatian and Serbian nationalists, declared his own statelet in the Bihać area, fragmenting further what was left of Bosnia.

By the summer of 1993, Bosnia was on the edge of annihilation. After the HVO attacked Muslims in the ancient Muslim-majority city of Travnik, the underarmed Bosnian army fought back; as the HVO retreated, many Croats fled Travnik to HVO-controlled territory. In many cases it was the HVO that forced Croats to leave areas controlled by the Bosnian army, although there were also cases in which Muslim militias forced Croats to leave.[17] The Bosnians were opposed to religious expulsions as a matter of policy; indeed, Bosnia was constitutionally defined as a multireligious nation. Yet the Owen-Stoltenberg rules of reality on the ground rewarded religious expulsions with territorial concessions and, in effect, punished any party that refused to engage in them.

As Bosnians struggled to survive, the only ones to come to their defense were a few contingents of *Mujahidin*, veterans of conflicts in Afghanistan and elsewhere in the Middle East. The volunteers came both to help save a Muslim population from extermination and to lead them back to what they believed was a more proper version of Islam. Even though most Bosnians resisted such missionary work, the militant and intolerant behavior of the *Mujahidin* became a propaganda bonanza for Serb and Croat nationalists and their European and North American supporters who had claimed that Bosnian Muslims were fundamentalists. By contrast, the many Greek and Russian volunteers fighting for the Republika Srpska aroused little attention in the West.[18]

In April 1993, in the Lašva Valley of Bosnia, the HVO launched a wave of terror. Entire families were burned alive in their homes. In the southern Herzegovinian town of Čapljina, Muslim civilians were raped and confined in concentration camps. The HVO openly collaborated with the Serb army in an assault on the town of Žepče.[19]

The "Convoy of Joy" has become the abiding symbol for the betrayal of Bosnia. In June 1993, the HVO and the Croatian army authorized a humanitarian convoy to pass through Croat military lines to relieve the city of Tuzla, in Bosnian government territory. Once the convoy had passed into HVO-controlled territory, the HVO attacked it. HVO militiamen shot the Muslim drivers or pulled them out of the trucks and slit their throats. The HVO invited local villagers to loot the trucks. For several days the convoy was attacked and pillaged as British UN peacekeepers, who were on the spot, observed but refused to intervene. Only when the peacekeepers themselves were attacked did they fire on the HVO.

Bosnian Muslims were caught in the middle of a family quarrel between Croat and Serb Christian nationalists. However violent that quarrel was between the two parts of the family, the violence was greater when displaced upon those considered to be alien. It is always dangerous for a third party to come near to an intrafamily dispute. The violence can easily be turned toward the alien; once the alien is dispensed with, the family can resume its dispute. The Serb-Croat dispute was bitter. Even so, for some Croats the Serbs were still fellow Christians, while Muslims are all Turks.

In 1993, Christoslavic hatred of Muslims was being stoked by Croatian President Franjo Tudjman and his anti-Muslim Minister of Defense Gojko Šušak. As the government-dominated news media in Croatia hammered home stereotypes about Muslims, some parts of Croatian society turned hostile. One Croatian writer recalled a cold reaction by friends in Zagreb when she declined to wear the jewelry crosses that had come into fashion; she was accused of subversive attitudes.[20] Many Muslim refugees were told they were no longer allowed to study or work in Croatia. In some cases, Muslims who did not eat pork or drink alcohol were called Turks and disowned by their own Catholic relatives.[21] Tudjman himself reviled Bosnian President Alija Izetbegović for not drinking alcohol. A 1992 article in the popular Catholic magazine *Veritas* rejoiced that the cross of Christ stood next to the Croatian flag, a Croatian bishop next to the Croatian minister of state, and "guardsmen wore rosaries around their necks."[22]

After finishing with Stolac in August 1993, the HVO turned to Počitelj. On August 23, Počitelj's sixteenth-century masterworks of Islamic art and architecture were dynamited and its Muslim population driven off to detention camps.[23] To mark the expulsion of the Muslims and destruction of the Islamic monuments, a huge cross was erected on the roadside next to the town.[24] Just as Serb religious nationalists first expelled the Muslims from Foča and Zvornik, then dynamited all the mosques, and then declared there never had been any mosques in the

Fig. 5.   Počitelj old town: Islamic monuments constructed in 1563 and destroyed by Croatian religious nationalists in 1993. From Husref Redžić, *Studije o Islamskoj arhitektonskoj baštini* (Sarajevo: Veselin Masleša, 1983).

towns, so the Herceg-Bosna authorities are now attempting to rewrite the history of Počitelj. In spring 1996, a conference was organized in nearby Čapljina on the "Historical Development of Croat Počitelj." There are reports that a Catholic church will be built on the ruins of the destroyed mosque.[25]

In the same month, images of skeletal prisoners at the HVO

concentration camp at Dretelj reminded the world of earlier images from the Serb nationalist camp of Omarska. The prisoners at Dretelj had been starved, forced to drink their own urine, and tortured sexually. As at Omarska, local criminals were invited in to kill Muslim captives.[26]

After watching the HVO and Croatian army attack Bosnian Muslims for more than a year and a half, the Western powers tired of the spectacle. Western diplomats threatened Croatia with a withdrawal of support and on March 18, 1994, the Clinton administration brokered an agreement between Bosnia and Croatia. The Croatian government ceased hostilities and agreed to a federation between Bosnian Croats and the Bosnian government, and a confederation between Croatia proper and the new federation of Bosnia-Herzegovina.[27]

THE MADONNA AND THE
CONCENTRATION CAMPS

In Croatia and central Bosnia, Catholic church leaders, particularly Cardinal Kuharić of Zagreb, Archbishop Puljić of Sarajevo, and Father Petar Andjelković OFM, the superior of the Franciscan Province of Bosnia, have specifically and courageously condemned the crimes of Croat religious nationalists. In Herzegovina, however, the Catholic clergy played a different, more troubling role.

The view of Slavic Muslims put forth by some Herzegovinian clergy differs little from nationalist Serb views. A local Herzegovinian priest offers a pilgrim to Medjugorje a portrait of Herzegovina under the Ottomans that differs little from the history of Ottoman occupation given by the Serb clergy: lurid tales of torture without acknowledgment of the long history and complexity of the relationship between the Franciscans and the Ottomans.[28] When European mediators attempted to reconcile the Catholic and Muslim population of Mostar, they were opposed by elements within the local Catholic clergy such as Tomislav Pervan, the provincial superior of 250 Franciscan friars in the Mostar region, who repeated the Tudjman propaganda that the Bosnian Muslims wanted an Islamic state. Friar Pervan went on to say that "Islamic states don't have free speech, democracy, or freedom of religion," ignoring the irony of such a statement made in the wake of the brutal persecution of Bosnian Muslims by Serb and Croat religious nationalists, in the name of Christian states.[29] In the Herzegovinian town of Bobani, a Franciscan priest, the Rev. Vinko Mikolić, compared the Bosnian government to the "Turkish occupiers." In the same town, the Catholic church features a large mural behind the altar showing the suffering of the Croat people, with portraits of a World War II Ustashe militiaman, Ranko Boban, hanging nearby. Portraits of the leader of Ustashe Croatia, Ante Pavelić, one of the most ruthless war criminals of the Nazi empire, are displayed in the homes of local Catholic priests.[30]

Not only Serb religious nationalists but Croat nationalists as well subscribed to the view of novelist Ivo Andrić that only weak and cowardly Slavs converted to Islam. Andrić drew on both the nineteenth-century Christoslavism of Serbian Orthodox Bishop Petar II (Njegoš), as well as an older tradition of Croat Christoslavism. In his dissertation, immediately after citing—as "the people's" judgment—Njegoš's caricature of Slavic Muslims as greedy and cowardly, Andrić cited Franciscan Friar Franjo Jukić as an exponent of the "spirit" of popular Christian perception:

"They [Bosnian Muslims] sprang from bad Christians who turned Muslim because only thus could they protect their land."[31]

As the visions at Medjugorje gained wider recognition, they were "nationalized" by Croat politicians. For example, the independence of Croatia was announced on June 25, 1991—the tenth anniversary of the apparitions. The Franciscans at Medjugorje favored an association between the Virgin and the independent Croat state and were proud of it.[32] Franciscans are especially prominent in Grude, the city in which the Christoslavic state of Herceg-Bosna was proclaimed. In 1993, as the HVO was turning Herzegovina into flames, a journalist reported that: "In the souvenir shops [of Medjugorje], statuettes of the Madonna were on sale with swastikas, Maltese Crosses and other Nazi regalia." The city had also become a major center for the warlords and gangsters known as the Herzegovinian mafia, who terrorized Muslims, Serbs, and any Croat who stood in their way. When the visions of the Virgin first occurred at Medjugorje, local Muslims (who also revere the mother of Jesus) came to visit the site. The religious nationalization of Medjugorje was complete when the HVO proclaimed that "anyone found sheltering Muslims in the Holy City would have their homes blown up."[33]

The continuing atrocities by the HVO were opposed by Cardinal Kuharić of Zagreb, who appealed to the Herceg-Bosna warlord Mate Boban to seek peaceful coexistence with the Muslims and warned (accurately) that those responsible for the violence could be charged in the future with war crimes. Boban responded to the cardinal's letter: "This is not a time of coexistence [with Muslims]. It is time for something else."[34] Despite his own earlier Croat nationalist statements dismissing the Ustashe atrocities of World War II and glorifying Croatia's thirteen-hundred-year Catholic history, by the summer of 1993 Kuharić was resisting religious nationalism of Boban and his hard-line Franciscan backers in Herzegovina, as well as the circle around Tudjman and Šušak.[35] On September 13, 1993, a new Catholic Bishop of Mostar was appointed, to whose installation ceremony at Neum (the only Bosnian town on the Adriatic Sea) Muslim clerics were invited and which they attended.[36]

The papal response is difficult to evaluate. Pope John Paul II called a conference at Assisi in January 1993 dedicated to seeking peace in the former Yugoslavia. In contrast to the statements, of the Serb Orthodox leaders, the Assisi conference participants did not single out for attention members of their own flock (in this case Catholics), but spoke with equal fervor of the suffering of all peoples in the region.[37] Even so, the Pope never publicly denounced the role of Herzegovinian clergy in supporting the violent religious nationalism of the Herceg-Bosna militias. Nor did the Pope, who has been forceful in his visits to Latin America in reshaping the hierarchy according to his own views, exert an effective force on the Mostar clergy or visit Mostar, a few minutes' flight from Rome, to demand an end to the persecutions.[38] Whether or not they could have been better supported by the Roman Catholic hierarchy, the moderate elements of the Bosnian Croat church and society had been marginalized by the late summer of 1993 and could only try to ameliorate, not stop, the ongoing persecutions.

Meanwhile, the struggle between the Bishop of Mostar and the Herzegovinian Franciscans was intensifying. The religious nationalists supported the Herzegovinian Franciscans and threatened to blow up the Mostar Cathedral. In November 1995, the

Map 4. Herzegovina

CROAT NATIONALIST OFFENSIVE, *1991–1993*

1991

June 25	Independence of Croatia declared on tenth anniversary of Medjugorje visions

1992

April	Bosnia-Herzegovina is recognized by the EC and the U.S. Croatian nationalists form the Croatian Defense Council (HVO)
May	Graz partition plan between Mate Boban and Radovan Karadžić
July	Mate Boban declares the Union of Herceg-Bosna
	Stjepan Kljuić ousted from elected post in the Croatian Democratic Union (HDZ)
October	Radovan Karadžić and HVO cease all hostilities
	Croat nationalist assault on Prozor
	Croat-Muslim fighting in Novi Travnik

1993

January	Vance-Owen plan is announced
April	HVO massacres at Ahmići and across the Lašva Valley
	Franjo Tudjman tours Herceg-Bosna to support the HVO campaign
June	Convoy of Joy
	HVO force near Travnik is rescued by the Serb army
	HVO and Serb army cooperate in besieging the Bosnian town of Maglaj
	HVO reign of terror against Muslims in Čapljina
August	Muslims driven from Stolac
	European mediators pressure Bosnians to accept the Owen-Stoltenberg plan
September	HVO concentration camp at Dretelj
	Bosnian army revenge atrocity at Uzdol

HVO destroys the old town of Počitelj and expels its
Muslims

October   Fikret Abdić declares an "Independent Republic" in the
Bihać region

November   HVO destroys the Mostar bridge on 55th anniversary of
Kristalnacht

Pope sent a special delegate, a papal nuncio, to urge the Franciscans of Čapljina to cede their parish to the bishop's control.
Anti-Muslim extremist Gojko Šušak, the Croatian Defense Minister, visited the meeting in an apparent show of support for the
Franciscans.[39]

On November 13, 1995, two high Croat officials in Herzegovina were indicted by the International Criminal Tribunal for
organizing the slaughter of Muslims in fourteen Muslim villages
in the Lašva Valley. After the indictments, Croatian President
Tudjman announced that rather than arresting indicted war-
criminal General Tihomir Blaškić, he was promoting him. Tudjman made the announcement in Dayton, Ohio, where he had
promised to cooperate with the International Criminal Tribunal
and to detain suspects for trial. The other suspect, Dario Kordić,
had been placed by Tudjman at the head of the HDZ in Herzegovina over more moderate candidates; after the Lašva Valley
atrocities, he was decorated for increasing Croatia's "position
and prestige."[40]

By November 1993, after eighteen months of shelling, first
by the Serb army and then by the HVO, the multireligious heritage of Mostar was reduced to rubble. As a final gesture, Christoslavic forces supported by Franjo Tudjman destroyed the Old

Fig. 6.   The Old Bridge (*Stari most*) in Mostar: symbol of a multi-religious heritage, constructed in 1561 and destroyed by Croatian religious nationalists in 1993. From Husref Redžić, *Studije o Islamskoj arhitektonskoj baštini* (Sarajevo: Veselin Masleša, 1983).

Bridge of Mostar, which had stood since 1561 as a symbol of Bosnia's role in bridging cultures. The destruction fit Tudjman's desire to be accepted by Europe and to cut his Catholic Croat nation off from any association with the "Orient" of Serbs, Muslims, and Jews. Tudjman depends upon the major Western European powers for economic, political, and cultural support. After "Europeanizing" Bosnia, he awaits his reward.

Herzegovinian Catholics call the Madonna of Medjugorje *Gospa* (Lady). Catholic theologians maintain that a true vision will lead to changed and morally responsible behavior on the part of those who experience it.[41] If the Madonna of Medjugorje did insist on peace one wonders why those who heard her message gave such little thought to the Muslims confined to concentration camps at Gabela, Čapljina, Dretelj, Ljubuški, and Rodoč, all within a few miles of Medjugorje. Did those busloads of pilgrims, filled with inner light and joy, hear the screams from the other side of the Medjugorje hills?

DIVING FROM THE BRIDGE

Amir Pašić is a native of Herzegovina. An architect and city planner, he won an international award in 1987 for his work in reconstructing the old city of Mostar. The historic core of the city, which had been in decline, was reconstructed with sensitivity to both historical detail and social viability. Residents of the old city were not priced out of their property. They were encouraged to open businesses and museums that would serve the tourists expected to come to a revived Mostar. The plan worked, and before the war broke out in neighboring Croatia in 1991, Mostar had a strong tourist economy and a vital old town.

When Mostar came under attack, Pašić escaped to Istanbul with detailed plans of the city. He now directs an institute with graduate students from around the world dedicated to rebuilding Mostar yet again, with attention to both historical detail and social vitality. When people start talking about religious and political exclusivity, he just changes the subject back to rebuilding this great city. He has given out invitations printed up for the reopening of the reconstructed city in the year 2004.

One Mostar tradition is the annual bridge dive. Daring young men and women would dive off the high-arched old Ottoman bridge, far down into the Neretva River. In the summer of 1994, in the wake of the siege, when east Mostar had been pummeled into ruin and its inhabitants starved, shelled, and confined to cellars for months, the people came out for the annual event. The spectators got out their swimsuits and sat along the banks of the river. An improvised, temporary bridge was placed over the blasted-out central section of the great bridge, and the divers dove.

CHAPTER SIX

MASKS OF COMPLICITY

ARMING THE AGGRESSOR

For almost two years, since the summer of 1992, the continuing atrocities in Bosnia had been denounced by officials with the UN High Commission for Refugees. Louis Gentile, the UNHCR head of operations in Banja Luka, was prompted to make the following statement: "It should be known, and recorded for all time, that the so-called leaders of the Western world have known for the past year and a half what is happening here. They receive play-by-play reports. They talk of prosecuting war criminals but do nothing to stop the continuing war crimes. May God forgive them, may God forgive us all."[1]

For months Gentile had been reporting on systematic atrocities against non-Serb civilians in Banja Luka. For months his appeals to stop the killings had been ignored by Western leaders. It is common to ask whether the West, the United Nations, or the Christian world failed in Bosnia, or worse, whether the Christian West was complicit in the evil that occurred there. Terms like "the West," however, are abstractions. The work of the UNHCR workers like Louis Gentile, Western news reporters, UN war crimes investigators, and some Western public officials may have prevented genocide from attaining even greater proportions. Despite these efforts, the conditions reported by Gentile were not only allowed to occur but were made possible by particular Western policy makers. Just as the ethnoreligious militants donned masks and face-paint to allow themselves to transform their former colleagues into disposable aliens and themselves into epic champions of their race and religion, so have many in the Western Alliance created their own masks to justify a policy that has allowed what Gentile called "beyond evil" to flourish. At the heart of the complicity was a policy that denied the Bosnians the right to defend themselves, while at the same time refusing to enforce UN resolutions authorizing NATO power to protect them.

A weapon is not a particular tool or device, but a disparity between one tool and another. Against a Goliath with a club, a slingshot is a weapon. Next to a tank, a slingshot is a toy. In 1991, the NATO nations armed the Serb militants, not with arms sales as in the Iran-Iraq war or the Rwanda genocide, but with a UN declaration.

During the cold war, the Yugoslav army, supported and financed by the Western powers, had stockpiled immense stores of weapons in hardened bunkers and had constructed weapons factories throughout Yugoslavia, especially in Bosnia-Herzegovina, in anticipation of a Soviet invasion that never came. In 1991, Serb nationalists seized control of most of those weapons. The advantage of the Serb army in heavy weapons over the Bosnians was estimated at anywhere from 20–1 to 100–1. When the Serb army attacked Sarajevo in the spring of 1992, the Bosnian government was so poorly armed that it was gangs of criminals and black marketeers—the only groups with the weapons and organization needed to set up barricades and capture Serb armaments—that saved parts of the city from the genocidal assault.[2]

On September 25, 1991, British Foreign Minister Douglas Hurd orchestrated passage of UN Security Council Resolution 713, an arms embargo on the former Yugoslavia by the UN Security Council, a resolution that the Milošević regime was seeking. The five permanent members of the Security Council—U.S., Britain, France, Russia, and China—all voted for the resolution. The embargo locked into place a radical arms disparity between the Serb army and Bosnian army; in effect, it armed the Serb militants.[3]

What occurred from April 1992 through October 1995 has been labeled a war and even a civil war. A war, however, is a conflict between armed adversaries. The Serb army took towns and villages that lacked significant military defenses. Where there was any Bosnian defense at all, Serb militants used heavy artillery to shell the defenders into submission. Once the town or village was taken, the killings of civilians would begin.

This was not war but organized destruction of a largely unarmed population. With weapons and weapons factories under their control and with the arms embargo in place and stubbornly maintained for years, Serb militants were able to carry out their program with impunity.

ORIENTALISM

In 1970, Yugoslavia was experiencing a form of *glasnost;* writers took up previously taboo subjects such as religion. A Sarajevo lawyer named Alija Izetbegović imposed a document entitled "The Islamic Declaration." The document, an anticommunist assertion of religious rights, spelled out the conditions for a just Islamic society and contained several provocative statements concerning the incompatibility of Islam with other systems. The principles of an Islamic state were discussed in an abstract manner, without specifying any particular nation. A few years later, Izetbegović wrote a more extensive work, *Islam between East and West,* which suggested two models—Islam and European liberal democracy—as antidotes to the problems besetting Europe at the time.[4]

When Izetbegović became president of Bosnia in 1990, many Bosnians had never read his Islamic Declaration. But Serb militants not only read it, they published a Belgrade edition of it and used it to claim that Bosnian Muslims were radical fundamentalists or "Islamists," that is, Muslims who desired a state based on Islamic religious law (*sharia*).

The charge that Bosnians were Islamists was combined with the charge that they were plotting to re-create the Ottoman rule over Bosnia. Serb radicals claimed that Bosnians wished for a state based on the leadership of religious scholars and a new Ottoman sultanate based upon imperial rule. Bosnian Muslims were accused of plotting to steal Serb women for their harems (Bosnian Muslims do not take more than one wife) and of drawing up lists of viziers (ministers in the Ottoman Sultanate) to rule the country.[5] Croatian Defense Minister Gojko Šušak claimed that 110,000 Bosnians were in Egypt studying to become fundamentalists.[6]

The representation of the Muslim as an alien "other" has been called Orientalism. During the Christian Middle Ages, Muslims were viewed as perverted heretics and frequently associated with Jews and persecuted with them. During the period of European colonialism, Western scholars, artists, and other intellectuals reflected the ideology of the age: the need for Western colonial rule to "civilize" barbaric Oriental lands. Orientalism abounds in contradictions. Muslims were portrayed as mysterious, sensuous, and sexually obsessed (the harem fantasy in Western writing). At the same time they were portrayed as sexually repressed, authoritarian, rote-learners, and lacking in all creativity and imagination.[7]

Religious nationalists in Croatia and Serbia used such Orientalist stereotypes both for home consumption and for the audience in the wider Christian world. Those who spread hate are seldom concerned about logical consistency, and stereotypes are not fashioned to appeal to reason but rather to semirepressed fears and hatreds. The contradictions of Orientalism appeared in a vicious and dehumanizing new form. Now Serb Orientalists had come up with the Islamist vizier, without the slightest embarrassment over the fact that modern Islamist ideologues believe in a state run by religious scholars and despise as corrupt and anti-Islamic the former imperial Ottoman structure with its sultans and viziers which collapsed in World War I. Similarly, the language of hate lacks even a basic concern with plausibility. Thus Šušak claimed that 110,000 Bosnian Muslims were studying fundamentalism in Egypt—a number that would represent 5 percent of the *entire* Bosnian Muslim population.

Religious nationalists in Serbia then charged a plot between Libya and Bosnian Muslims. During the 1970s Yugoslavia and Libya had been partners in the nonaligned block of nations that refused allegiance to either the Western Alliance or the Soviet Bloc. Through cultural, educational, and economic interchanges, many Yugoslavs of all ethnic and religious backgrounds worked or studied in Libya, including Bosnians such as Haris Silajdžić, who went on to become Prime Minister of Bosnia.

According to the religious nationalists, Silajdžić and other Bosnians who had visited Libya were trying to set up a fundamentalist *Jamahariyya* ("People's State," a word used by Libya's Qaddafi to describe his regime) without noting the difference between Qaddafi's Arab nationalism (based on the socialist ideas of Jamal Abdul Nasser of Egypt) and modern Islamist militants (who oppose Qaddafi and whom Qaddafi suppresses).

According to Tanjug, the news service controlled by Slobodan Milošević, one of the most enthusiastic supporters of Milošević's Yugoslavia has been none other than Muammar Qaddafi, President of Libya. By December 3, 1994, Tanjug was reporting on the visits to Libya of high-level Serbian officials. Praise for close cooperation between the two states, both of them outcasts from the international community, resounded through Tanjug reports.[8] The same Serb nationalists who attacked Bosnian Muslims for alleged involvement with Libyans were posting Tanjug's effusive reports on Serbo-Libyan cooperation.[9]

In 1994, Bosnian Minister of Culture Enes Karić defended a Muslim cleric who had discouraged mixed marriages and criticized the playing of enemy (i.e., Serb) music. His provocative statements were denounced by a wide range of government and extragovernment leaders, including Haris Silajdžić, the Prime

Minister. Yet Karić's statements were enough to set off announcements by Western observers that multireligious Bosnia was now dead and that Bosnia should therefore be partitioned along ethnoreligious lines.[10]

Particularly galling to many Bosnians is the phrase, popular among diplomats and newscasters, "Muslim-dominated government of Bosnia-Herzegovina." The Bosnian executive branch of government is made up of two Catholic Christians, two Serb Orthodox Christians, and three Muslims; the Bosnian parliament and diplomatic corps contain Muslims, Jews, Serbs, Croats, and atheists. It is true that Muslims are in the majority in Bosnia and that, as large numbers of Croats and Serbs choose or are compelled by their own nationalist leaders to live under all-Croat and all-Serb governments in Herceg-Bosna and the Republika Srpska, the percentage of Muslims has increased. Yet Bosnians ask why there are not references to the "Protestant-dominated government of the United States" or the "Anglican-dominated government of Britain."

Behind much of the official, governmental propaganda were academics. University of Belgrade Professor Miroljub Jevtić, for example, wrote of the imminent threat to Europe posed by Muslims and also wrote of Balkan Muslims as having the blood of the martyrs of Kosovo on their hands—an almost direct copy of the blood-libel, that European Jews had the blood of Christ on their hands, used to persecute Jews from the time of the First Crusade in 1096.[11] Dr. Aleksandar Popović wrote of Islam as a "totalitarian" religion because it embraces all aspects of life.[12] His use of the term "totalitarian" evokes Stalinist and Nazi totalitarianism, mentions of which are still painful in the former Yugoslavia. Belgrade academician Darko Tanasković described Bosnia as the scene of a struggle between fundamentalist Muslims on the one hand and Serbs dedicated to keeping Church and State separate on the other. He thereby reversed the reality in which a clericalist Republika Srpska had eradicated every trace of peoples and cultures outside of Serbian Orthodox Christianity, while the Bosnian government struggled to maintain a multireligious culture.[13]

The refusal of European governments to either defend Bosnians against genocide or allow them to obtain arms to defend themselves has been based in part on stereotypes about Islam. The attitudes of policy makers in Europe and North America are also influenced by a nativist backlash against immigrant communities, especially non-Christian immigrant communities, and an environment of increasing global tensions between some Muslim governments and the West.[14] As Croatian President Franjo Tudjman noted, he had taken his mission to Europeanize Bosnian Muslims from the expressed desires of Western European leaders. Serb President Slobodan Milošević was equally desperate to play up to European leaders and be accepted by them. In his 1989 Kosovo speech Milošević stated that Prince Lazar's battle six hundred years before had been a battle to defend Europe from Islam, that Serbia was the bastion of European culture and religion, and that Serbia's future actions would demonstrate that now as in the past, Serbia was always a part of Europe. Tudjman and Milošević felt a duty as Europeans to destroy the Bosnian Muslims and felt that doing so would facilitate their acceptance by Europe.[15]

Central to the Orientalist stereotype is a confusion in the presentation of Islam between religious observance and religious militancy. While few would argue that the militant wing of the

Irish Republican Army represents all observant Catholics, the association of observant Muslims with religious militancy is widespread. Some defenders of Bosnia have fallen into this trap, arguing that Bosnian Muslims are not "real Muslims" since many of them eat pork or drink alcohol and dress in Western fashion. The implicit logic seems to be that if Muslims in Europe eat pork, they deserve to exist. Desperate to counter false charges that they were fundamentalists, there were Bosnian Muslims who used the same logic, arguing that some of them also ate pork and drank alcohol, or were religious skeptics. Ironically, while European powers out of prejudice against Muslims and fears of fundamentalism tried to prevent Bosnia from attaining arms to defend itself, support in the Islamic world was slow in coming, partly because some Muslim leaders viewed Bosnians as not rigorous enough practitioners of Islam. A particularly sad absurdity awaited many Bosnian refugees in Western nations. Having been driven out of home and country for being Muslim, the refugees sometimes find themselves castigated for not observing what certain Muslims in the West deem proper Islamic observance, dress, or behavior.[16]

The stereotypes of Orientalism did not have to be subtle to be effective. However crude the presentation of Islam, however filled with interior contradictions, they provided a justification for many among Christian Croat and Serb populations for what was done to their Muslim neighbors, and they worked outside the region to militate against any effective, coordinated action by Western powers to stop the aggression.

As evidenced by those commentators who immediately assumed that the terrorist behind the Oklahoma City bombing was a Muslim, when it turned out the suspect was a follower of the

Christian Identity movement, a militant anti-Islamic prejudice has now pervaded much of Western society, subduing any popular sentiment for protecting "them," the religiously "other" in Bosnia.[17] Tragically, the betrayal by Western powers of Bosnian Muslims into the hands of genocide will only strengthen the argument of Islamic militants that the West is by nature inimical to Islam, thus further polarizing elements of Muslim and Christian populations.[18]

BALKANISM

Bosnian Muslims are also objects of a dehumanizing discourse about Balkan peoples which portrays Bosnians as Balkan tribal haters outside the realm of reason and civilization.

"They have been killing each other with a certain amount of glee in that part of the world for some time now," asserted former U.S. Secretary of State Lawrence Eagleburger in July 1995 just after the betrayal of Srebrenica.[19] The phrase "in that part of the world" provides to the domestic audience an immediate, nongeographical excuse to feel alienation: these people are not our concern because they are "other," "foreign," "different." In view of the domestic audience's deep-seated (though not always admitted) prejudices against non-Christians in general and Muslims specifically, vague references to "that part of the world" tap into both anti-Balkan and anti-Islamic sentiments.

"Ancient Balkan hatreds" has become a standard cliché in debate on Bosnia. The Balkans are historically and geographically too close to the Orient (read Islam) to be a true part of Europe, we are told. The 1992 book by Robert Kaplan, *Balkan Ghosts*, referred to the border with Turkey as Europe's "rear door."[20] The book popularized the caricature of Balkan peoples as locked in unending hate and revenge.

Balkanism is the distorted depiction of the people of southeastern Europe as barbaric with the implication that violence, even genocide, is inevitable there and part of the local culture. Balkanist comments were pervasive after the revelations of the horrors of Omarska in August 1992. Western officials had been holding back news of such camps.[21] The press revelations caught the major players off guard. Western leaders came under pressure by the press and public to liberate the killing camps. During this period, all the major figures of the foreign-policy team of U.S. President George Bush repeated Balkanist stereotypes.[22]

One stereotype was the superhuman Serb warrior. In World War II Serbs had tied down many Nazi divisions, we were told by Pentagon planners and by experts at military think tanks. No effort was made to distinguish between the anti-Nazi fighters of World War II, who were a multiethnic and multireligious group, and the Serb militias of fifty years later. Ignored also was the decidedly unheroic behavior of the Serb military in 1992: attacks with massive heavy weaponry against lightly defended villages and retreats when faced with serious military confrontation.

Public comments from the U.S. Defense Department also violated a key military principle: Never tell an aggressor what you may and may not do. Even if you are not going to act, never let an aggressor know what to expect. The comments from the Pentagon on the uselessness of air power to deter genocide and on the impossibility of stopping it with anything less than massive casualties were a signal that the U.S. and the NATO powers would not respond, no matter how heinous the assault—a "green light" for further genocide.[23]

In September 1995, the NATO powers tried air strikes. After three weeks of very selective bombing, the siege of Sarajevo was broken and NATO became concerned that further strikes would utterly destroy the Serb army in Bosnia. For three years, experts had declared the Serb army to be invincible and impervious to air power. After three weeks of air strikes, NATO feared that the same Serb army would collapse, causing a "destabilizing" shift in the balance of power.[24]

BALKANISM AS A MASK

How Balkanism functions as a code for political decisions can be seen in the statements of U.S. President Bill Clinton. As candidate for president in 1992, Bill Clinton proposed the use of NATO air power to save Bosnians from "deliberate and systematic extermination based on their ethnic origin."[25]

On February 10, 1993, President Clinton still acknowledged massive human rights violations but spoke of "containing" the conflict. Containment had been the policy of the Bush, Mitterrand, and Major administrations. The policy served, in effect, to turn Bosnia over piece by piece to Serb and Croat army conquest. On April 25, 1993, Clinton proclaimed that "Hitler sent tens of thousands of soldiers to that area and was never successful in subduing it." He was ignoring the fact that the Bosnians had never asked for Western ground troops, only for a lifting of the arms embargo and for air support.[26] On May 7, 1993, U.S. Secretary of State Warren Christopher returned from Europe with a Balkanist stereotype to explain the refusal by the NATO powers to stop the killings. In testimony before the U.S. Congress, he referred to "ancient antagonisms" and spoke of the Bosnian catastrophe as a "problem from hell."[27]

Another Balkanist claim, advanced by Serb President Slobodan Milošević, Bosnian Serb President Radovan Karadžić, and the British government, was that the violence was a "civil war," an "interior affair," or an "ethnic war." Among the most zealous Balkanists were the Serb nationalists, who asserted that the Bosnian conflict was part of an age-old pattern of ethnic war, that outsiders could not understand it and should leave the people of Bosnia to solve it for themselves (while keeping in place the arms embargo).[28] By May 1993, Clinton was calling the conflict a civil war, even though Croat and Serb forces had crossed the borders into Bosnia and were fueling the violence. Clinton next spoke of a "conflict" in Bosnia that is "ultimately a matter for the parties to resolve." On February 10, 1994, Balkanism reached its conclusion: "Until these folks get tired of killing each other," Clinton said, "bad things will continue to happen."[29] The stage was set for Srebrenica.

After Srebrenica, the U.S. Senate passed by an overwhelming margin the bipartisan Dole-Lieberman bill requiring the United States unilaterally to lift the arms embargo against the Bosnians. Both the vote and the speeches that accompanied it were a historic bipartisan repudiation of the foreign policy of an American president still in office.[30] The Europeans had threatened to withdraw their peacekeepers from Bosnia if the arms embargo were violated. Clinton had promised to send U.S. troops to aid in any evacuation of peacekeepers. A withdrawal would have led to a crisis in Bosnia before the 1996 presidential elections.

The Clinton administration was finally moved to act. Backed

by NATO air strikes on Serb army munitions dumps and communication facilities in Bosnia, Assistant Secretary of State Richard Holbrooke led negotiations that resulted in the Dayton peace agreement of November 22, 1995. Soon after, Deputy Secretary of State Strobe Talbot denounced the idea that the Bosnia tragedy was the inevitable result of "ancient hatreds"—the Balkanist stereotype that had been propounded by the same administration for two years.[31]

The Balkanist mask, donned and removed by the Clinton administration, was put back to work by the isolationist wing of the Republican party. All of Bosnia (and its four million human lives) was not worth one American soldier, exclaimed one candidate for the Republican presidential nomination.[32] One congressman proclaimed that "they have been fighting" in the Balkans for fifteen hundred years, oblivious to the fact that none of the major religious and ethnic groups in Bosnia had yet settled in the Balkans by that time. The culmination of the Balkanism frenzy was reached by Congressman William Goodling of Pennsylvania, who announced it "all began in the fourth-century split of the Roman Empire."[33] These congressmen had now embraced the mythology propounded by British policy makers and pundits such as Sir Crispin Tickell, who claimed that the hatreds among Yugoslav peoples extended back "thousands of years."[34]

PASSIVE VIOLENCE AND
FALSE HUMANITARIANISM

Western policy makers also manipulated the language of pacifism to justify maintaining an arms embargo against the Bosnians while refusing to use force to help them. The same leaders have authorized arms sales throughout the world. British Foreign Secretary Douglas Hurd stated that to lift the arms embargo would be to create a "level killing field."[35] When the existence of the concentration camp at Omarska was revealed in August 1992, President Bush, proud author of Operation Desert Storm against Iraq, consistently refused to advocate lifting the arms embargo on the grounds that more arms in the area would increase the violence.

NATO policy makers had a moral and legal duty to uphold Article 51 of the UN Charter guaranteeing the right of a nation to defend itself, as well as the 1948 Geneva Convention requiring all signatory nations not only to prevent genocide but to punish it. By refusing either to allow the Bosnians to defend themselves or to use NATO power to defend them, these leaders engaged in a form of passive violence, setting the parameters within which the killing could be and was carried out with impunity.[36]

Despite the extraordinary efforts of many individuals and small congregations, influential Christian church leaders and organizations also opposed both lifting the embargo and the use of NATO force to save the Bosnians and have offered little in the way of an alternative.[37] The position of many church groups that the best way to stop the violence was by "tightening" the arms embargo neglected the fact that the Serb army had enough weapons and weapons factories to last years. One of the few influential Christian leaders to speak out against the acquiescence of major church leaders and organizations in the assault on Bosnia has been Adrian Hastings, emeritus professor of theology at Leeds University. Hastings remarks that "If those in need are mostly Muslims who have lived peaceably for generations with their Christian neighbors but are now being destroyed by nominal Christians, that is all the more reason for Christians to come to the rescue." He remarks on the silence of the archbishops of Canterbury, York, and Westminster and the British Council of Churches in view of the greatest moral outrage in Europe since World War II. He then draws a historical parallel: "Bishop George Bell of Chichester was a lonely voice 50 years ago when he spoke up for the Jews. Where is a Bishop of Chichester today?"[38] Sarajevo Archbishop Vinko Puljić, who has so courageously struggled for a multireligious Bosnia, approaches the topic with devastating understatement: "I think we had expected much more energetic voices against injustice from Western churches."[39] While it is true that differing churches have widely different views on the issue of just war and justified use of force, what was indisputable was the reluctance of major Christian church leaders to call the crimes in Bosnia what they were, genocide, and to demand a stop to them. To the extent that church statements showed only a generalized concern over suffering in Bosnia without an urgent demand to stop genocide, they can be justly accused of refusing to speak truth to power, or in Hastings's term, of speaking platitudes.

To the passive violence of the Western policy makers was added a false humanitarianism. By focusing the UN mission on the supply of humanitarian aid while refusing to stop the campaign of genocide, the UN Security Council created a system that put UN peacekeepers as suppliers of humanitarian aid to Bosnia—as hostages. Whether or not they were actually detained by radical Serb militias was not important. They could be detained at will and thus served as hostages whether or not they were confined. The Serb army was able to violate with impunity dozens of UN resolutions demanding free flow of humanitarian aid, liberation of concentration camps, access to camps by war crimes investigators, and protection of civilians.[40] By requiring a dual key for any action by NATO (approval by both the UN military and civilian commanders and the NATO commander), the Security Council prevented any effective deterrence to hostage-taking. Some people were fed who would otherwise have starved but, as Bosnians commented, they were being fed for the slaughter.

For three years the UN struggled to get a basic minimum of food to the enclaves of Srebrenica and Žepa. After some peacekeepers were taken hostage and others threatened with being taken hostage, the people in the safe areas who had been forbidden adequate weapons to defend themselves and had been kept alive by UN humanitarianism were turned over to the Serb army for mass killings.[41] In September 1995, when NATO did use air strikes to break the siege of Sarajevo, total casualties to NATO forces were two French pilots missing. Had those strikes, or a credible threat of strikes, been used to prohibit any genocidal act by any party in 1992, not only would untold numbers of Bosnians (of all religions) have been saved, but the lives of more than two hundred UN peacekeepers as well.

It is impossible to know the personal motivations of those who for three years manipulated a language of pseudopacifism and false humanitarianism to justify a policy that rewarded aggression and punished its victims; who recognized Bosnia's sovereignty and pledged to defend it, then broke their own pledges; who declared a "no-fly zone" in October 1992, refused to authorize any enforcement for months, then refused to enforce it anyway; who declared six cities safe areas but refused to protect them; and who authorized "all necessary means" to get humani-

Fig. 7. British UN General Michael Rose (*right*) shares a laugh with Serbian General Ratko Mladić (*left*) as Mladić's forces close in on UN designated safe areas. Reuters/Stjepanovic, 1995.

tarian convoys through to starving civilians but refused to use the means available.[42]

For some, the degradation of the notion of peacekeeping is encapsulated in a particular incident. In the summer of 1992, UN peacekeepers under the command of Canadian General Lewis MacKenzie frequented the rape camp known as Sonja's Kon-Tiki, in the town of Vogošća near Sarajevo. Even after they learned that the women at the Kon-Tiki were Muslim captives held against their will, abused, and sometimes killed, UN peacekeepers continued to take advantage of the women there and to fraternize with their Serb nationalist captors. Only 150 yards

away from Sonja's, scores of Muslim men were being held in inhuman conditions, but the peacekeepers took no notice.[43]

For others, the degradation of the peacekeeping role culminated on January 8, 1993. A French contingent of UN peacekeepers was escorting the Bosnian Deputy Prime Minister Dr. Hakija
Turajlić into Sarajevo. They were stopped at a Serb army check-
point. When the Serb soldiers asked the French peacekeepers
to open up the armored car—against their orders and with the
certain knowledge of what would follow—they complied, then
stood aside and watched as a Serb soldier shot the unarmed
Dr. Turajlić dead. When the same French peacekeepers came
home to France, they were decorated for heroism.[44]

A Serbian religious nationalist put into one formula the ma-
nipulations of the language of nonviolence and humanitarianism
that have been so often used by Western policy makers in regard
to Bosnia and by doing so demonstrated the moral equalizing to
which such language leads. The nationalist claimed that Christianity was superior to Islam because Christianity forbids all
violence, even in self-protection. When asked why he justified
as self-defense the violence of Serb nationalists, he responded:
"We are all sinners."[45]

MORAL EQUALIZING

"There are no angels in this conflict" has been a slogan used for
the refusal to stop the killing—as if angels, rather than human
beings, deserve our empathy and support. In July 1992, British
Foreign Secretary Douglas Hurd patronized victims along with
perpetrators: "Where there is no will for peace we cannot supply

it."[46] The Balkanist stereotype was continually used to imply that all sides were equally guilty.

No party in any war has ever been free of blame. But the blame-on-all-sides position falsified important differences between the methodical genocide carried out by Serb nationalists, the predatory aggression of Croat nationalists, and individual crimes committed by Bosnian soldiers, crimes that were not related to any overall criminal policy and that have been punished.[47]

Moral equalizing led to political equalizing. After the London Conference of 1992 affirmed the territorial integrity and legitimacy of Bosnia, NATO powers shifted to a competing language in which the Bosnian government was one of three "warring factions."[48] When Bosnian leaders held out against aspects of peace plans that rewarded the atrocities of Serb and Croat nationalists with territorial concessions and left Bosnia open to future destruction, Western diplomats leaked statements to the effect that the Bosnians were "sore losers" and would not accept the fact that they had "lost"—as if genocide were some kind of football game.

In 1993, David Owen stated that Serbs had controlled 60 percent of pre-war Bosnia, a claim used by Serb militants to justify their claim that most of Bosnia should be given to the 31 percent of the country that was Serb.[49] The last land registers before the war, however, showed 50 percent of Bosnia was public land and that Serb landowners controlled 23 percent. In April 1995, Thorwald Stoltenberg made the astonishing announcement that Bosnian Muslims were actually Serbs; it was a Serb extremist dream-come-true. If Bosnian Muslims were Serbs, then they had no reason to reject Serb military occupation and since (according to the extremists) Serbs were either Orthodox Christian or traitors, there was no reason Bosnian Muslims shouldn't be treated as traitors.[50] The two men entrusted by the Western powers to protect the sovereignty of Bosnia were adopting the most spurious and fatal claims of the radical religious nationalists among the Serbs.

Moral equalizing could be achieved by portraying all sides as inhuman savages; it could also be achieved by ignoring atrocities. According to a senior fellow at the Brookings Institution and a senior advisor to Yasushi Akashi, the chief of the UN operation in Bosnia, the problems in Bosnia were not the result of age-old tribal hatreds but rather the effects of organizational breakdown—within both international and Yugoslav institutions—following the cold war. There was no crime and, it was implied, no one really was responsible.[51]

A final way of avoiding moral distinctions was to demonize an entire people. Phrases such as "Serb aggression" and "Serb atrocities" ignore any Serb opposition to genocide. The group demonization is based upon a view of the Serb people as a homogenous mass—a view shared by Serb militants. For Republika Srpska President Radovan Karadžić, for example, any Serb who does not support the attack on Bosnia is not a true Serb and any criticism of Karadžić's policies is a criticism of "Serbs" in general.

Peter Brock published a piece in the journal *Foreign Policy* asserting that the Western media had exaggerated the atrocities committed by Serbs while refusing to report atrocities against Serbs.[52] The article ignored the massive evidence in the human rights reports and war crimes investigations of organized genocide by the Serb militants. Multiple flaws in the Brock article were soon demonstrated. Even so, it was a propaganda bonanza for Serb religious nationalists.[53] For many Serbs and others who wish to believe that the genocide was a fabrication of Western media, the Brock article was a citation from an establishment journal. At the base of the Brock article was the notion that criticism of the leadership of the Republika Srpska was a slur against *all* Serbs; Radovan Karadžić couldn't have said it better.

NATIONAL INTERESTS

Western officials such as U.S. Secretaries of State Lawrence Eagleburger and Warren Christopher had trouble seeing a vital interest in acting to prevent genocide in Bosnia, beyond "containment" of the violence within the boundaries of Bosnia. At this time, it is still unclear whether the Dayton accords will be enforced or whether the NATO operation to support them will be degraded in the manner of the UN mission from 1992 to 1995. The outcome will affect the security of peoples and nations outside of Bosnia in profound ways.

In 1948, the first Arab-Israeli war left 750,000 Palestinian refugees. The "Palestinian problem" led to three more major Middle East wars, the destruction of Lebanon, East-West geopolitical conflict, proliferation of nuclear weapons by Israel and its enemies, and billions of dollars in U.S. foreign aid to the Middle East. In July 1995 there were more than twice as many Bosnian refugees as there were Palestinian refugees in 1948, and they have suffered atrocities beyond description. The consequences of allowing Bosnia to be destroyed will begin to appear in the second and third generations of children born in refugee camps, and they will be incalculable.

GENOCIDE IN BOSNIA, *1992–1995*

1989	
June 28	Milošević speaks at the 600th anniversary Kosovo celebration
1991	
September 25	UN Security Council Resolution 713: Arms embargo on all parties in the former Yugoslavia
1992	
March 27	Republika Srpska declared
April 6–7	Bosnia-Herzegovina is recognized by the EC and U.S.
April 3–17	Serb military begins genocide in Zvornik, Višegrad, Foča, and Bijeljina areas
April 21	Siege of Sarajevo begins
May	Bosnian government pleads in vain for military help or a lifting of the arms embargo
May 17	Serb army destroys Oriental Institute in Sarajevo
May 19	Yugoslav Army claims it is "withdrawing" from Bosnia, transferring soldiers and weapons to the control of the Bosnian Serb army
May 27	Bread-line shelling in Sarajevo
May 30	UN Security Council Resolution 725: Sanctions against Yugoslavia (Serbia and Montenegro)
June 19	Union of Herceg-Bosna declared
August 3	Bosnian President Izetbegović appeals in vain for an end to the arms embargo
August 4–6	Televised pictures of Omarska and Trnopolje concentration camps
August 25–28	London Conference: NATO nations affirm Bosnia's territorial integrity
	Serb army burns the National Library in Sarajevo

1993

January 2	Unveiling of the Vance-Owen plan
January 8	UN gives over the Bosnian Deputy Prime Minister to Serb soldiers, who kill him on the spot
January 15	Water-line shelling in Sarajevo
March–April	Serb army takes Cerska and threatens Goražde, Srebrenica, and Žepa
April 16	UN Security Council Resolution 819: Declares Srebrenica a safe area
May 5	The Republika Srpska rejects the Vance-Owen plan
May 22	Bihać, Tuzla, Žepa, Goražde, and Sarajevo declared safe areas along with Srebrenica
June– September	Owen-Stoltenberg partition of Bosnia, based on a map drawn by Tudjman and Milošević
June 30	UN Security Council rejects a proposal to lift the arms embargo
July	Joint Croat-Serb nationalist attacks on Bosnian Muslims
August 23	HVO forces destroy Počitelj's Old Town and expel its Muslims
September 6	Izetbegović pleads for the UN Security Council to lift arms embargo
September 27	Fikret Abdić declares an autonomous state in the Bihać pocket
November 9	HVO destroys the Mostar Old Bridge
November 17	UN War Crimes Tribunal authorized

1994

February 5	Marketplace shelling in Sarajevo; NATO pressure leads to temporary relief from shelling
April 4–15	Serb army shells Goražde, enters the safe area, and burns Muslim homes. British UN General Michael Rose refuses to protect the safe area

May	Contact Group plan to partition Bosnia with 49 percent of the territory to go to the Republika Srpska
August–	
September	Vojkan Djurković phase of expulsions and religious terror in Banja Luka and Bijeljina
September–	
November	Yugoslavia claims it has closed its border with Bosnia
November	Bihać attacked by Serb forces from Bosnia and Croatia, and by Abdić rebels. British UN General Michael Rose renounces further NATO air strikes to protect Bihać

1995

July 11–21	UN hands over safe areas of Srebrenica and Žepa to Serb army; mass killings ensue
July 26	U.S. Senate passes Dole-Lieberman bill to lift arms embargo against Bosnia
July–August	Croatian regular army crushes the Serb Krajina Republic in "Operation Storm"
August 28	Second Sarajevo marketplace shelling leads to NATO bombing
November 22	Peace agreement initialed in Dayton, Ohio

At the end of the cold war, NATO changed its mission from defense against the Soviet Union to protecting the peace and security of Europe. Failure to fulfill that mission in Bosnia will weaken and may destroy an alliance that has been critical to stability in Europe and to which all the NATO nations have contributed enormous resources.

Sarajevo is at the center of ethnic and religious fault lines that stretch around the world: the Slavic and Orthodox Christian world extends to the east and northeast; the Muslim and Turkic worlds extend to the east and southeast across central Asia and to the west along North Africa; the Catholic world extends to the west and northwest from Austria to Latin America; the Protestant world begins its arc not far north of Sarajevo. Rewarding genocide in Bosnia will send a message to the many potential antagonists: strike first and strike ruthlessly and you will get what you want.

In 1994, the extremist Hutu leadership of Rwanda was plotting genocide. They had every reason to expect that if genocide could be carried out with impunity in Europe, right in front of NATO, it could be carried out in Central Africa, far from any force like NATO. A final failure in Bosnia will send an ominous message to any other group in the world (and there will be many) who might contemplate genocide.

A geopolitical cold war between Islam and the West would be more intractable and more dangerous, perhaps, than the cold war between the West and the Soviet Bloc. Muslims around the world were stunned by Western acquiescence in the genocide, and by the passivity of pro-Western Islamic governments. A final failure in Bosnia will only strengthen the claim of Islamic militants who argue that the West wishes to destroy Islam. It will weaken the position of Muslims who seek peaceful relations with the Western world.

Religious violence has broken out globally: a Buddhist group's poison gas attack against Tokyo; the April 1995 Oklahoma City bombing by followers of the Christian Identity movement; the attack on Muslim holy sites by Hindu militants; the attack on the World Trade Center in New York City by Islamic radicals; the celebration by Jewish militants of the mass murder of Muslim Arabs in Hebron and the killing of Prime Minister Yitzhak Rabin in Israel. Rewarding genocide in Bosnia will make such violence a model for success.[54]

For some, it may well be in the national economic interest for a major arms producer like the United States to allow or even foster such strife and conflict. It assures markets for a major export item, keeps a military industrial complex in a state of readiness, and keeps a large army as a safety valve in a time of increasing unemployment; a conflict with the Islamic world would create a new global enemy; outside enemies help interior cohesion. The practitioners of *realpolitik* do not make these arguments so baldly, but they intimate them. Ultimately, whether preventing genocide is in our national interest depends on our definition of "interest"; that definition depends in turn upon what kind of nation and what kind of world we wish to inhabit.[55]

NOT TWO CENTS

"I don't give two cents about Bosnia. Not two cents. The people there have brought on their own troubles." This statement by *New York Times* columnist Thomas Friedman was made on June 7, 1995. It marks the logical end of moral equalizing, the equating of the victim and the perpetrator and the devaluing of both.[56]

In theological terms, the moral and political equalizing was embodied in the statement by the Serb Church spokesman that "everyone in this war is guilty."[57] The ramifications of such a statement go beyond theological doctrines of original sin. The notion that everyone is guilty in the Bosnian conflict is a generalized statement that leads downslope to the conclusion that

Bosnian people are in some sense getting what they deserve. Indeed, the view that the victims of genocide deserve what they get is more often a subtext of the language of moral and political equalizing; only rarely does an influential columnist such as Thomas Friedman articulate the message directly. In the less restrained world of Internet newsgroups, posters often state a version of the slogan, "Let them keep on killing one another and the problem will solve itself," a statement that is a more honest version of the phrase popular among political commentators: "Contain the problem to Bosnia and let it burn itself out."

Albert Speer, the architect of much of Nazi Germany's industrial machine, spent twenty years in prison. In his memoirs, he stated that he never accepted responsibility for the evil he had caused despite the vast number of victims. Then he saw a photo of a family being taken to a death camp. With that glimpse of suffering on an individual scale, he began to understand the evil of which he had been part.[58]

In Bosnia, witnesses to the violence have focused on individual cases in order to touch somehow a world that seemed not to wish to care. A reporter noted that after the second Sarajevo market massacre on August 28, 1995, a Bosnian child turned to her mother saying "Mommy, I've lost my hand," as her mother, herself grievously wounded, moaned "Where is my husband, I've lost my husband." After the Serb army shelling of a Sarajevo suburb in 1992, a reporter wrote of a young boy found next to his dead mother, repeating, "Do you love me, Mommy?" After the Srebrenica shelling massacre of 1993, in which the Serb army opened fire on a group of Muslim civilians waiting to be evacuated by the United Nations, an official with the UN High Commission for Refugees told of a young girl who had half her face

Fig. 8.   Who was she? Refugee from Srebrenica after the safe haven
was turned over to the Serb army in July 1995. AP/Wide World
Photos.

blown away. He said that her suffering was so intense, he could do nothing but pray that she would die soon, which she did.[59]

In some cases, images that intimate rather than demonstrate have allowed people to see beyond the masks to what is at stake in Bosnia. A young woman from Srebrenica hanged herself after the enclave was turned over to the Serb army; a picture of her allowed U.S. Senator Dianne Feinstein, who had been using the language of Balkanist "ancient animosities" mythology to excuse the violence, to understand the human element of the genocide. Feinstein asked a series of questions about the young woman: What was her name, where was she from, what humiliations and depravations did she suffer, had she been raped, did she witness loved ones being killed? It was what the picture left unsaid that allowed the senator to look beyond the linguistic masks of "warring factions" and "guilt on all sides" to the reality that this young woman was most likely not warring, not guilty, not an ancient antagonist or hater, and that her act was "not the act of someone who had the ability to fight in self-defense."[60]

The violence in Bosnia was a religious genocide in several senses: the people destroyed were chosen on the basis of their religious identity; those carrying out the killings acted with the blessing and support of Christian church leaders; the violence was grounded in a religious mythology that characterized the targeted people as race traitors and the extermination of them as a sacred act; and the perpetrators of the violence were protected by a policy designed by the policy makers of a Western world that is culturally dominated by Christianity.

In the case of religious genocide, moral distinctions are particularly difficult to maintain; the basis of much moral thinking is to be found within religions, but in religiously motivated violence, religions are being manipulated to motivate and justify the evil. One response is to reform religions from within, in dialogue with other religions. Religious leaders of each tradition need to better understand and more clearly explain the full humanity of those who embrace other religions and the variety and richness within other traditions. Another response is to begin with a basic premise—that needless, willfully inflicted human suffering cannot and should not be explained away. The two responses may complement one another.

A counterreading to the manipulation of the Good Friday story by religious nationalists might be found in the refusal of "doubting Thomas" to accept the risen Jesus until he had put his hands into the wounds. There are those who will refuse to accept the suffering of their fellow human beings even if they were to put their hands into the wounds; in the case of Bosnia the doubters might include Western political leaders and a segment of the public.

The story of Thomas may be a story about how difficult it is to recognize the wounds of another and how such recognition is necessary in order to see the resurrected Jesus. The Bosnian Muslim has been the "other" for much of the Christian world. The genocide in Bosnia was grounded in a particular version of the Good Friday story; it remains to be seen whether other readings of that story will contribute to a decision to stop the genocide, and whether that decision will occur before it is too late.

CHAPTER SEVEN

THE BRIDGE

THE WOUNDING SKY

Before Aida Mušanović spoke of the cloud of ashes that hung over Sarajevo for three days after the Serb army burned the National Library, she told another story. She had gone to the Oriental Institute, one of the central resources for the history and development of Bosnian culture. It was the day after the institute had been completely destroyed by Serb army gunners. She stood on the ground floor of what used to be a six-floor building and looked up at the open sky.

Bosnian culture has always resisted being reduced to a single religion or ethnicity. In pre-Ottoman times, Bosnia was the home of three churches: Orthodox, Catholic, and the independent Bosnian Church. Since Ottoman times, Islam, Orthodoxy, and Catholicism have made up the large pattern of Bosnian cultural heritage. After the expulsion of the Jews from Spain in 1492, many Sephardic Jews who had been offered refuge in the Ottoman Empire came to Bosnia; Ashkenazi Jews from northern and eastern Europe also settled in Bosnia. The Roma (Gypsy) population of Bosnia-Herzegovina is divided between adherents of Islam and Christianity.

The specific character of Bosnia's heritage is reflected in its tradition of love lyric, among the world's most sophisticated. The native love song is the *sevdalinka*, which can be composed in Croatian, Bosnian, and Serbian and written in either the Latin alphabet, Cyrillic alphabet, or as Adžamijski (Slavic in the Arabic alphabet).[1] The *sevdalinka* involves the timeless lyrics of unrequited love. It is called "the woman's song" because by convention it is sung by a woman to her male beloved. The woman poses as a male lover in the song, singing to his female beloved. This complex gender interplay is further enhanced when male singers sing the woman's song. There is one account of six Muslim *ulema* or religious scholars on their way to the pilgrimage in Mecca, singing *sevdalinkas*.

The love lyric is about love, but it is also about loss and exile. During the shelling of Sarajevo, one of the most popular lyrics, based on an ancient *sevdalinka*, concerned Mt. Trebević, the mountain above Sarajevo from which Serb army gunners were shelling the city. In the old *sevdalinka*, Mt. Trebević was the mountain of the love fairy. The love song took on new meaning during the siege of 1992–1995, when Sarajevans listened to a *sevdalinka*-based popular song and love lament in which the fairy atop Trebević mountain calls out: "Is Sarajevo where it used to be?"

In addition to composing *sevdalinkas* in South Slavic, Bosnian poets composed them in the languages of the Ottoman empire: Ottoman Turkish, Persian, or Arabic. They also combined the native *sevdalinka* themes with themes from the Ottoman Islamic world and from the Petrarchan sonnet. Many poets composed in all the languages of the region. Some of the more popular poems, composed in Persian or Ottoman Turkish (or in interlocking verses of Persian and Ottoman Turkish), were translated into South Slavic, and in some cases the South Slavic versions are now better known than the Persian and Ottoman Turkish originals. The manuscripts containing this intricate multilingual tradition of Bosnian love lyric were one part of the cultural treasure that went up in flames on May 17, 1992.

Bosnia has a culture rich in transitions and translations. Those looking for the essence of culture and language in ethnic, racial, or religious purity will find Bosnia incomprehensible. On the other hand, those who see culture as a creative process that by its very nature involves intermingling and creative tension among different elements will treasure Bosnia-Herzegovina.

Sarajevo was at the center of such a pluralistic culture. Its mosques, synagogues, Catholic and Orthodox churches stand side by side. Its people are skilled at languages and navigating the concourses of differing traditions—as many discovered when they visited the city for the Winter Olympics in 1984. Bosnia-Herzegovina could be a bridge between the increasingly polarized spheres of East and West and could play an important role in preventing a war between the majority Christian world and the majority Islamic world, a reversion to the Crusades. It is the polarized world of the Crusades that religious nationalists presuppose and desire and that the complex culture of Bosnia-Herzegovina contradicts.

The sounds of that polarized world are clear in the lyric sung by Radovan Karadžić's soldiers, accompanied by the *gusle*—the

stick fiddle used with classical South Slav epics—as they trained
their guns down from the mountains above Sarajevo:

Oh, beautiful Turkish daughter
Our monks will soon be baptizing you,
Sarajevo, in the valley,
The Serbs have you encircled.[3]

THE EXECUTION OF CULTURE

In the fall of 1995, former U.S. Secretary of State Henry Kissinger proclaimed that "there is no Bosnian culture." The context for Kissinger's claim was his proposal that Bosnia should be
partitioned between Serbia and Croatia and that the Muslims
(and presumably anyone else who did not want to be part of
ethnically pure Greater Croatia and Greater Serbia) should be
placed in a "Muslim state." Partitioning Bosnia and putting the
Muslims in a religious ghetto was the original goal of the Serb
and Croat nationalists.[4]

Those who have done the most to disprove Kissinger's claim
that there is no Bosnian culture are Ratko Mladić and Mate Boban, the Serb and Croat nationalists who devoted such extraordinary energy to destroying the vast testimony to Bosnian
culture: the National Library, the Oriental Institute, and the
National Museum, all in Sarajevo; the archives of Herzegovina;
music schools; local museums; graveyards; ancient bridges and
clocktowers; entire historic districts; covered marketplaces; and
of course thousands of churches, synagogues, and mosques, from
masterworks of South Slavic architecture to the humble, local
houses of worship.

One incident, recounted by the Bosnian writer Ivan Lovrenović, captures the frenzy of this campaign of cultural annihilation. A Serb army officer had entered the home of a Sarajevan artist, who happened to be Serb. Among the works of art, he saw a piece that depicted a page from the Qur'an. Infuriated, he had all the artwork taken out into the street, lined up, and shot to pieces with automatic weapons fire.[5]

What is behind such a seemingly lunatic obsession with destroying culture? Why would Croat and Serb nationalists spend almost four years destroying a culture that did not exist in the first place? The four years of destruction were an attempt to eliminate something that does exist and continues to exist. Testimony to that existence is to be found in the people and cultural world that has survived, and in the empty spaces throughout Bosnia-Herzegovina where so many human lives and cultural monuments used to be.

The armies of the Serb and Croat religious nationalists targeted Bosnian culture, monuments, cultural leaders, teachers, and students, so that someday advocates of religious apartheid in Bosnia could declare: "There is no Bosnian culture." People looking at the parking lots where mosques and churches and art museums and music schools and libraries and manuscript collections once stood would say: "I guess Kissinger was right." The argument then becomes plausible. As the mayor of the newly "cleansed" and 100 percent pure Serb Orthodox city of Zvornik said, after all of the city's mosques had been dynamited, "There never were any mosques in Zvornik." If there is no Bosnian culture, why not divide Bosnia between Croatia and Serbia, and herd the Muslims into a central ghetto?

The same reasoning was used by advocates of apartheid in South Africa. There was no African culture, they said, so why not put Africans on reservations called homelands and institute an apartheid state? The same approach was used during the extermination of the American Indian nations. There was no Native American culture, so why not "cleanse" the American Indians and put the survivors on reservations?

Since the First Crusade in 1096, non-Christian communities in Europe have been subject to annihilation. Throughout the Crusades, Jewish communities were attacked and burned, visited with the kind of atrocities that have occurred in Bosnia-Herzegovina. In 1492, exactly five hundred years before the beginning of the attack on Bosnia, Queen Isabella of Spain ordered her kingdom "cleansed" of its Jewish population. In 1609, those to be "cleansed" were the Moriscos, all those who kept the customs of the Muslims of Spain, whether or not they were practicing Muslims. A new word, "pogrom," came into our vocabulary to explain the fate of Jewish communities in eastern Europe for several centuries. Then there was the Holocaust. To advocate the driving of Bosnian Muslims into a Muslim state surrounded by two heavily armed nationalist armies that have tasted blood is to advocate, if a ruthlessly consistent European history tells us anything, the probable destruction of that people. Those who advocate a ghetto for Bosnian Muslims may suggest that the UN and NATO would give the ghetto security guarantees—like those given to the "safe area" of Srebrenica.

Like culture in the United States, Bosnian culture cannot be defined by the linguistic and religious criteria of nineteenth-century nationalism. Just as Americans share a language with the British and Australians, so Bosnians share a language with Serbs and Croats. Just as the United States has no single, official church, so Bosnia is made up of people of different religious confessions, and within those confessions, vastly different perspectives. If Bosnia has no culture, then the United States has no culture. If Bosnia should be partitioned into religiously pure apartheid states, then the same logic leads to the idea, proposed by the Christian Identity movement, that the United States should be divided into apartheid states of different races and religions.

CREATION IN THE FIRE

After recounting her experiences of the destruction of culture in Sarajevo, Aida Mušanović explained the exhibit she was organizing, entitled Expo/Sarajevo 92. It consists of eighteen engravings made by distinguished Sarajevan artists during the worst of the shelling of Sarajevo. The names of the artists (Serb, Croat, and Muslim) and the styles of their art reflect the mosaic of cultures, religions, and influences that comprises Sarajevo. Radoslav Tadić's work, "Echo 92," shows the silhouette of a building in which Catholic, Serbian Orthodox, and Muslim architectural and sacred figures blend into, grow out of, and complement one another. Mustafa Skopljak's "The Cry" offers piercing emotion transmuted through semi-anthropomorphic shapes reminiscent of those of Joan Miró. Sead Čizmić's "Sarajevo Sera" depicts a calm evening with a Mediterranean atmosphere, with a darkness on the horizon. Zoran Bogdanović's "Homage to Alija Kućukalić" is calm solemnity, a grief too deep for words or movement. Nusret Pašić's "Witnesses to Existence" depicts human figures in elongated shapes partially reminiscent of German expressionism.[6]

The artists decided to use engraving not only because prints are replaceable and thus not vulnerable to total destruction but also because of the social aspect of engraving. Because of the shelling, the artists were often forced to stay overnight or for several nights at a time in their studio (an old evangelical church). In their catalogue comments the artists trace the line of teachers and traditions that religious nationalists wished to destroy.

Why would people risk their lives to produce a work of art? Why did that doctoral candidate at the University of Sarajevo give her young life to try to carry some small part of the cultural heritage of Bosnia out of the flames of the National Library?[7] Several months after the death of her father at the hands of a sniper, the student's sister in Canada received in the mail some letters from the dead father; because of the siege of Sarajevo they had been delayed en route. At the time of their delivery, she said, she had not been able to open them. I do not know what the letters might have said, whether they discussed the death of his daughter. From the testimony of hundreds of Bosnians, I imagine one theme would be this: It is not tolerable to live as a captive, to sneak along alleys and walls to receive a UN food handout. To live is to create. To create or protect culture is an act of living.

One participant in the discussion of Expo/Sarajevo 92 suggested that the engravings do not represent a cultural reality that could exist independently and prior to them.[8] Rather, it may be that through such art a culture like that of Bosnia—a culture not defined by notions of ethnic and religious purity—can exist. In the act of creating culture, the overlapping boundaries and claims of different languages, religions, and traditions can find a space in which otherwise competing worlds are on common ground.

When Slobodan Milošević stood at the Kosovo field in 1989, he told the crowd that Serbia "was a fortress defending European culture and religion." The Serbian Orthodox Church leaders and academics in Belgrade speak of a defending wall against the Asiatic aliens. Croat religious nationalists destroyed the Mostar bridge as they "Europeanized" Bosnian Muslims. After the Dayton treaty proposed a unified Sarajevo, Radovan Karadžić demanded a walled Sarajevo patterned on the Berlin of the cold war.

Those who want a wall between Europe and an allegedly alien and inferior "Orient," a wall between Christian and Islamic worlds, face one problem: the stubborn propensity of Bosnians to think in terms of bridges instead of walls and their courageous effort to save or rebuild their bridges. Cultures are hard to kill. Fire meant to destroy them may steel them instead.

A DANCE

In a city in North America, a family of exiles from Sarajevo had invited a group of friends to a dinner party before they moved to another city. The family, of mixed religious background—primarily Serbian Orthodox, with relatives in the Muslim and Croat Catholic communities—had struggled to survive for three years of separation and persecution. Guests included Serbs, Croats, and Muslims from Bosnia as well as Americans of many religions and ethnic backgrounds.

At such events there is a moment when the evening comes together in a special way. That moment occurred as someone put popular music from Sarajevo on the cassette player. The song was an old *sevdalinka* in popular music form. Jasminka, who had spent three years in exile struggling to reunite her family, stood up and began to dance. Soon her daughter joined her. At such times, as separation is mourned and reunion celebrated, joy and sorrow have a way of blending into one.

NOTE ON SOURCES

PRINCIPLES OF CREDIBILITY

The charge of genocide almost always generates disputes over data and numbers killed and charges that the other side engaged in equal atrocities. False charges of genocide can be used to foster and motivate actual genocide, as Chapter 3 demonstrates.

Even the most clearly established cases of genocide, such as the Holocaust or the genocide perpetrated by the Khmer Rouge in Cambodia, have frequently been denied. Given the human tendency to deny, evade, excuse, or ignore something as profoundly evil as genocide, a few denials in the right place at the right time can effectively disrupt efforts to halt genocide in progress.

The claims in this book are based on the following types of sources: (1) human rights reports by organizations that are not attached to any government, that have reported on human rights practices of any and all governments, and whose credibility has been established by vindication of their reporting over long periods of time; (2) evidence collected by the International Criminal Tribunal in The Hague (authorized by the United Nations on November 17, 1993) and indictments issued by the tribunal; (3) eyewitness accounts by refugee workers in Bosnia, who have no political interest in either maximizing or minimizing the abuses they witnessed; (4) interviews by this author with Bosnian refugees and survivors; (5) reports in the press insofar as they are corroborated by evidence from one or more of the first four categories; and (6) negative evidence, revealed in glaring contradictions within the denials of atrocities by those alleged to have committed them or in the refusal by those accused to allow access to independent investigators or to cooperate with the International Criminal Tribunal.

Of special importance is the corroboration of evidence from more than one source and more than one kind of source. It is possible even for trained human rights investigators to make a mistake in a particular case. Cross-corroborated evidence and evidence gathered not from a single incident but from a pattern are more reliable. An example of how cross-corroboration works can be found in the case of the Čelopek Cultural Center killings near Zvornik. Survivors from Zvornik testified that Serb militiamen detained, raped, tortured, and killed Muslim civilians at the Čelopek Cultural Center outside town. This evidence was later corroborated by a trial in Yugoslavia, reported by the dissident Serb journalists of *Vreme News Digest*, in which an alleged perpetrator admitted the crimes but excused them on the grounds that he was drunk. Later, when the issue of possible involvement by the Yugoslav secret police was raised, the Yugoslav government shut down the trial. Serb nationalist authorities in Zvornik have refused to cooperate with or grant access to International Criminal Tribunal investigators and human rights groups. It is often difficult to prove rape and torture to those who discount the testimonies of survivors, but the physical testimony of dynamited mosques is hard to dispute. The accounts of genocide in Zvornik, as elsewhere, weave accounts of attacks on persons with descriptions of the systematic destruction of mosques. When it turns out that every mosque in Zvornik and every mosque in the Republika Srpska has been destroyed, the evidence of systematic, organized genocide is reinforced.

Negative evidence is important in view of demands that the point of view of the other side be respected and heard and that coverage should be "balanced." The point of view of Serb and Croat religious nationalists has indeed been taken into account very carefully; it has impeached itself in the following ways: (1) through internal contradiction based on obvious stereotypes and ignorance, as in the accusations by Serb religious nationalists that Bosnians are Muslim fundamentalists who aim to establish an Islamic state ruled by religious scholars, on the one hand, and are plotting to reestablish the viziers and other accouterments of imperial Ottoman rule, on the other; (2) through contradictory responses to the same accusation, as when Serb authorities defended shelling refugees in Srebrenica in 1993 by saying they were shooting at a Bosnian tank and accidentally hit the refugees, while at the same time maintaining that there was no shelling at all but that the incident was staged by Bosnian and UN officials using the bodies of Serbs who had been tortured to death; (3) through a pattern of repeated falsehoods, as with the three-year history of denial by Republika Srpska officials that ethno-religious expulsions were taking place or that refugee convoys were being blocked in the face of massive eyewitness testimony to the contrary; (4) through glaring falsehood in individual instances, such as the claim by Yugoslav diplomat Vladislav Jovanović in his December 1995 letter to the UN Security Council that the thousands of Bosnian Muslims missing from the safe areas of Žepa and Srebrenica were killed by their own soldiers, despite overwhelming evidence to the contrary; or the Croatian government's claim that the property of Muslims in Prozor was damaged during a fire fight, when photos and eyewitness accounts showed burned-out Muslim businesses and residences scattered throughout town next to undamaged businesses and residences of Catholic Croats; and (5) through refusal to allow claims to be verified, as has been the case throughout the Republika Srpska: Serb nationalists claimed that prisoners were treated according to the Geneva conventions but refused access to the International Red Cross, war crimes investigators, and other human rights monitoring organizations.

Religious nationalists in the former Yugoslavia have specialized in the control of the media. Atrocities by their own forces are never mentioned; alleged atrocities by their enemies are repeated continually. Are there people of good will in these territories who truly believe the views presented to them with such an air of authority? Is it possible for them not to have noticed the interior contradictions in such propaganda or how the boasting of local militia leaders in their own town or village contradicts it? In writing a book like this one, I take it as a moral challenge to be open to the possibility that I have been deceived and to reexamine continually the account I give. To those who maintain total skepticism, however—and with it, reject any moral responsibility to stop the genocide if it is occurring—I would say this. The possibility of deception can never be ruled out completely, but the willingness to accept an unpleasant, even devastating truth, when we are faced with it, is necessary if we are to become truly human.

SOME BASIC SOURCES

Publications by Governments and International Organizations

Amnesty International: *Bosnia-Herzegovina: Gross Abuses of Basic Human Rights* (New York: 1992); *Bosnia-Herzegovina: Rana u duši—A Wound to the Soul* (New York, 1993).

Helsinki Watch: *War Crimes in Bosnia-Hercegovina* (New York: Human Rights Watch, 1992); *Letter to President of Serbia and JNA Chief of Staff* (New York, 1992); *War Crimes in Bosnia-Hercegovina*, Vol. 1 (New York, 1992); *War Crimes in Bosnia-Hercegovina*, Vol. 2 (New York, 1993); *Abuses Continue in the Former Yugoslavia: Serbia, Montenegro and Bosnia-Hercegovina* (New York, 1993); *Prosecute Now!: Helsinki Watch Releases Eight Cases for War Crimes Tribunal on Former Yugoslavia* (New York, 1993); *Procedural and Evidentiary Issues for the Yugoslav War Crimes Tribunal: Resource Allocation, Evidentiary*

Questions and Protection of Witnesses (New York, 1993); *Abuses by Bosnian Croat and Muslim Forces in Central and Southwestern Bosnia-Hercegovina* (New York, 1993); *The War Crimes Tribunal: One Year Later* (New York, 1994); *War Crimes in Bosnia-Hercegovina: Bosanski Šamac* (New York, 1994); *War Crimes in Bosnia-Hercegovina: U.N. Cease-Fire Won't Help Banja Luka* (New York, 1994); *Sarajevo* (New York, 1994); *"Ethnic Cleansing" Continues in Northern Bosnia* (New York, 1994); *War Crimes Trials in Former Yugoslavia* (New York, 1995).

UN Security Council: *Annex I: European Community Investigative Mission into the Treatment of Muslim Women in the Former Yugoslavia, Report to the European Community Foreign Ministers,* Vol. S/25240, February 3, 1993 (New York: United Nations, 1993).

U.S. Congress: *Genocide in Bosnia-Herzegovina: Hearing Before the Commission on Security and Cooperation in Europe, One Hundred Fourth Congress,* Vol. CSCE 104-1-4 (Washington, D.C.: U.S. Government Printing Office, 1995).

U.S. Department of State: "War Crimes in the Former Yugoslavia": This consists of eight U.S. State Department War Crimes Commission Reports found in *U.S. Department of State Dispatch,* 3.39, 3.44, 3.46, 3.52 (1992); 4.6, 4.15, 4.16, 4.30 (1993). This author has edited the reports into a form more easy to cite, by numbering each entry. The edited versions are available on the World Wide Web:

URL:http://www.haverford.edu/relg/sells/reports.html/

Electronic Bulletin Boards

Tribunal Watch World Wide Web Site on Major War Criminals/Suspects: Information and documents are from Helsinki Human Rights Watch, International Criminal Tribunal in The Hague, UN Special Committees for War Crimes in the former Yugoslavia, and other international organizations and sources including referenced articles from newspapers:

http://www.cco.caltech.edu/~bosnia/criminal/criminals.html

United Nations International Criminal Tribunal for the Former Yugoslavia:

http://www.igc.apc.org/tribunal/

Court TV: War Crimes Tribunal Page (especially useful for description of the tribunal jurists and personnel):

http://www.courttv.com/casefiles/warcrimes/

Human Rights Watch/Helsinki Watch:

gopher://gopher.igc.apc.org:5000/11/int/hrw/helsinki/bosnia

Commission of Experts on the Former Yugoslavia Established Pursuant to Security Council Resolution 780 (1992):

http://www.cij.org/cij/commission.html

War Crimes Investigators' Open Source, Factual and Legal Resources:

http://www.his.com:80/~cij/investigations.html

Reports of Tadeusz Mazowiecki, Special Rapporteur on Human Rights to the United Nations:

http://www.haverford.edu/relg/sells/reports/mazowiecki.html

Physicians for Human Rights:

gopher://gopher.igc.apc.org:5000/11/int/phr

ICRC Operations in Western and Central Europe and the Balkans (with details on the Manjača and Mostar-area camps):

http://www.icrc.ch/unicc/icrcnews.nsf/

Efforts to Resist Cultural Genocide and Destruction of Manuscripts:

http://www.applicom.com/manu/ingather.htm

AN EXAMPLE OF SOURCE CROSS-CORROBORATION: OMARSKA

The Omarska camp offers one example of how the various sources can be used in cross-corroboration. Following are the sources used by this author in depicting the camp at Omarska. Similar cross-corroborated evidence was used in discussion of the other camps and killing sites.

U.S. Department of State: "War Crimes in the Former Yugoslavia: Submission of Information to the United States Security Council in Accordance with Paragraph 5 of Resolution 771 (1992)." The original publications of these reports are difficult to cite, since they are scattered over eight issues of a publication. The citation below is based upon an index prepared by Aida Premilovac and Michael Sells and posted, with the full text, on the World Wide Web site listed above: 1:20, 2:13, 2:15, 2:16, 2:17, 2:24, 3:4, 3:7, 3:8, 3:9, 3:11, 3:12, 3:17, 3:18, 3:21, 3:24, 3:36, 4:3, 4:9, 5:15, 6:1, 6:2, 6:6, 6:7, 7:7, 7:14, 7:16, 8:6, 8:10, 8:13, 8:14.

Helsinki Watch: *War Crimes in Bosnia-Hercegovina* vol. 1 (New York, 1993), 87; vol. 2 (1994), 163.

Indictments: (1) The International Criminal Tribunal for the Former Yugoslavia, The Prosecutor of the Tribunal

[Richard Goldstone], Against Dušan Tadić, a.k.a. "Dule"
Goran Borovnica, *Indictment*. Includes eight sets of charges,
each set detailing up to fifty-four specific incidents. Tadić
was a local official allegedly invited into the Omarska camp
on a regular basis to commit atrocities. (2) The International
Criminal Tribunal for the Former Yugoslavia, The Prosecutor of the Tribunal [Richard Goldstone], Against Željko
Meakić [Commander of Omarska] and eighteen other named
Omarska personnel. Includes thirteen sets of charges.

Books, Reports, Diaries, and Interviews: Roy Gutman, *Witness
to Genocide* (New York: Macmillan, 1993); Rezak Hukanović,
"Eyewitness to Hell: A Survivor's Diary of the Serb Concentration Camp at Omarska," *The New Republic*, 12 February 1996, 24–29; Ed Vulliamy, *Seasons in Hell* (New York:
St. Martin's Press, 1994); Radovan Karadžić's public statements on Omarska; Televised reports (ITN) of visits to
Omarska and Trnopolje; Reports by the UN High Commission for Refugees for the Banja Luka region (site of
Omarska); Published interviews with Omarska survivors and
survivors of nearby camps where some Omarska prisoners
were transferred; Personal interviews with refugees whose
family members were last seen being taken to Omarska.

NOTES

CHAPTER ONE

1. Aida Mušanović, "Bosnian Culture under Siege: Artistic Responses" (paper presented at the 1995 Annual Gest Symposium on the Cross-Cultural Study of Religions, "Art, Religion, and Cultural Survival," Haverford College, October 29, 1995).

2. On Passover, April 15, 1995, the *Haggadah* was ceremonially opened for the third time since it entered the National Museum's collection a hundred years ago, during an interreligious service at which Jews, Croats, Serbs, Muslims, and other Bosnians reaffirmed their commitment to a multireligious society. See Roger Cohen, "Bosnia's Jews Glimpse Book and Hope," *New York Times*, 16 April 1995. For the *Haggadah*, see Mirza Filipović, ed., *The Sarajevo Haggadah* (Sarajevo: Svjetlost, 1988).

3. András Riedlmayer, *Killing Memory: Bosnia's Cultural Heritage and Its Destruction*, Haverford: Community of Bosnia Foundation, 1994, videocassette.

4. Riedlmayer, *Killing Memory;* and *idem*, "The War on People and the War on Culture," *New Combat* (Autumn 1994): 16–19; B. Bollag, "Rebuilding Bosnia's Library," *Chronicle of Higher Education* (13 January 1995): A35–37; *Warchitecture* (Sarajevo: OKO, 1994); Karen Detling, "Eternal Silence: The Destruction of Cultural Property in Yugoslavia," *Maryland Journal of International Law and Trade* 17 (Spring 1993): 41–74. See also the essay by the Serbian architect who served as mayor of Belgrade from 1982 to 1986 and who has been kept under house arrest for his opposition to radical Serb nationalism: Bogdan Bogdanović, "Murder of the City," *New York Review of Books* 51 (27 May 1993): 20.

For a scholarly exposition of the "Colored Mosque of Foča," dynamited and turned into a parking lot in 1992, see Andrej Andrejević, *Aladža džamija u Foči* (Belgrade: Institute for the History of Art, 1972).

5. For Bosnia's religiously pluralistic art and architecture, see Mirza Filipović, ed., *The Art in Bosnia-Herzegovina (The Art Treasures of Bosnia and Herzegovina)* (Sarajevo: Svjetlost, 1987); and idem, *Yugoslavia* (Sarajevo: Svjetlost, 1990).

6. Carol Williams, *New York Times,* 28 March 1993; and Roger Cohen, *New York Times,* 7 March 1994, "In a town 'cleansed' of Muslims, Serb Church Will Crown the Deed." For an account based upon the eyewitness testimony of José Maria Mendiluce, an official of the UN High Commission for Refugees in Zvornik, see the video series *Yugoslavia: Death of a Nation* (BBC/Discovery, 1995) and the accompanying book, Laura Silber and Allan Little, eds., *Yugoslavia: Death of a Nation* (New York: TV Books, 1995): 222–25. See also the eight *U.S. State Department Reports on War Crimes in the Former Yugoslavia Submitted to the United Nations Security Council in Accordance with Paragraph 5 of Resolution 771 (1992),* which have been published under the title "War Crimes in the Former Yugoslavia" in the *U.S. Department of State Dispatch* 3.39 (28 September 1992): (first report) 732–35; 3.44 (1992): 802–6 (second report); 3.46 (16 November 1992): 825–32 (third report); 3.52 (28 December 1992): 917–22 (fourth report); 4.6 (8 February 1993): 75–79 (fifth report); 4.15 (12 April 1993): 243–52 (sixth report); 4.16 (19 April 1993): 257–69 (seventh report); 4.30 (26 July 1993): 537–48 (eighth report). The incidents in these eight reports are not numbered, but listed by dates, which makes them difficult to reference. I have edited them, adding incident numbers, and indexed them by number, for clear citation. See the World Wide Web at URL: http://www.haverford.edu/relg/sells/reports.html/.

These reports are village by village reports of crimes against humanity researched and written in response to UN Resolution 771 demanding access for international organizations to detention camps in the former Yugoslavia and authorizing the collection of information on human rights violations (see n. 22 below). They are not to be confused with the annual State Department reports on human rights in countries around the world, which are far less detailed. In all subsequent references to the eight reports I will simply refer to the eight U.S. State Department Reports on War Crimes in the Former Yugoslavia, and give the number of the report and the incident number. In the three years since these reports have been compiled, the validity of the testimony has been verified continually by independent investigations. For Zvornik then, the testimonies are found in the following reports and incidents: 1:19, 3:13, 4:11, 5:11, 6:15, 6:45, 7:16, 8:16, 8:22, 8:28, 8:63. See also Helsinki Watch, *War Crimes in Bosnia-Hercegovina* (New York: Human Rights Watch, 1994), vol. 2, 220 ff, "Forced Displacement."

7. For one of the clearer accounts of these events, see *Yugoslavia: Death of a Nation*; this video series and accompanying book are based upon interviews with the principals in the drama, including Serb and Croat nationalists who are proud of their role in destroying Yugoslavia and quite explicit about the various stages in their program.

8. David Owen, *Balkan Odyssey* (New York: Harcourt Brace Jovanovich, 1995), 10, 40.

9. For the details in the events of 1991 and early 1992, see Paul Shoup, "The Bosnian Crisis in 1992," in Sabrina Petra Ramet and Ljubisa S. Adamovich, eds., *Beyond Yugoslavia: Politics, Economics, and Culture in a Shattered Community* (Boulder: Westview Press, 1995), 155–88.

10. Izetbegović replied to the Assembly that Karadžić's words "illustrate why others refuse to stay in this Yugoslavia." The exchange took place on October 14, 1991. See Silber and Little, *Yugoslavia: Death of a Nation,* 215.

11. President Milošević of Serbia had made it clear he was willing to go to great lengths to secure a peace and to remove sanctions on Serbia and Montenegro that had been imposed by the United Nations. The protégé of Serb President Slobodan Milošević, the militia leader Arkan, was implicated in the expulsions and brutalities. Yet Milošević was issued a visa to the United States not conditioned upon the release of this last remnant of Bosnian non-Serbs in the Banja Luka region.

12. See Richard Rubenstein, "Silent Partners in Ethnic Cleansing:

The UN, The EC, and NATO," *In Depth: A Journal for Value* 3.2 (1994), 51 ff. Even after the camps were revealed in news reports, Western nations refused to act promptly to save lives. The Serb authorities offered to release the prisoners if Western nations would take them as refugees. For several critical days, many Western nations delayed. As a result of the delay, many prisoners are thought to have perished.

13. See the eight U.S. State Department Reports on War Crimes in the Former Yugoslavia 1:20, 2:13, 2:15, 2:16, 2:17, 2:24, 3:4, 3:7, 3:8, 3:9, 3:11, 3:12, 3:17, 3:18, 3:21, 3:24, 3:36, 4:3, 4:9, 5:15, 6:1, 6:2, 6:6, 6:7, 7:7, 7:14, 7:16, 8:6, 8:10, 8:13, 8:14. Other, corroborating testimonies on Omarska are so extensive that, rather than listing them in this note, I have offered a separate discussion of them above in the Note on Sources. For an extended account by one survivor, see Rezak Hukanović, "Eyewitness to Hell: A Survivor's Diary of the Serb Concentration Camp at Omarska," *The New Republic*, 12 February 1996, 24–29.

14. Roy Gutman, *Witness to Genocide* (New York: Macmillan, 1993), author's note. Cf. Edward Vulliamy, *Seasons in Hell* (New York: St. Martin's Press, 1993), 97–111, 320–41.

15. Thus, Serb nationalists call the language spoken in Bosnia "Serbian" and consider Bosnian Muslims and to some extent even Bosnian Croats to be Serbs who have fallen away from their true identity. Similarly, Croat nationalists speak of the language as "Croatian." Caught in between the two nationalist terminologies, which are based on visions of an identity among religion, language, and nation, Muslims in Bosnia and those Croats and Serbs who do not identify with Croat and Serb visions of a Greater Croatia and a Greater Serbia now speak of the Bosnian language. As the conflict continues, the artificial differences in the languages are reinforced by a politically correct vocabulary for each grouping. Certain key words can determine whether one is speaking Serbian, Croatian, or Bosnian—even though, from the standpoint of linguistic comprehension, all three are the same language.

16. Some scholars believe the tribes that later became the Croats

and Serbs migrated originally from Central Asia and gradually became absorbed by the Slavic cultural and linguistic worlds.

17. Areas of mass killings carried out against Muslim civilians include Sanski Most, Ključ, Banja Luka, Prijedor, Kotor Varoš, Bosanski Šamac, Zvornik, Vlasenica, Zaklopača, Rogatica, Višegrad, Gacko, and Trebinje (by Serb nationalists); and Stolac, Čapljina, Počitelj, Ahmići, Stupni Do, Prozor, and Vitez (by Croat nationalists).

18. There were also major differences between Muslims in villages and those in the cities. For a glimpse into one Muslim community in Bosnia, see Tone Bringa, *Being Muslim the Bosnian Way: Identity and Community in a Central Bosnian Village* (Princeton: Princeton University Press, 1995).

19. For the background and implications of the designation of the "Muslim" national category in Bosnia, see Noel Malcolm, *Bosnia: A Short History* (New York: New York University Press, 1994), 119 ff.

20. See the interview in *Vreme News Digest* 213 (30 October 1995).

21. This summary is based upon personal interviews with Osman and Sabiha and upon Osman's article, written under the pen name Orhan Bosnević, "The Road to Manjača," in Rabia Ali and Lawrence Lifschultz, eds., *Why Bosnia? Writings on the Bosnian War* (Stony Creek, Conn.: The Pamphleteer's Press, 1993), 103–13.

22. In August 1992, in response to the media revelations about the concentration camps, the UN Security Council enacted Resolution 771 authorizing the collection and collation of human rights data, under which the U.S. State Department authored and submitted its eight reports. In September 1992, the United Nations Human Rights Commission appointed Polish Prime Minister Tadeusz Mazowiecki as Special Rapporteur for Human Rights in the Former Yugoslavia. The United Nations Commission of Experts was established at the request of the UN Security Council on 6 October 1992, Security Council Resolution 780. The Commission of Experts was empowered to gather evidence but not to prosecute. In a separate resolution on 25 May 1993 (Resolution 827) the Security Council authorized the establishment of an In-

ternational Criminal Tribunal on War Crimes with prosecutorial powers. The U.S. State Department human rights investigation group, the Rapporteur, the Commission of Experts, and the International Criminal Tribunal are, therefore, separate entities. The U.S. State Department, the Rapporteur, and the Commission of Experts have turned over to the tribunal their information, and some of that information is available to the public (see n. 6 above and Note on Sources above). The International Criminal Tribunal, based in The Hague, has made its own information available in two forms: in public indictments and in Rule 61 hearings that expose further evidence against indicted criminals who have not yet been taken into custody.

23. The following depiction is based on the sources listed in the previous note, detailed articles on war crimes in the journal *Vreme News Digest*, written by Serb human rights activists, and other sources listed below under each aspect of the "ethnic cleansing" program.

24. The first week of August saw mass killings at Manjača, but at other periods the killings were less frequent and methodical than at camps such as Omarska. See the eight U.S. State Department Reports on War Crimes in the Former Yugoslavia: 1:1, 1:25, 1:42, 2:26, 3:24, 6:1, 6:6, 6:11, 7:14, 7:16, 8:6, 8:14, 8:17, 8:23, 8:24, 8:51; Helsinki Watch, *War Crimes in Bosnia-Hercegovina* (New York: Human Rights Watch, 1994), vol. 2, 133 ff.

25. For the persecution of Muslims in Višegrad, see Peter Maass, *Love Thy Neighbor: A Story of War* (New York: Knopf, 1996), 8–15; Chris Hedges, "From One Serbian Militia Chief, A Trail of Plunder and Slaughter," *New York Times*, dateline Višegrad, 21 March 1996, A1, A8.

26. Such centers included the Drina River bridge at Višegrad, the Drina bridge at Foča, the stadium at Bratunac, and schools, mosques, stadiums, and roadsides throughout Serb-army occupied Bosnia-Herzegovina. For the killings and other abuses at Foča, see the eight U.S. State Department Reports on War Crimes in the Former Yugoslavia: 2:28, 4:8, 5:18, 6:14, 7:4, 7:5, 7:17, 7:19, 7:20, 7:21; Helsinki Watch, *War Crimes in Bosnia-Hercegovina*, vol. 2: 237, 257. Particularly

well documented are the killings that took place at the Čelopek cultural center near Zvornik. See the exposé in *The Weekend Australian*, 2–3 March 1996. One of the many Serbian militia taking part in the Zvornik killings was a group called the Yellow Wasps. Dušan Vuković, a member of the Yellow Wasps, was arrested and tried in Serbia for crimes in Zvornik, in an attempt by the Milošević government to show that it was capable of prosecuting Serbs for crimes in Bosnia. The trial was delayed, however, when questions about the relationship of Vuković and the Yellow Wasps to the Serbian secret police began to emerge. Vuković has acknowledged rape and multiple killings and even his defenders admit that he may have been involved in the killing of over one hundred civilians. See *Vreme News Digest* 156 (19 September 1994); 157 (26 September 1994); 164 (14 November 1994); 166 (28 November 1994); 178 (27 February 1995); 200 (31 July 1995).

27. An example of the first type occurred on May 16, 1992, in the village of Zaklopača in eastern Bosnia, where up to a hundred Muslims were killed as the Serb militias entered the town, which had previously disarmed itself under the orders of local Serb nationalist officials. See Helsinki Watch, *War Crimes in Bosnia-Hercegovina*, vol. 1: 50–53; Malcolm, *Bosnia: A Short History*, 245. An example of the second type was the days-long spree of rape, torture, and murder in the village of Liskovac. See Sally Jacobs, "Terrified, trapped in Bosnia: After a murderous attack, Liskovac Muslims want to leave," *Boston Globe*, 8 August 1993.

28. The ICRC appeal was made during the ethnic terror associated with Vojkan Djurković, an associate of the Serb militia leader Arkan. The appeal was made by International Red Cross president Cornelio Sommaruga. UN human rights rapporteur Tadeusz Mazowiecki also demanded a stop to the persecutions. The UN chief of civil affairs in Bosnia, Sergio de Mello, said Republika Sprska leader Karadžić had given him guarantees that the evictions would halt, but the expulsions and atrocities continued. See the Associated Press report of 9 September 1994 and *New York Times*, 18 October 1994. Many of those evicted were sent to the Lopare slave labor camp near Brčko.

29. From the testimony at the International Criminal Tribunal in The Hague, Netherlands.

30. Susan Brownmiller, *Against Our Will: Men, Women, and Rape* (New York: Simon and Schuster, 1975).

31. See the Pulitzer Prize winning reports of Roy Gutman, which appeared originally in *New York Newsday* and have been included in Gutman, *Witness to Genocide*, 157–63.

32. Other major sites of organized rape include the camps at Trnopolje and Manjača, various locales in Višegrad, Rogatica, Vogošća, Grbavica (a district in Serb army–occupied Sarajevo), Zvornik, Vlasenica, and the nearby camp at Sušica. The most notorious area of organized rape by Croatian religious nationalists was the Čapljina region of Herzegovina. See the eight U.S. State Department reports, the reports of Helsinki Watch, and the other sources listed above in the Note on Sources.

33. See Paul Mojzes, *Yugoslavian Inferno* (New York: Continuum, 1994), 231: "*Muslimanka sva u krvi, Srbin joj je bio prvi*" ("The Muslim woman is all bloody; a Serb was the first to spoil her"). The Serbian Guard militia boasted of gang-raping a 13-year-old Muslim girl in the Bosnian town of Gacko, attaching her to a tank, and riding around until there was nothing left of her but the skeleton. The boast was made public by Danica Drašković, wife of Vuk Drašković, who founded the Serbian Guard. See Norman Cigar, *Genocide in Bosnia: The Policy of "Ethnic Cleansing" in Eastern Europe* (College Station: Texas A & M University Press, 1995), 104–5.

34. See the discussion of Kosovo in Chapter 3 for detailed examples.

35. Božidar Popović, commander of the concentration camp at Manjača, in comments to Richard Cohen, *Philadelphia Inquirer*, 19 December 1992.

36. See the illuminating conversation of Peter Maass with a Bosnian Serb woman who maintains the absolute truth of the allegation about the harem plot that was broadcast on the radio. Maass, *Love Thy Neighbor*, 112–14.

37. The Qur'anic phrase chanted five times a day from the mosque

is: *la ilaha ill Allah.* The word "Allah" is a personal name believed to be derived from a combination of *al* (the) and *ilah* (god). Thus the testimony means: no "ilah" but "allah," or no god but God.

38. For just one example, see the U.S. State Department Report on War Crimes in the Former Yugoslavia 7:19, recounted by a woman who survived the atrocities at Foča.

39. "The Convention on the Prevention and Punishment of the Crime of Genocide," 78 U.N.T.S. 277, adopted by Resolution 260 (III) A of the General Assembly of the United Nations on December 9, 1948.

40. Rafael Lemkin, *Axis Rule in Occupied Europe: Laws of Occupation, Analysis of Government, Proposals for Redress* (New York: Howard Fertig, 1973), 79. See also L. L. Bruun, "Beyond the 1948 Convention: Emerging Principles of Genocide in Customary International Law," *Maryland Journal of International Law and Trade,* 17.2 (Fall 1993): 196–98.

41. The denials are usually based on the assumption that anything less than Auschwitz is not genocide. The 1948 Geneva Convention banning genocide was an effort, however, to avoid the conflation of all organized destruction of people with the Holocaust, while still learning from it. See for example Charles Krauthammer, "Drawing the Line at Genocide," *Washington Post,* 11 December 1992. Krauthammer denies that violence in Bosnia was genocidal but never mentions the criteria for genocide set in the Geneva Convention or in the definition by Lemkin. See also George Kenney's denial as cited in Owen, *Balkan Odyssey,* 80.

42. See n. 22 above for a list of the major sources of information. Charged with genocide for activities in Bosnia-Herzegovina are Republika Srpska President Radovan Karadžić, Serb army General Ratko Mladić, Bosnian Serb Security Chief Mićo Stanišić, Dušan Sikirica, commander of the Keraterm killing camp in Prijedor, Goran Jelišić, commander of the Brčko-Luka killing camp, and Željko Meakić (a.k.a. Mejahić), commander of the Omarska killing camp near Prijedor. A Rule 61 hearing has been held on the case of Dragan Nikolić, com-

mander of the Sušica camp, who has been indicted on multiple counts of crimes against humanity.

The term "genocide" was invented as a response to the Holocaust and has been inscribed within the articles of international law. During the cold war period, the genocides that existed (in Guatemala and Uganda, for example) were partially protected by a cold war rivalry that prevented coordinated international efforts to enforce the Geneva Convention. With the end of the cold war, the genocides in Bosnia and Rwanda have led to the creation of an International Criminal Tribunal in The Hague and have become the focal point for the effort to reestablish the Convention of 1948 criminalizing genocide and to provide judicial, diplomatic, and economic disincentives to those who would practice it.

43. UN Security Council Resolution 819. On May 6, 1993, the Security Council passed Resolution 824, declaring Bihać, Sarajevo, Žepa, Goražde, and Tuzla as safe areas along with Srebrenica.

44. In addition to the International Criminal Tribunal indictments, and evidence presented to the UN Security Council (including satellite and spy plane photos of Muslim prisoners held in stadiums and of mass graves), there have been investigative reports in the press. See the reports of David Rohde of the *Christian Science Monitor*, who was captured by the Serb military as he investigated a mass grave (16, 17, 20, and 21 November, 1995); Rohde's reports on Srebrenica are available on the World Wide Web at http://www.haverford.edu/relg/sells/srebrenica/srebrenica.html. See also the special report, "Srebrenica: The Days of Slaughter," *New York Times*, 29 October 1995.

CHAPTER TWO

1. For the development of the notion of "the Jews as Christ killer" see Cecil Roth, "The Mediaeval Conception of the Jew," in *Essays and Studies in Memory of Linda R. Miller*, ed. Israel Davidson (New York: Jewish Theological Seminary of America, 1938), 171–90; Jeremy Cohen, *The Friars and the Jews: The Evolution of Medieval Anti-Judaism* (Ithaca:

Cornell University Press, 1992); and *idem*, "The Jews as Killers of Christ in the Latin Tradition, from Augustine to the Friars," *Traditio* 29 (1983): 1–28. For the wider ideological and institutional forms of persecution, see R. I. Moore, *The Formation of a Persecuting Society* (New York: B. Blackwell, 1987).

2. For the legacy of Kosovo in the Serb tradition, see Thomas A. Emmert, *Serbian Golgotha: Kosovo, 1389* (New York: East European Monographs, 1990) and Wayne S. Vucinich and Thomas A. Emmert, eds., *Kosovo: Legacy of a Medieval Battle* (Minneapolis: University of Minnesota Press, 1991).

3. The power of passion commemoration, for good or evil, is not limited to Christianity, of course. In the passion of Shiite Islam, Husayn, the grandson of the Prophet Muhammad, is being opposed in his rightful role as leader and guide (Imam) of the Islamic community by the wicked Caliph Yazid. Yazid's army surrounded Husayn and his family and followers at the battle of Karbala in 680. Husayn and most of his family were killed in cruel fashion by the Caliph's soldiers. Each year the martyrdom of Husayn is reenacted during the commemorations known as the *ta'ziyya*. Some Islamic radicals used the *ta'ziyya* performances in Iran to demonize Americans, Jews, Bahais, and others as the killers of Husayn in a manner similar to the way Serb radicals used the Kosovo passion play to demonize Slavic Muslims. For example, see Ruhollah Khomeini, *Imam Khomeini's Last Will and Testament* (Washington, D.C.: Embassy of the Democratic and Popular Republic of Algeria, Interests Section of the Islamic Republic of Iran, 1989).

4. Some believe that the migrating South Slavic tribes that settled in Bosnia were led by and named after Iranian ruling castes, but little is known about this period.

5. See Alexander K. A. Greenawalt, "The Nationalization of Memory: Identity and Ideology in Nineteenth Century Serbia" (bachelor's thesis, Princeton University, 1994), 34–63. For Karadžić's interest in Herder, see ibid., 45.

6. Vuk Stefanović Karadžić, *Srpske narodne pesme* (Belgrade: Prosveta, 1985).

7. Greenawalt, "The Nationalization of Memory," 54.

8. Anne Elizabeth Pennington and Peter Levi, *Marko the Prince: Serbo-Croat Heroic Songs* (London: Duckworth, 1984), 15.

9. Milorad Ekmečić, "The Emergence of St. Vitus Day," in Vucinich and Emmert, *Kosovo: Legacy of a Medieval Battle*, 335. Cf. Greenawalt, "The Nationalization of Memory," 54.

10. Greenawalt, "The Nationalization of Memory," 53.

11. For the development of the Kosovo legend in the literature of chronicles and sermons, from the fifteenth to the nineteenth centuries, see Emmert, Serbian Golgotha, 61–142.

12. From the point of view of the Lazar legend, the religious element in nineteenth-century Serbian nationalism is far more important than works like Benedict Anderson's *Imagined Communities* might lead us to expect. While linguistic purification was crucial to the nineteenth-century construction of the Serb nation, the religious element was also crucial. See Greenawalt's "The Nationalization of Memory," 20–33, for an explicit critique of *Imagined Communities* on this point.

The difference between historical event and the literary construction of "age-old antagonism" can be seen in the contrast between Vuk Branković and Marko Kraljević. Marko was a Serb vassal of the Ottomans and yet he is celebrated within the tradition of Serb heroic poetry. Vuk Branković (who many historians believe did not betray Lazar at Kosovo) has been identified with the Judas figure and used as a coded symbol since the nineteenth century to stigmatize Slavic Muslims.

13. Bishop Petar II Petrović (Njegoš), *The Mountain Wreath (Gorski vijenac)*, trans. and ed. Vasa D. Mihailovich (Irvine, Calif.: Charles Schlacks, Jr., 1986). The explicitly Christological patterning of Njegoš's portrayal of the Kosovo myth was echoed in other art and literature produced or collected during the late nineteenth-century Romantic period. A description of a particular fragment of poetry, known (among other epithets) as the "Last Supper," depicts Lazar's banquet on the eve of the battle. Lazar's Last Supper is represented in Adam Stefanović's lithograph "The Feast of the Prince [Lazar]" with Lazar in the center of the banquet table surrounded by figures posed as Christ's dis-

ciples, with light suffusing the prince, and the traitor Vuk brooding in the background (see Fig. 1) (Ljubica Popovich in Vucinich and Emmert, *Kosovo: Legacy of a Medieval Battle*, fig. 21, p. 287).

14. Njegoš, *Mountain Wreath*, verses 95, 284.

15. See George Bush, "Remarks and an Exchange with Reports on Departure from Colorado Springs," 6 August 1992. *Public Papers of the Presidents of the United States. George Bush, 1992–93, Book II: August 7, 1992, to January 20, 1993* (Washington, D.C.: Office of the Federal Register, National Archives and Records Administration, 1993), 1393.

16. Christopher Boehm, *Blood Revenge: The Enactment and Management of Conflict in Montenegro and Other Tribal Societies* (Philadelphia: University of Pennsylvania Press, 1984).

17. Bishop Nikolaj Velimirović, *Religija Njegoševa* (Belgrade: Izdanje S.B. Cvijanovica, 1921), 166.

18. Branimir Anzulović, *The Triumph of the War God: Violence in Serbian Life and Culture* (unpublished manuscript, 1995), chap. 17.

19. Emmert, Serbian Golgotha, 134.

20. The Reverend Dr. Krstivoj Kotur writes of the Kosovo story as a Good Friday story, "with suffering, death, resurrection, and ascension, which experiences accrue to the poet from the ancient cosmic-ontological spiritual motivation." Kotur cites with approval the characterization of the Kosovo legend as "a nationalized Christ-epic: sacrifice, physical death, a defeat now in exchange for a future ascension to Heaven; Lazarus perishes, the heroes with him; even the traitor is there, and the premonition of treachery is at hand, as well, during the Last Supper." Kotur writes of Christian belief as a battle, of the day before St. Vitus's day—the eve of Vidovdan—as the Last Supper, of Vuk Branković as Judas, of Lazar as Christ, of Miloš as St. Peter, of Kosovo as an analogy of Golgotha, the mount on which Jesus was crucified.

See Rev. Dr. Krstivoj Kotur, *The Serbian Folk Epic: Its Theology and Anthropology* (New York: Philosophical Library, 1977) and Vladimir Dvorniković, *Karakterologija Jugoslavena* (Characteristics of the Yugoslavs) (Belgrade, 1930), 969.

21. Pavle Zorić in Alek Vukadinovic, ed., *Kosovo 1389–1989: Special*

Edition of the Serbian Literary Quarterly on the Occasion of 600 Years since the Battle of Kosovo (Belgrade: Serbian Literary Quarterly, 1989), 79.

22. Ivo Andrić, *The Development of Spiritual Life in Bosnia under the Influence of Turkish Rule* (Durham: Duke University Press, 1990), 20. Andrić's dissertation was composed in German and presented to the dean of the faculty of philosophy at the Karl-Franz University in Graz, Austria on May 14, 1924, under the title *Die Entwicklung des geistigen Lebens in Bosnien unter der Einwirkung der türkischen Herrschaft.*

23. Ibid., 12.

24. Ibid., 16 ff. For careful revision of the Bogomil thesis see John Fine, *The Bosnian Church: A New Interpretation* (Boulder: East European Quarterly, 1975; distributed by Columbia University Press).

25. John Fine dismantles national mythologies that portray Slavic Muslims, Croats, and Serbs as unchanging entities. See John Fine, "The Medieval and Ottoman Roots of Modern Bosnian Society," in M. Pinson, ed., *The Muslims of Bosnia-Herzegovina: Their Historic Development from the Middle Ages to the Dissolution of Yugoslavia* (Cambridge: Harvard University Press, 1993), 1–21. Both Fine and Noel Malcolm, *Bosnia: A Short History* (New York: New York University Press, 1994) show that the Orthodox Christians in Bosnia only in the postmedieval period came to identify themselves explicitly as Serbs.

26. Ivo Andrić, *The Bridge on the Drina*, trans. Lovett F. Edwards (New York: Macmillan, 1959; Chicago: University of Chicago Press, 1977). *Na Drini ćuprija* was originally written in 1942.

27. Ibid., 35–37.

28. Ibid., 37–52. See the comments by John Matthias, "Introduction," in *The Battle of Kosovo*, trans. John Matthias and Vladeta Vuckovic (Athens, Ohio: Swallow Press/Ohio University Press, 1987, 15–16). Matthias chooses the Andrić impalement scene as the single image "most resonant of the suffering by the Christian Slavic population during the long night of Turkish rule in the Balkans." One American reader told this author that by the time she finished the impalement scene of *The Bridge on the Drina*, she was trembling all over; the horror of the scene never left her.

29. Prince Vlad was a Vlach, an ethnic group closely intertwined with Serbs and allied with Serbs through the shared Orthodox Christian faith. Prince Vlad is a hero to some supporters of the Republika Srpska.

30. They are also characterized by monodimensional characters. Muslim Slavs fall into one of a series of types: the evil Turk, the good Turk (dull, uncreative, but not cruel), and the janissary (brilliant, gifted, with the sadness of the loss of Christian essence always in his soul). These types are portrayed through the voice of an omniscient narrator who presents their thoughts through a stereotyped notion of Islam. Also in *The Bridge on the Drina* (written in 1942 while Gypsies were being exterminated in Europe), Gypsies are portrayed generically as vile.

31. In addition to a revival in the cult of Njegoš, the late 1980s experienced a revival of interest in Andrić from both Serb and Croat nationalists. For the revival and nationalistic politicization of the works of Andrić and Njegoš, see Sabrina Petra Ramet, *Balkan Babel: Politics, Culture, and Religion in Yugoslavia* (Boulder and Oxford: Westview Press, 1992), 28–29 and Misha Glenny, *The Fall of Yugoslavia* (London: Penguin, 1992), 22. This brief reading of Njegoš and Andrić cannot do justice to the range of their work. It is meant to demonstrate that religion is a key element in the tragedy and to identify how that element is used.

32. For the *gusle* verses and the statement of Karadžić, see the film *Serbian Epics,* produced and directed by Paul Paulikawski (BBC, 1992).

33. Milovan Djilas, *Njegoš: Poet, Prince, Bishop* (New York: Harcourt Brace Jovanovich, 1966), 310–96.

CHAPTER THREE

1. For the Serbian art and monuments of Kosovo, see the sumptuously illustrated collection of essays, *Kosovo,* comp. William Dorich, ed. Basil W. R. Jenkins and Anita Dorich (Alhambra, Calif.: Kosovo Charity Fund, 1992).

2. The Islamic tradition of Albania differs from that of the Slavic Muslims of Bosnia. The differences between Albanian Muslims and Bosnian Muslims would not be recognized within the stereotypes of

religious nationalists. For a scholarly discussion of Albanian Islam, see Frances Trix, *Spiritual Discourse: Learning with an Islamic Master* (Philadelphia: University of Pennsylvania Press, 1993).

3. Marko Mladenović, "Counter-Revolution in Kosovo, Demographic Policy and Family Planning," in Alek Vukadinović, ed. *Kosovo 1389–1989: Special Edition of the Serbian Literary Quarterly on the Occasion of 600 Years since the Battle of Kosovo* (Belgrade: Serbian Literary Quarterly, 1989), 141–50, cf. Milan Komnenić, "The Kosovo Cataclysm," in Vukadinović, *Kosovo 1389–1989*, 67–80. For the pervasiveness of this claim among Serb nationalists, see Robert Duff, "The Resurrection of Lazar," *The Spectator*, 8 July 1989.

4. Branko Kostić, "The Yugoslav Programme on Kosovo," in Gordana Filipović, *Kosovo: Past and Present* (Belgrade: Review of International Affairs, 1989), 309.

5. "Memorandum on the Position of Serbia in Yugoslavia" (Belgrade, 1986). The document was authored by members of the Serbian Academy of Sciences and Arts, but the names were not made public, and the Memorandum was never officially published but leaked to the nationalists in the media.

6. For the problems of the 1974 constitution analyzed from a scholarly perspective, see Vojin Dimitrijević, "The 1974 Constitution and Constitutional Process as a Factor in the Collapse of Yugoslavia," in *Yugoslavia: The Former and the Future*, ed. Payam Khavan and Robert Howse (Washington: The Brookings Institute, and Geneva: The United Nationalist Research Institute for Social Development, 1995), 45–74.

7. Milan Komnenić in Vukadinović, *Kosovo 1389–1989*, 69. The denunciation of Albanians is from a speech given by Milan Komnenić at the meeting "Serbians and Albanians in Yugoslavia Today," April 26, 1988. It was incorporated into a memorial volume on the 600th anniversary of the battle of Kosovo, as a special issue of the *Serbian Literary Quarterly*.

8. See Branka Magaš, *The Destruction of Yugoslavia: Tracking the Break-up 1980–92* (London: Verso, 1993), 49–73.

9. Mihajlo Marković, then a professor at the University of Pennsylvania and a founder of the philosophical journal *Praxis*, was exposed by Michele Lee with his allegations unproved. See Magaš, *The Destruction of Yugoslavia*, 57–58; and *Vreme News Digest* 208 (25 September 1995).

10. A. Dragnich and S. Todorovich, *The Saga of Kosovo: Focus on Serbian-Albanian Relations* (Boulder: East European Monographs, 1984), 170–72.

11. Amnesty International, *Yugoslavia: Ethnic Albanians—Victims of Torture and Ill-Treatment by Police* (New York, 1992). Cf. Helsinki Watch reports on Kosovo for the years 1986, 1989, and 1990. In addition to lacking any evidence, the genocide charges were filled with interior contradictions. Serb nationalists insisted that Albanians were never prosecuted in Kosovo for individual crimes against Serbs, yet in one complaint a Serbian nun denounced the sentences leveled against a group of teenagers convicted of setting a fire; the sentences ranged from five years to twelve years (Rada Saratlić in Vukadinović, *Kosovo 1389–1989*, 151–61). In an article entitled "Violated Culture" (Petar Šarić in Vukadinović, *Kosovo 1389–1989*, 159–61), a Serb nationalist claimed that the lack of road signs to monasteries implied an ominous intent on the part of the Albanian populace and that the lack of signs in the Cyrillic alphabet was a manifestation of "cultural violation." The writer recalled that a traveler in Serbia proper had expressed surprise "that no road sign or name of the city, dwellings or a river was in Cyrillic writing." He concluded, "It is not hard to imagine what the situation in Priština, Djakovica, Prizren, Uroševac [towns in Kosovo] is. . . ." After implying that the lack of Cyrillic signs in Kosovo is an aspect of the Albanian policy to "violate" Serb culture, the Serb nationalist states (as if it bolstered his own case) that a traveler could find no Cyrillic signs in Serbia proper, dominated and controlled by Serbs.

12. Holy Council of Bishops, 1969, in G. Filipović, *Kosovo: Past and Present*, 354–55.

13. Appeal by the Clergy in G. Filipović, *Kosovo: Past and Present*, 355–60.

14. Ibid., 360–63.

15. *Srbobran*, 2 November 1988.

16. Njegoš, *Mountain Wreath*, verses 131–32.

17. Komnenić in Vukadinović, *Kosovo 1389–1989*, 70.

18. Ibid., 71. A participant in the events has offered the following synopsis of the manipulation of Kosovo genocide claims (Azem Vllasi in *Vreme News Digest* 208 (25 September 1995). The author asked police for crime figures and found that the lowest number of cases in Yugoslavia was in Kosovo and Montenegro. There were five interethnic murders in all of Kosovo during the period from 1981 to 1987, two in which Albanians murdered Serbs and three in which Serbs murdered Albanians. Cf. Mark Thompson, *A Paper House: The Ending of Yugoslavia* (New York: Pantheon, 1992): 129–30. In reference to calls for the expulsion from Kosovo of 360,000 alleged Albanian immigrants, the police files showed a total of 813 Albanian immigrants in Serbia.

The manipulation of the term "genocide" during the Kosovo dispute came full circle in 1995. After NATO air strikes were called against Serb army anti-aircraft positions and munitions dumps, Serb Orthodox clergy and activists railed against this alleged genocide of the Serbian people. See *Srbobran*, September–October 1995.

19. Adam Puslojić, "On the Way," in Vukadinović, *Kosovo 1389–1989*, 114.

20. Stepinac was tried after the war for complicity in the crimes of the Ustashe regime, but his conviction was marred by Tito's attempt to pressure Stepinac into forming a Catholic Church in Croatia more independent of the Vatican. See Richard West, *Tito and the Rise and Fall of Yugoslavia* (New York: Carroll and Graf, 1995), 212–361. The most famous clerics involved in World War II atrocities were Catholic Archbishop of Sarajevo Ivan Šarić, an anti-Semite and admirer of Ustashe chief Ante Pavelić, and Franciscan Friar Filipović-Majstorović, known as "Brother Devil," a killer in the Jasenovac camp. For the role of Catholic leaders in the protection of Ustashe criminals after the war, see M. Aarons, M. and J. Loftus, *Unholy Trinity: The Vatican, the Nazis, and*

Soviet Intelligence (New York: St. Martin's Press, 1991). For the Croatian bishops' refusal (with the significant exception of Bishop Pihler) to address the Ustashe genocide, see Paul Mojzes, *Yugoslavian Inferno* (New York: Continuum, 1994), 129–35 and Gerald Schenk, *God with Us: The Role of Religion in Conflicts in the Former Yugoslavia* (Uppsala: Life and Peace Institute, 1993).

21. Interview, *Sixty Minutes*, 17 June 1995.

22. Milovan Djilas, *Wartime* (New York: Harcourt Brace Jovanovich, 1977), 139. For Tito's recollection of his shock at the massacre of Foča Muslims, see V. Dedijer, *Novi prilozi za biografiju Josipa Broza Tita*, 1 (Zagreb: Mladost, 1980), 557; trans. Paul Garde, *Vie et mort de la Yougoslavie* (Paris: Fayard, 1992), 81.

23. Vuk Drašković, *Nož* (Knife) (Belgrade: Zapis, 1982). One Serb commented that on reading Drašković he would become enraged and go out immediately to attack Croats and Muslims; see Norman Cigar, *Genocide in Bosnia: The Policy of 'Ethnic Cleansing' in Eastern Europe* (College Station: Texas A & M University Press, 1995), 25.

24. Muharem Durić and Mirko Carić, *"Kako srpski nacionalisti odmažu srpskom narodu i šta prati mošti kneza Lazara"* (How Serbian Nationalists Are Hindering the Serbian People and What Accompanies the Relics of Prince Lazar), *Politika*, 17 September 1988, 7. Cited and translated in Cigar, *Genocide in Bosnia*, 35. Cf. Milan Milošević and Dragoslav Grujié in *Vreme News Digest* 145 (4 July 1994): "At about the same time the Serbian Orthodox Church carried the relics of Grand Duke Lazar (the leader of the Kosovo battle) around the Serb lands, and religious services were held over the remains of the victims of genocide of a half a century ago that were retrieved from mass graves for that purpose."

25. V. Gagnon, "Roots of the Yugoslav Conflict," *International Organizations and Ethnic Conflict*, ed. M. J. and S. T. Esman (Ithaca: Cornell University Press, 1995), 180–97, especially 191–92.

26. Ivo Banac, "Serbia's Deadly Fears," *New Combat* 3 (Autumn 1994): 36–43.

27. Cigar, *Genocide in Bosnia*, 78.

28. For these instances and others, ibid., 80.

29. Cited in *Vreme News Digest* 170 (26 December 1994). At this stage, the Serb militias allowed camera crews to videotape their work. For the video footage, commentary by Mendiluce, and Šešelj's discussion of his and Serb President Slobodan Milošević's roles in what he calls the "separations" at Zvornik, see *Yugoslavia: Death of a Nation* (BBC production aired 26–30 December 1995 on "Discovery Journal"), part 3.

30. These last two positions are also part of an international discourse of complicity discussed in Chapter 6.

31. See *Yugoslavia: Death of a Nation*, part 3, for an interview with Miroslav Šolević, the Serb nationalist who helped stage the incident and is proud of his achievement. Cf. Laura Silber and Allan Little, *Yugoslavia: Death of a Nation* (New York: TV Books, 1995), 37–38. See also Beverly Allen, *Rape Warfare: The Hidden Genocide in Bosnia-Herzegovina and Croatia* (Minneapolis: University of Minnesota Press, 1996).

32. These events received little journalistic notice at the time. Among the available descriptions, see Barney Petrovic, "Serbia Recalls an Epic Defeat," *Guardian*, 29 June 1989, 9; Robert Duff, "The Resurrection of Prince Lazar, *Spectator*, 8 July 1989, 9–11.

33. Noel Malcolm, *Bosnia: A Short History* (New York: New York University Press, 1994), 213 ff and *Vreme News Digest* 145 (4 July 1994).

34. Misha Glenny, *The Fall of Yugoslavia* (London: Penguin, 1992), 39.

CHAPTER FOUR

1. See Klanwatch, *Intelligence Report*, 79 (August 1995) and 80 (October 1995) and "Neo-Nazi Novel a Blueprint for Hate," in the Southern Poverty Law Center, *SPLC Report*, 25.3 (September 1995), for detailed information on William Pierce's *The Turner Diaries* and its role in the Christian Identity and militia movements. For branches of self-

styled Christian militancy, see Ronald Holmes and Stephen Holmes, *Murder in America* (Thousand Oaks: Sage Publications, 1994), 55–70. McVeigh tried to call Pierce just before the destruction of the Oklahoma City Federal Building.

2. V. Gagnon, "Roots of the Yugoslav Conflict," *International Organizations and Ethnic Conflict*, ed. M. J. and S. T. Esman (Ithaca: Cornell University Press, 1995), 180–97, especially 195–96.

3. The role of Milošević in the destruction of Yugoslavia and in the violence in Bosnia was discussed in a book by a former political ally of his, Borisav Jović, *The Last Days of the Socialist Federation of the Republic of Yugoslavia*. See Jane Perlez, "Serb Chief Painted as Warmonger by Ex-Aide," *New York Times*, 16 December 1995.

4. These groups are mentioned in Misha Glenny, *The Fall of Yugoslavia* (London: Penguin, 1992), but to understand their close cooperation with the Yugoslav army and security forces, one needs to consult *Vreme News Digest* (1993–1995, *passim*) and see the comments of the militia leaders themselves in Laura Silber and Allan Little, eds. *Yugoslavia: Death of a Nation* (New York: TV Books, 1995), 222–50. An example of the cooperation between the regular army and the irregular genocide squads occurred after the Yugoslav army took the city of Vukovar in 1991. Colonel Veselin Šljivančanin was filmed refusing the International Red Cross access to over 200 prisoners that had been taken from the hospital at Vukovar. Also on camera are Chetnik irregulars, with beards, backpacks, and rifles. According to one of the few survivors, the prisoners were handed over by the Yugoslav army to the irregulars for torture and execution. A mass grave has been found at the nearby village of Ovčara. Šljivančanin has been indicted by the International Criminal Tribunal.

5. Jezdimir Vasiljević is considered to be one of Arkan's financial backers. After his bank collapsed, he fled with the savings of thousands of innocent Serb civilians (*Vreme News Digest*, 1993–1994, *passim*).

6. U.S. Department of State Report on War Crimes in the Former Yugoslavia 4:12.

7. For other examples, see Norman Cigar, *Genocide in Bosnia: The Policy of "Ethnic Cleansing" in Eastern Europe* (College Station: Texas A & M University Press, 1995) 84.

8. See the comments by Radovan Karadžić, who considers all Serbs living in Bosnian government areas to be "ethnic hostages" (David Binder, "Bosnian Serb Leader Says His People Fight Out of Fear and in Self-Defense," *New York Times,* 5 March 1993). The Croat population in eastern Bosnia was small, so that Serb extremists were mainly preoccupied with what they called the "separation" of Muslims from Serbs.

9. Ljuljeta Goranci, "1,300 Weeping Muslims Forced from Homes in Serb-Held Bosnia," Associated Press, *Philadelphia Inquirer,* 19 September 1994. In the article, Vasvija Mulasalihović, 39, is quoted as saying that the leader of the expulsions, Vojkan Djurković, told her and other women whose sons, brothers, and husbands were being taken away that they should go to Tuzla (in Bosnian-government controlled territory) and attain the expulsion of 150 Serb families. Upon doing that, they would get their loved ones back.

10. The practice was later adopted by Croat commanders of camps for Muslims. See Chapter 6, below.

11. For a chronicle of the economics of looting in Serbia and in the Republika Srpska, see *Vreme News Digest* 104 (20 September 1993); 108 (18 October 1993); 147 (18 July 1994); and 156 (19 September 1994).

12. Cigar, *Genocide in Bosnia,* 65.

13. The effect of such dehumanization was clear at Srebrenica, where before the Dutch UN battalion handed over the town to the Serb army, a Dutch soldier expressed contempt for Muslims because they were "smelly." It evidently did not occur to him that people living in concentration-camp conditions are not able, as part of a deliberate policy, to practice normal hygiene.

14. In interviews with the author, Haverford College, 1993.

15. When Sanski Most was retaken by the Bosnian army in the fall of 1995, a mask was found that had been used during killing sprees carried out against Muslim civilians.

16. Dragan Nikolić, Rule 61 Hearing, International Criminal Tri-

bunal, The Hague, 10 October 1995. The *müfti* (Muslim religious leader) of Banja Luka has survived the persecution there and acknowledged those courageous Serbs who sheltered or rescued their Muslim and Croat neighbors.

17. Serbian-Americans have tended either to remain silent or to support the religious nationalists. For a denunciation of the Serbian-American refusal to recognize and condemn the slaughter organized by Serb religious nationalists in Bosnia, see George Mitrovich, "Serbian-Americans should Condemn Nazi-style Savagery," *Philadelphia Inquirer*, 2 September 1993.

18. Dr. Mirko Pejanović, President of the Serb Civic Council of Bosnia and a member of the collective seven-member presidency of the Republic of Bosnia-Herzegovina, in an interview in Washington by Umberto Pascali of *Executive Intelligence Review*, 19 September 1995.

19. On the newsgroup soc.culture.bosna-herzgvna from 1993 to 1995.

20. See Serbian Republic News Agency (SRNA) report of 20 November 1995 for Karadžić's presentation of Obilić decorations in Bijeljina and 3 December 1995 for the Obilić awards in the district of Nevesinje.

21. Paul Holmes, Reuters, 15 May 1993, "Serbian Extremists Gather in Bosnia to Honour Fighters": "In Knezina, a mountain village 60 km (40 miles) east of Sarajevo, Šešelj invested 18 Chetnik fighters with the old Serbian title of 'military duke' (*vojvoda*) at a candlelit ceremony in the small stone monastery of the Sacred Lady. . . . The battlegrounds reeled off in the citation included towns shattered by Serb artillery and purged of non-Serbs in almost two years of war—Brčko, Srebrenica, Foča and Višegrad in Bosnia. . . . They kissed a silver crucifix and a copy of the bible before they were blessed by Father Voja, a Serbian Orthodox priest."

22. SRNA, dateline Banja Luka, 20 November 1995.

23. Vojislav Maksimović, "Podseća na robovanje" (It is Remindful of Slavery), *Evropske Novosti*, 27 January 1994, 18, cited and translated by Cigar, *Genocide in Bosnia*, 61. For the role of Maksimović at Foča, see

Gutman, *Witness to Genocide*, 157–63. Cf. BBC broadcast, 7 January 1994, from the Belgrade Newspaper *Borba* (5 January 1994), "Foča Becomes Srbinje"; BBC, 3 October 1994, "Serbian Orthodox Patriarch Meets Karadžić on Tour of Bosnian Serb Republic," based upon the Yugoslav Telegraph Service news agency, Belgrade, 30 September 1994; Inter Press Service, 13 January 1995. For the term "Srbinje" used during expulsions, see the *Cleveland Plain Dealer*, 2 April 1995.

24. Duško Doder, Special to the *Boston Globe*, "On Serb Holy Day, Hellfire for Foes," 10 February 1993. For the Mirko Jović remark, see Cigar, *Genocide in Bosnia*, 35. Many examples could be given. Thus, after the slaughter of Muslims from the safe area of Srebrenica, a Serb priest disagreed with local Serbs who condemned the killings, stating that he would gladly kill a "Turk." *New York Times*, 29 October 1995.

25. For Bishop Atanasije's remark, see Cigar, *Genocide in Bosnia*, 30. The remark is part of an interview published in Rajka Radivojić, "Zavodjenja za Golešplaninu" (Leading Astray to Mount Goleš), *Intervju*, 9 December 1988, 27).

26. In *Glas Crkve*, cited by Cigar, *Genocide in Bosnia*, 31–32.

27. Metropolitan Christopher, *The Historical Background of the Contemporary Situation of the Orthodox Church in Yugoslavia* (Belleville, Mich.: Firebird Video, 1992), videocassette.

28. Interview in *Evropske Novosti*, 4 March 1993, 10, cited in Cigar, *Genocide in Bosnia*, 66. Zvornik was the first Muslim-majority city in Bosnia to become 100 percent "cleansed" of Muslims and to have a new church commissioned in memory of this accomplishment.

29. Christopher Bennett, *Yugoslavia's Bloody Collapse: Causes, Course and Consequences* (New York: New York University Press, 1995), 126–29.

30. *Los Angeles Times*, 12 August 1995.

31. Cited in Cigar, *Genocide in Bosnia*, 59.

32. The SS officer was Edwin Neuwirth, who treated Zhirinovsky to two days at his retreat in the Austrian Alps; see Craig Whitney, "Russian Rightist Angers Germans," *New York Times*, 24 December 1992. For Zhirinovsky in Bijeljina, see *Washington Post*, "Bosnian Serbs Hail Russian Nationalist," 1 February 1994, A16.

33. See the three articles in *Vreme News Digest* 178 (27 February 1995): Alexander Cirić, "Turbo Land: Machine Gun Wedding (with Singing)"; Dejan Anastasijević, "Željko Ražnjatović Arkan: The Groom," and idem, "Ceca Veličković: The Bride." See also Roger Cohen, "Serbia Dazzles Itself: Terror Suspect Weds Singer," *New York Times*, 20 February 1995; and John Kifner, "An Outlaw in the Balkans Is Basking in the Spotlight," *New York Times*, 23 November 1993.

34. Rev. Djordje Ilić cited in B. Demick, "Bosnian Serbs Nurture Anger: A Town United in Acrimony," *Philadelphia Inquirer*, 26 September 1995, A1, A9. Demick goes on to show how Father Ilić's teachings affect a young Serb man, Drago Konstantinović. Konstantinović grew up with Muslims and Croats as friends and dated a Muslim girl named Amela. He is shown kissing Father Ilić's ring and states to the journalist that if he saw his former Muslim and Croat friends now, he would kill them.

35. See Milan Milošević, "Conflict within the Serbian Church: Pavle versus Atanasije," *Vreme News Digest* 221 (25 December 1995). The politicians who had protested atrocities against Muslims in Trebinje and Gacko were none other than Dobrica Ćosić and Vuk Drašković, whose virulent anti-Muslim writings had created the climate for the atrocities; but Ćosić and Drašković at least were able to reject the worst extremes committed by their militias and followers, while Bishop Atanasije's support of extreme religious nationalism has never wavered.

36. BBC Monitoring Summary of World Broadcasts, 7 July 1994, "Yugoslavia: Serb Bishops Appeal for Rejection of Contact Group's Maps" (Tanjug news agency, Belgrade, 5 July 1994). In urging rejection of the peace plan, the synod stated that it was speaking not just as a political party, but as "Christ's church of this God-loving people at a time of serious temptations for our history and the history of humankind"— to the people it has guided upon "Christ's Via Dolorosa for centuries."

37. Radovan Karadžić interview, on Paul Paulikawski, *Serbian Epics* (BBC, 1994). For Nikolaj's argument, advanced in his condemnation of the Dayton accords, see *SRNA Bulletin*, 26 November 1995. In fact, the first Orthodox church in Sarajevo was built in the 1530s at the order of

the Ottoman governor, almost a century after the Turkish conquest of the region.

38. Kalajić is a mentor for the White Eagles militia (*Beli orlovi*), associated with some of the most inhuman atrocities in Bosnia; it is commanded by a historian on Kosovo, Dragoslav Bokan, and Mirko Jović, the chairman of the Serbian Popular Renewal Party. See Dragoš Kalajić, "Kvazi Arapi protiv Evropljana" (Semi-Arabs versus Europeans), *Duga*, 13–19 September 1987, 14–15, translated and cited by Cigar, *Genocide in Bosnia*, 26. For the genetically caused flaws supposedly resulting from this "special gene" of Ottoman soldiery, see Cigar, *Genocide in Bosnia*, 26–27. In a September 1995 issue of *Duga*, Kalajić also celebrates Serb army destruction of Bosnian cities, claiming that since Homer, true Europeans have hated cities.

39. See "The Extraordinary Session of the Holy Episcopal Synod of the Serbian Orthodox Church in Response to the False Accusations against the Serbian People in Bosnia-Herzegovina," *Pravoslavni misionar*, June 1992, 250–51, cited by Cigar, *Genocide in Bosnia*, 89; and Memorandum of the Holy Episcopal Synod's session of May 14–20, 1992, *Pravoslavlje*, 1 June 1992, 2, in Cigar, *Genocide in Bosnia*, 78.

40. *Los Angeles Times*, 12 August 1995, reporting on a statement made in a recent issue of the weekly *Pogledi*.

41. See the statement from the Syndesmos Conference on Nationalism and Culture held in St. Petersburg in July 1994, quoted in *In Communion: Journal of the Orthodox Peace Fellowship of the Protection of the Mother of God*, 1995, 6.

42. Edward Sorel, "Religion in the News," *The Nation*, 11 October 1993, 380. See also Martin Peretz, "Cape Cod Diarist: Symbolic Politics," *The Nation*, 5 September 1994, 50. Peretz compares Karadžić's honor to Pope John Paul II's awarding of the Knight of the Ordine Piano for "outstanding service to Church and society" to Kurt Waldheim, the former Nazi officer in Yugoslavia who lied about his Nazi connections and later was elected president of Austria. (Waldheim was awarded the Order of King Zvonimir by Ustashe leader Ante Pavelić for

his work with Nazi Group E, which supervised massacres in the Kozara region of Bosnia). See also Marlise Simons, "At a Crossroads, Rifts Pull at Orthodox Churches," *New York Times*, 5 November 1995.

43. For a summary of this appeal, see *Syndesmos, The World Fellowship of Orthodox Youth*, Orthodox Press Service 70 (31 August 1995). Among the signatories were Bishop Kallistos Ware of Diokleia (UK), Professor Olivier Clement (France), Professor Nicholas Lossky (France), and James Forest (USA), Secretary of the Orthodox Peace Fellowship.

44. See James Forest, "We Drink the Same Water and Pray to the Same God, an Orthodox Response to the War in Former Yugoslavia," *In Communion: Journal of the Orthodox Peace Fellowship of the Protection of the Mother of God*, 1995, 1–3. After opposing a succession of peace plans and supporting Karadžić and Mladić, Pavle refused to oppose the Dayton accords. For this he was condemned by other Serb bishops for betraying the Serb cause. Belgrade, December 20, 1995, from a report by Serb independent agency BETA.

45. Živica Tucić quoted in *Los Angeles Times*, 12 August 1995.

46. For Milošević's language of battles to come, see Silber and Little, *Yugoslavia: Death of a Nation*, 72.

47. Cigar, *Genocide in Bosnia*, 33. Other slogans included "I'll be the first, who'll be second, to drink some Turkish [Muslim] blood?" "Europe, remember who we are fighting for," and simply, "We want arms."

48. See the "Serbian Pride" t-shirts advertised in *Srbobran*, 19 April 1989, with designs including the maiden of Kosovo and various versions of the CCCC flag upon a shield on the breast of the double eagle.

49. Mark Juergensmeyer, *The New Cold War* (Berkeley: University of California Press, 1993), 4–5.

50. For a few examples, see Martin Marty and Scott Appleby, eds., *Fundamentalisms Observed* (Chicago: University of Chicago Press, 1991); Bruce Lawrence, *Defenders of God* (New York: Harper and Row, 1989); John Voll, in John Esposito, ed., *Voices of Resurgent Islam* (New York: Oxford University Press, 1984); and Juergensmeyer, *The New Cold War.*

51. The denial of the religious element in the genocide in Bosnia is

pervasive. For just one example, see Susan Woodward, *Balkan Tragedy: Chaos and Dissolution after the Cold War* (Washington, D.C.: The Brookings Institution, 1995), 243: "The victimization of Muslims through ethnic cleansing was also a result of the political contest behind the wars, not ethnic or religious hatreds."

52. Rezak Hukanović, "Eyewitness to Hell: A Survivor's Diary of the Serb Concentration Camp at Omarska," *The New Republic*, 12 February 1996, 29. For accounts of such forced singing at other concentration camps and torture centers, see the eight U.S. State Department Reports on War Crimes in the Former Yugoslavia 2:5, 5:11.

53. An extended investigation of this nexus of issues might begin with Gavin Langmuir's important study, *History, Religion, and Antisemitism* (Berkeley: University of California Press, 1990).

54. In the realm of the visual arts, for example, see Petar Palavicini's relief, "The Mother of the Jugovići" and Ljubinka Jovanović's work of the same title (Ljubica D. Popovich in Wayne S. Vucinich and Thomas A. Emmert, *Kosovo: Legacy of a Medieval Battle* (Minneapolis: University of Minnesota Press, 1991), figs. 34 and 35, pp. 300–301.

CHAPTER FIVE

1. See András Riedlmayer, "Killing Memory: The Targeting of Libraries and Archives in Bosnia-Herzegovina," *MELA Notes: Newsletter of the Middle East Librarians Association* 61 (Fall 1994): 3. See also Riedlmayer, *Killing Memory: Bosnia's Cultural Heritage and Its Destruction* (Haverford: Community of Bosnia Foundation, 1994), videocassette.

2. For the Islamic monuments in Bosnia-Herzegovina and a report on their destruction, see Amir Pašić, *Islamic Architecture in Bosnia and Hercegovina* (Istanbul: Research Centre for Islamic History, Art, and Culture, 1994). Of 29 major Islamic monuments in Mostar, dating from 1552 to 1651, Pašić lists 27 as totally destroyed.

3. See Riedlmayer, *Killing Memory*.

4. Franjo Tudjman, *Bespuća povijesne zbiljnosti* (Wastelands of Historical Reality) (Zagreb, 1990), 318–19.

5. Franjo Tudjman, *Nationalism in Contemporary Europe* (Boulder: East European Monographs, 1981; distributed by Columbia University Press), 162–63, cited by Richard West, *Tito and the Rise and Fall of Yugoslavia* (New York: Carroll and Graf, 1995), 364. Cf. Richard West, "An Apologist for Hitler," *The Guardian*, 21 October 1991, 23.

6. Warren Zimmerman, "The Last Ambassador: A Memoir on the Collapse of Yugoslavia," *Foreign Affairs* 74.2 (Spring 1995). Zimmerman recounts a meeting with Tudjman during which Tudjman "erupted into a diatribe against Izetbegović and the Muslims of Bosnia." Tudjman accused them of being fundamentalists trying to establish a beachhead in Europe and appealed to "civilized nations" to stop them.

7. Interview with *Le Figaro*, 25 September 1995. See also Christopher Hitchens, "Minority Report," *The Nation*, 18 December 1995.

8. See Laura Silber and Allan Little, eds. *Yugoslavia: Death of a Nation* (New York: TV Books, 1995), 131–32.

9. Edward Vulliamy, *Seasons in Hell* (New York: St. Martin's Press, 1994), 221–34; John Burns, "Croats Wield the Guns in 'Cleansed' Bosnian Town," *New York Times*, 30 October 1992.

10. András Riedlmayer, "The War on People and the War on Culture," *New Combat* 3 (Autumn 1994): 23, quoted from a UNHCR report of August 23, 1993.

11. See Mary Craig, *Spark from Heaven: The Mystery of the Madonna of Medjugorje* (Notre Dame: Ave Maria Press, 1988), 67–103; Wayne Weible, *Medjugorje: The Message* (Orleans, Mass.: Paraclete Press, 1989), 274–95; Mar Bax, *Medjugorje: Religion, Politics, and Violence in Rural Bosnia* (Amsterdam: VU Uitgeverij, 1995).

12. The World War II Bishop of Mostar, Dr. Alojzije Mišić, was horrified by the methods used by the Ustashe in carrying out forced conversions. Stepinac's response to the letter was to blame the Serbs for their own persecution. See West, *Tito*, 94–96. Mišić described how mothers, girls, and children under eight were taken from six railway wagons and thrown alive down the cliffs into ravines.

13. Vulliamy, *Seasons in Hell*, 214–24.

14. The relationship between the Vance-Owen map and the HVO

military operations against Bosnian Muslims is clearly illustrated in a booklet drawn up by the followers of Mate Boban in defense of the "cleansing" campaign against Muslims: Croatian Community of Herceg-Bosna, *Ethnic Cleansing of Croats in Bosnia and Herzegovina 1991–1993* (Mostar, August 1993). The booklet uses the Vance-Owen map in claims that Herceg-Bosna is entitled to land inhabited by Muslims and, at the very time of its publication, being purged of Muslims.

15. In his own account, Owen vehemently maintains that the original Vance-Owen plan was subverted by the U.S. State Department. He acknowledges that he and Stoltenberg then tried to persuade the Bosnian Muslims to accept a plan based upon a revised version of the Milošević-Tudjman map, but insists that the plan should not be called the "Owen-Stoltenberg" plan. See David Owen, *Balkan Odyssey* (New York: Harcourt Brace Jovanovich, 1995), 89–225. It may be true, as Owen maintains repeatedly, that the U.S. State Department helped kill the Vance-Owen plan, but Owen refused, continually, to confront the reality that after months of stalling, it was the Bosnian Serb parliament that killed the Vance-Owen plan formally. The Serb government in Pale allowed the Vance-Owen plan to be used as a pretext for avoiding a credible use of force to stop the genocide, and then, when they were finally forced to make a decision, they rejected it, first by refusing to endorse it and then by engineering a referendum of Bosnian Serbs in which the plan was presented as a sell-out and overwhelmingly defeated. Whatever the virtues of the Vance-Owen plan itself, Owen cannot bring himself to confront the reality that the Bosnian Serb side had no incentive to accept a just peace plan as long as it could carry out its aggression with impunity, backed secretly by the regular Serb army and openly by Serb militias, against a Bosnian opponent that was vastly inferior in military strength.

16. In addition to the attack against the Bosnian Muslims at Prozor, the HVO had also engaged in a campaign of cultural destruction and religious expulsion against Orthodox Serbs. An HVO team destroyed the sixteenth-century Orthodox monastery of Žitomislići, south of

Mostar, for example, and blew up the Orthodox Cathedral in Mostar, as well as destroying scores of smaller, village Orthodox churches. It should be emphasized immediately that such actions do not mean that all sides are equally to blame: the Bosnian government never engaged in systematic cultural annihilation.

17. HVO soldiers pushed from Travnik and Vareš by the Bosnian army took refuge with the Serb army, indicating their common agenda with the Serb army even as they presented themselves as allies of the Bosnians.

18. In addition to the volunteers from Serbia, Montenegro, Russia, Greece, and other nations with large Orthodox Christian populations, there were Orthodox members of the UN peacekeeping forces who used their position to thwart UN resolutions and aid the Serb militants. In one case, Colonel Viktor Loginov, a Russian officer in UNPROFOR, stated in a December 1992 interview published in the Russian newspaper *Ruski vjesnik* that Russia and Serbia were brothers in a Christian Orthodox war of self-defense against the Vatican and other conspiratorial anti-Orthodox powers. At the same time he was a member of UNPROFOR, Loginov took on a highly paid position with Arkan's Serbian Volunteer Guard and used his position with the UN to smuggle fuel and supplies to Arkan. See Vlastimir Mijovic, "Big Brother is Backing You," in Ben Cohen and George Stamkoski, eds., *With No Peace to Keep: United Nations Peacekeeping and the War in the Former Yugoslavia* (London: Grainpress, 1995), 142–47.

19. See Chuck Sudetic, "Serbs and Croats Mount Joint Attack on Muslim Town," *New York Times*, 28 June 1993, A3. Serb and Croat religious nationalists also cooperated on the siege of nearby Maglaj. Only two years earlier, that Serb army now being aided by the Tudjman-backed HVO had been annihilating the Croatian city of Vukovar.

20. Dubravka Ugrešić, *Have a Nice Day*, trans. Celia Hawkesworth (New York: Viking, 1994), 236–37.

21. From an interview conducted by the author in November 1995 with a Bosnian Muslim refugee. The Bosnian refugee and his family had

come to Croatia to stay with a Croatian relative. When they refused to eat pork, they were called Turks and thrown out onto the street.

22. Josip Beljan, "Priznata vjernost" (Recognition of Faithfulness), *Veritas* 9–10 (September–October 1992): 24–25, translated by Paul Mojzes, *Yugoslavian Inferno* (New York: Continuum, 1994), 130.

23. See Pašić, *Islamic Architecture in Bosnia and Hercegovina*, 218, who lists the following works of major importance annihilated by late summer 1993: Šišman Ibrahim Paša Mosque, Šišman Ibrahim Paša Medresa (school complex), Šišman Ibrahim Paša Han (market complex), Šišman Ibrahim Paša Hamam (Turkish-bath complex), and the Gavran-Kapetanović House.

24. Eyewitness report by correspondent Francois Raitberger, "NATO Lifeline to Bosnia Revives Croatia Port," Reuters, 9 February 1996.

25. For reports on the conference at Čapljina, see BBC Summary of World Broadcasts, 14 February 1996, reporting on a broadcast from Radio-TV Mostar, 13 February 1996. For the report on plans to build a Catholic church on the ruins of the mosque, see Reuters, 17 March 1996; and BBC Summary of World Broadcasts, 6 March 1996, citing a report in the Sarajevo newspaper *Večernje novine* of 5 March 1996. There is no independent confirmation of these reports, but the Herceg-Bosna authorities have not denied them. There is also a report that the Herceg-Bosna authorities wish to change the name of Počitelj to Komušin, again following the example of Serb nationalists who changed the name of Foča to Srbinje. See TWRA press agency, dateline Mostar, 14 February 1996.

26. See Vulliamy, *Seasons in Hell*, 320–41. Vulliamy was among the first press witnesses to Omarska and the Herzegovinian Croat camps.

27. See Owen, *Balkan Odyssey*, 268.

28. Weibel, *Medjugorje*, 105–6. The priest's views are enthusiastically reinforced by the narrator and author, Wayne Weibel.

29. "Croats Accused of Terrorism," *Toronto Globe & Mail*, 5 February 1996, A1, A7.

30. See Mike O'Connor, "Bosnian Croats Resist Peace Accord," *New York Times*, 13 February 1996.

31. Ivo Andrić, *The Development of the Spiritual Life in Bosnia under the Influence of Turkish Rule* (Durham: Duke University Press, 1990), 16.

32. West, *Tito*, 383.

33. Vulliamy, *Seasons in Hell*, 260; Bax, *Medjugorje*, 78.

34. OMRI (Open Media Research Institute) Daily Report, 28 May 1993.

35. For Kuharić's religious nationalism in 1991 and his claim that "only a handful of Serbs" were killed in the Ustashe state during World War II, see West, *Tito*, 372 and the London daily *The Times*, 25 August 1991. For the Boban-Šušak controversy, see OMRI Daily Report, 8 June 1993, 14 June 1993, 28 July 1993, 27 August 1993. While some view Kuharić as genuinely concerned with peaceful coexistence, others have suggested that the Croatian Catholic hierarchy was upset with Boban for losing territory in his attacks on Muslims and for trading other traditionally Catholic territory to Serb nationalists. For a discussion of the various readings of the Boban-Kuharić dispute, see Gojko Berić, "Catholic Church: Setbacks in Bosnia Fuel Boban-Church Conflict," *Balkan War Report* 21 (August/September 1993): 15.

36. OMRI Daily Report, 17 September 1993.

37. See The Catholic Church, *Assisi 1993: Giovanni Paolo II per la pace in Bosnia ed Erzegovina* (Citta del Vaticano: Libreria Editrice Vaticana, 1993). Earlier Vatican documents did focus on the death and destruction suffered by Catholic Croats, especially in Dubrovnik, while still wishing peace for all parties. See *La Crisi Jugoslava: Posizione e azione della Santa Sede* (1991–1992) (Citta del Vaticano: Libreria Editrice Vaticana, 1992).

38. Pope John Paul II visited the Sudan in February of 1993 and protested vigorously the persecution of Christians by the military regime. Alan Cowell, "Pope, in the Sudan, Assails Religious Persecution," *New York Times*, 10 February 1993.

39. Šušak is alleged to have ordered the assassination of moderate

Croat police officials in an effort to provoke war with Serbia in 1991 and to have instigated HVO attacks on Muslims in 1993. For Šušak's role in 1991, see *Yugoslavia: Death of a Nation* (BBC, 1995), part III and Silber and Little, eds., *Yugoslavia: Death of a Nation* 140–46. For Šušak's ties to the Herzegovinian Franciscans, see the account by Gordan Nuhanović, *Globus* 259 (24 November 1995). The Nuhanović article discusses three days of negotiations between Herzegovinian Franciscans and Mostar's bishop. It states that the meeting was called by the Pope and convened by the papal nuncio for Bosnia-Herzegovina, Francesco Monteresi, and that it included a verbal threat, a first in the 700-year-old history of Franciscans in Herzegovina, to shut down the Franciscan order in the province.

While a meeting of Franciscans was in process to discuss the problem, Gojko Šušak (a frequent and welcome guest at Mostar's monasteries) and the director of Croatian Intelligence Service (HIS) Dr. Miroslav Tudjman rang the bell. They had arrived from a celebration of four years of Herceg-Bosna at Grude, founding site of Herceg-Bosna. Originally from the Medjugorje area (before he emigrated to Canada to make his fortune), Šušak is considered an important man around town.

40. OMRI Daily Digest, No. 223, Part II, 15 November 1995, "Croatian President Promotes Indicted War Criminal." See the article by Dubravko Grakalić and Davor Ivanković in *Globus* (258) 17 November 1995, which lists the awards given to Dario Kordić on the day of statehood as the Order of Prince Branimir with Neckband, for "particular merits in advancing the international position and prestige of the Republic of Croatia and its relations with other countries"; the Order of Nikola Šubić Zrinski "for a heroic deed in the war"; and the Order of Petar Zrinski and Frano Krsto Frankopan with Silver Braid, "for contribution to the maintenance and development of the Croatian state-forming idea, the establishment and betterment of the sovereign state of Croatia." In December 1995, Croat authorities further violated the Dayton accords by releasing Ivica Rajić. Rajić was indicted by the International Criminal Tribunal for crimes against humanity, including

the mutilation and burning-alive of Muslim children at the village of Stupni Do.

41. The relationship of the truth of a vision to its moral efficacy in the lives of those who experience it is also argued by William James, *Varieties of Religious Experience* (New York: Longmans, Green, 1902).

CHAPTER SIX

1. Louis Gentile, *Toronto Globe & Mail*, 13 January 1994. A similar comment by Gentile was quoted by Anthony Lewis, *New York Times*, 25 January 1994: "The leaders of the Western world have received a play-by-play report of what is going on here. It is unforgivable that it has been allowed to go on month after month." See also *New York Times*, 15 February 1994, opinion page. Other UNHCR officials who have been denouncing the systematic atrocities have been Kris Janowski, Larry Hollingsworth, and José Maria Mendiluce.

2. The three most famous gangsters went by the nicknames of Caco, Ćelo, and Juka. When the Caco and Ćelo gangs began abusing residents of Sarajevo, they were arrested by Bosnian police on October 24, 1993. Ćelo (Colonel Ramiz Delalić) and his gang were arrested, but Caco (Colonel Mušan Topalović) was killed during the violence surrounding his arrest.

3. See Mark Almond, *Europe's Backyard War: The War in the Balkans* (London: Mandarin, 1994), 243; Winston Nagan, "Bosnia: A Question of Genocide," talk given 12 September 1994 in Gainesville, Fla.; Carol Hodge, "Hurd Mentality: Britain's Foreign Secretary Bows out in Shame," *The New Republic*, 7 August 1995, 18. Croatia was less affected by the embargo because it could purchase arms on the black market in Eastern Europe. The embargo thus only really harmed the Bosnians; any attempt to send arms to Bosnia would have to run a double gauntlet of Croatian blackmail and "surcharges" and the NATO arms blockade. The most obvious donor of weapons for Bosnia would have been the NATO powers themselves; the arms embargo allowed

them to refuse to arm Bosnians with the excuse that it would be illegal to supply them.

4. "The Islamic Declaration" was not published in the original Serbo-Croatian until 1990: *Islamska deklaracija* (Sarajevo, 1990). An English version appears in the *South Slav Journal*. For the later, more modulated position, see Alija Izetbegović, *Islam between East and West* (Indianapolis: American Trust Publications, 1984). Again, the Serbo-Croatian version appeared after the English version: *Islam izmedju Istoka i Zapada* (Sarajevo, 1988).

5. Amila Buturovic discusses the link between the curse of Kosovo (in which anyone who did not fight at Kosovo would be bereft of children) and the gynocidal assault against Slavic Muslims who were, precisely, viewed by Serb nationalists as Kosovo traitors. Amila Buturovic, "Nationalism and Rape: Gendering 'Ethnic Cleansing' in Bosnia-Herzegovina," paper presented at the conference "The Crisis in Bosnia," 7 November 1995, Keene State College, Keene, N.H.

6. Interview by Batsheva Tsur in the *Jerusalem Post*, 13 November 1992, cited by Cigar, *Genocide in Bosnia*, 124.

7. For the link between anti-Muslim and anti-Jewish prejudice, see Allan Cutler and H. Cutler, *The Jew as an Ally of the Muslim* (South Bend: Notre Dame University Press, 1986). This use of the term "Orientalism" was popularized by the influential book of Edward Said, *Orientalism* (New York: Pantheon Books, 1978). For a specific example of the history of Orientalist scholarship, see Michael Sells, "The Qasida and the West: Self-Reflective Stereotype and Critical Encounter," *Al-'Arabiyya*, 20 (1987): 307–57.

8. Since May 1992, Yugoslavia has been made up of the two Serb-majority republics of Serbia and Montenegro and has been dominated by Serbian President Slobodan Milošević. In the 25 July 1994 Tanjug news agency release, dateline Tripoli, Yugoslav President Zoran Lilić was reported to have arrived in Tripoli for a friendly visit where he was received "with honors customarily reserved for outstanding officials from friendly countries." Colonel Qaddafi made an unscheduled visit to

the Yugoslavian president, a visit that was considered by the reporter to be a special compliment. See also the Tanjug reports for July 24–27, September 18, and December 5, 1994.

9. Similarly, when the NATO nations refused to lift the arms embargo on Bosnia, the Bosnians accepted military aid from nations such as Iran and the Sudan that were willing to break the embargo. Serb nationalists and Western politicians pointed to such desperate moves as evidence of the militant fundamentalism of the Bosnian Muslims. Yet when Iran was caught breaking the economic embargo against Serbia (with an effort to smuggle a massive oil-drilling complex directly to the Milošević regime), the Serb nationalists in Belgrade escaped being labeled militant Islamic fundamentalists. See Ray Bonner, "U.S. Scrambles to Keep Oil Rigs from Reaching Serbia," *New York Times*, 7 April 1995.

10. See Tanjug reports from the first week of October 1994 for synopses of such articles from the French weekly *L'Evenement de Jeudi*, the Paris daily *Le Figaro*, and the Paris daily *Liberation*, from which the Belgrade daily *Politika* carried an anti-Muslim article as a feature. The point here is not that the Bosnian government or Bosnian Muslim religious leaders should not be criticized, but that the criticism should be kept in perspective. There are some who wish to introduce Islamic symbols into Bosnian public life, but then Christian symbols, slogans, and pledges pervade the public rituals, currency, and public monuments of European and North American nations.

Given the enormity of the assault on Bosnia, the Bosnian people have shown restraint by refraining from retaliation or generic condemnation of all Serbs or all Christians. In World War II, the U.S. government put Japanese-Americans in detainment camps without any due cause and without Japan having occupied any U.S. soil; what might have happened to Japanese-Americans had Japan "ethnically cleansed" 70 percent of the United States? The Bosnian government never considered putting all Serbs in their territory into detention camps.

11. See the translations in H. T. Norris, *Islam in the Balkans* (Co-

lumbia: University of South Carolina Press, 1993), 295–96; and Norman Cigar, *Genocide in Bosnia: The Policy of "Ethnic Cleansing" in Eastern Europe* (College Station: Texas A & M Press, 1995), 29. Cigar provides a series of Jevtić's stereotypes about Muslims.

12. Aleksandar Popović, *Les Musulmans Yougoslaves, 1945–1989: mediateurs et metaphores* (Lausanne: L'Age d'Homme, 1990), 1–10. If the term "totalitarian" is to be applied to Islam because the religion is not restricted to private life, then it also must be applied to Halakhic Judaism, much of Evangelical Christianity, and much of classical Hinduism, Roman Catholicism, Confucianism, and Shintoism.

13. Darko Tanasković, "Religion and Human Rights in the Contemporary Balkans," *The Mediterranean Review*, Winter 1995, 81–96.

14. See Luciano Cheles, Ronnie Ferguson, and Michalina Vaughan, eds., *The Far Right in Western and Eastern Europe* (London: Longman, 1995), chapter 2, "The Dark Side of Nationalism," and chapter 11, "The Extreme Right in France"; and Hans-Georg Betz, *Radical Right-Wing Populism in Western Europe* (New York: St. Martin's Press, 1994), chapter 3, "Immigration and Xenophobia."

15. The speech appears in the Serbian daily *Borba*, 29 June 1989, 1.

16. David Owen recounts of Bosnian President Alija Izetbegović that "there was no outward and visible sign that he was a Muslim. He, his son and his daughter dressed and acted as Europeans"—as if it were surprising that Muslims, who have been inhabiting Europe for twelve centuries, would appear European, or if there were a contradiction between appearing Muslim and appearing European. See David Owen, *Balkan Odyssey* (New York: Harcourt Brace Jovanovich, 1995), 39.

17. For just one example of the construction of Muslims as anti-Western caricatures, see David Pryce-Jones, *The Closed Circle: An Interpretation of the Arabs* (London: Weidenfeld & Nicolson, 1989) and the review of that book by Conor Cruise O'Brien, "Sick Man of the World," in *The Times*, 11 May 1989. O'Brien states: "Muslim threats and incitements following the publication of Salman Rushdie's *The Satanic Verses* have brought home to many people in the West just how inimical to Western values Islamic society actually is." After offering a list of stereo-

types about Muslims, O'Brien states that "It [Muslim society] looks re-pulsive because it *is* repulsive from the point of view of Western post-Enlightenment values [emphasis O'Brien's]." O'Brien adds: "It remains true that Arab and Muslim society is sick, and has been sick for a long time." After citing a Muslim reformer's statement that the remedy for the ills of Islam is the Qur'an, O'Brien ends: "Unfortunately the sick-ness gets worse the more the remedy is taken." It would be unimagin-able to find such a venomous, purely bigoted portrayal of Christianity, Judaism, or any other major religion in the pages of a leading Western newspaper. It would be naive to think that the attitudes represented by O'Brien did not play a role in the acquiescence by British society and Western society more generally in the assault on Bosnian Muslims.

18. For the anti-Muslim basis of keeping the arms embargo, see Roger Cohen, "West's Fears in Bosnia," *New York Times,* 13 March 1994, and Chris Hedges, "In the Truce Line, a Vast New Divide," *New York Times,* 11 February 1996. Hedges writes: "The possibility that there would be an overtly Islamic state in Europe, allied with Iran, is one of the main reasons the French opposed the establishment of Bosnia in the first place." Willy Claes, NATO Secretary General during much of the Bosnian conflict, wrote of the fundamentalist Islamic threat and of NATO as an alliance committed to "defending the basic principles of civilization that bind North America and Western Europe." See "NATO Chief Warns of Islamic Extremists," *Toronto Globe & Mail,* 3 February 1995. Cf. Edgar O'Ballance, *Civil War in Bosnia 1992–94* (New York: St. Martin's Press, 1995), 79. While policy makers and diplomats do not speak publicly of their motives for allowing the assault on Bosnia to continue with impunity for three and a half years, those not in public office are more open. The Internet discus-sion groups (soc.culture.bosna-herzgvna, alt.current-events.bosnia, soc.culture.yugoslavia) offer postings angrily questioning why Christians should come to the aid of Muslims. The construction by some Western ideologues of a "green threat" of Islam and the self-fulfilling prophecies of a clash of civilizations, and the mirror construction by some Islamic militants of a Western great Satan—and the way in which the two ex-

three weeks of selective bombing had utterly disoriented the Serb army. See Owen, *Balkan Odyssey*, 336. Owen begins the discussion by saying that Serb General Ratko Mladić "did not fold up with the first wave of NATO bombing as so many commentators had confidently predicted" (as if those arguing for the "lift and strike" option had specified a one-week period). Owen then goes on to admit that after three weeks of the campaign, the communications system of the Serb army was disrupted and the balance of power on the ground shifted in favor of the Bosnian and Croat coalition.

25. Bill Clinton, campaign speech, August 6, 1992, cited by Hanna Rosin in Andrew Sullivan, *Accomplices to Genocide* (Entire August 7, 1995, issue of *The New Republic*) (Washington, D.C.: The New Republic, 1995).

26. President Bill Clinton, cited by Rosin in ibid., 14.

27. As quoted in the Associated Press report by Barry Schweid, *Philadelphia Inquirer*, 19 May 1993, A3. According to the account in Elizabeth Drew, *On the Edge: The Clinton Presidency* (New York: Simon & Schuster, 1994), 157–63, Christopher and his aide Tom Donilon were major figures in persuading Clinton to give up his commitment to the "lift and strike" plan to stop the genocide and to turn to a policy of containment.

28. For the efforts of British Foreign Secretary Douglas Hurd and others in Britain to portray the genocide as a "civil war," see Noel Malcolm, *Bosnia: A Short History* (New York: New York University Press, 1994), 239. Cf. A. M. Rosenthal, "Why Only Bosnia?" *New York Times*, 30 May 1995: "What to do now? . . . Keep American troops out and the [arms] embargo on—against all parties. Tell Bosnians to deal with their own fate, asking for Western diplomatic help if they want it." Rosenthal's solution would likely have led to the rest of Bosnia suffering the fate of Srebrenica.

29. "Our interest is in seeing, in my view at least, that the UN does not foreordain the outcome of a civil war." President Bill Clinton, May 14, 1993, cited by Rosin in Sullivan, *Accomplices to Genocide*, 14. The other Clinton quotes above are taken from the same source. Ser-

bian President Milošević maintained that the Yugoslav army was not involved in Bosnia. By the admission of his assistant, Borisav Jović, the alleged "withdrawal" of the Yugoslav army from Bosnia had been a ruse, a "fast one," and the Serbian government in Belgrade continued to arm, direct, and pay the salaries of Serb soldiers in Bosnia. See *Yugoslavia, Death of a Nation* (BBC, 1995), part III, and Laura Silber and Allan Little, eds., *Yugoslavia: Death of a Nation* (New York: TV Books, 1995), 217–18.

30. For the Senate speeches on S. 21, "The Bosnia and Herzegovina Self-Defense Act of 1995," known as the Dole-Lieberman bill to lift the arms embargo, see the *Congressional Record*, 18–20 July 1995, 10178–10367.

31. Strobe Talbot, "Remarks to the World Affairs Council of Pittsburgh," December 14, 1995. Whether the Clinton administration is committed to enforcing the Dayton accords or merely using them to keep genocide in Bosnia out of the election campaign is a controversial question. The NATO troops are to be withdrawn after the 1996 elections, and there are deep doubts whether or not the Western powers will fulfill their commitment to establish a viable framework for peace during the NATO stay in Bosnia.

32. Senator Phil Gramm in his campaign comments, November 1995.

33. For the notion that "they have been fighting for fifteen hundred years" see Congressman Manzullo of Illinois, address on the House floor, 29 November 1995. For the view that the problem goes back to the fourth-century split in the Roman empire, see Congressman William Goodling, 30 November 1995. Goodling boasted of his background as a history professor while making his speech. For a short piece pointing out the many historical errors in Goodling's speech, see Anthony Bazdarich, "An Open Letter to the Voters of the 19th Congressional District of Pennsylvania," *Zajedničar*, December 20, 1995.

34. See Noel Malcolm, "Impartiality and Ignorance," in Ben Cohen and George Stamkoski, eds., *With No Peace to Keep: United Nations*

Peacekeeping and the War in the Former Yugoslavia (London: Grainpress, 1995), 121.

35. See Carol Hodge, in Sullivan, *Accomplices to Genocide*, 18. For the U.S. arms export industry, see William Hartung, *And Weapons for All: How America's Multibillion Dollar Arms Trade Warps Our Foreign Policy and Subverts Democracy at Home* (New York: Harper Collins, 1995).

36. Bosnian President Izetbegović repeatedly urged Western leaders to either lift the arms embargo or intervene to stop the genocide. In a September 6, 1993 speech to the UN Security Council he pleaded: "Defend us or allow us to defend ourselves. You have no right to deny us both."

37. The Associated Press reported from Geneva on November 24, 1994, that the World Council of Churches, made up of Protestant and Orthodox churches, "demanded renewed enforcement of the U.S. arms embargo to all sides in the conflict."

38. Adrian Hastings, "A Crime that Puts the Church to Shame," *The Guardian*, 3 July 1993.

39. Quoted in the London daily *The Independent*, 17 December 1995.

40. For a list of all the relevant UN Security Council resolutions, see Cohen and Stamkoski, eds., *With No Peace to Keep*, 177–84. For a succinct exposé of the activities of the UN in Bosnia, see David Rieff, "The Institution That Saw No Evil," *New Republic*, 12 February 1996, 19–24.

41. At Srebrenica, British diplomats first watered down the safe area resolution. Next, Yasushi Akashi and other UN officials refused to use all necessary means to get convoys through to the enclave, turning it into an abode of hunger and misery. Then Akashi issued a UN report suggesting that Srebrenica be abandoned—a clear green light to the Serb army. On June 5, 1995, the Serb army violated the safe area and drove two thousand desperate refugees into the center of town, but the UN refused to enforce its mandate to deter attacks. The Dutch officers drank a toast with General Mladić and wrote him a document stating

the civilians had been treated properly, while Mladić had a pig slaughtered before the Dutch commander's eyes as an example of what happened to his "enemies" and as Mladić was having thousands of Srebrenica residents led away for slaughter. The Dutch soldiers retreated in their armored vehicles, running over and killing a number of desperate residents trying to flee the killings. When they returned to the Netherlands, they were decorated for heroism.

42. Of the refusals to protect the UN-declared safe areas, British General Michael Rose's refusal to protect Goražde in April 1994 was among the more ingenious. As the Serb army shelled and killed civilians in the city and burned outlying villages, Rose stated that he had not been authorized to "protect" the safe area, only to "deter" attacks on it. Yet it was Rose who had refused to use a credible threat of NATO air strikes to deter the Serb army from violating the enclave in the first place. See *Yugoslavia: Death of a Nation* (BBC, 1995), part IV.

In November 1993, the Serb armies entered the safe area of Bihać and were on the verge of taking it. Rose and French General Bertrand Lapresle finalized the destruction of any credible NATO deterrence. As the Croatian Serb army violated the no-fly zone and the international border by launching air strikes on Bihać from the Udbina air base in Croatia, Rose and Lapresle authorized an air strike on the Udbina runway—a militarily useless target. The runway was soon repaired, and Lapresle demonstrated to the Serb army just how far he was willing to go to make NATO air power ineffective. It has since been revealed that at the same time, the CIA had intercepted a message from British special forces (SAS) in the area. The SAS were supposed to give NATO coordinates for the air strikes against Serb artillery and anti-aircraft batteries, but they deliberately held back the coordinates or gave false coordinates to thwart the effectiveness of any NATO strikes. See Ed Vulliamy, "How the CIA Intercepted SAS Signals," *The Guardian*, 29 January 1996.

43. See Roy Gutman, "Witnesses Claim UN Forces Visited Serb-Run Brothel," *New York Newsday*, 1 November 1993. Branislav Vlaco, the Bosnian Serb commander of the camp from May to November,

confirmed that UN peacekeepers from various nations frequented Sonja's, but claimed the women there were not captives, but rather "women of low morals." Gutman's account of the captivity of the women at the camp, the gang rapes in which UN personnel took part, and the fraternization of UN personnel with those running the camp are based on the testimony of nine Muslim men from the area who had been held in the bunker and three Muslim women who had been held at Sonja's, two of whom had been raped. The UN ultimately was forced to investigate and a number of UN peacekeepers were disciplined, but the UN refuses to make public its report on the incident. Borisav Herak, a Bosnian Serb militiaman who admitted to raping and killing women at the camp, also charged that General MacKenzie himself visited the camp. Gutman was able to prove this charge wrong; other UN officers may have been mistaken for MacKenzie.

During this same period, General MacKenzie gave numerous interviews in which he patronized the Bosnians and ignored the genocide. After he retired, he was paid $18,000 a day by Serbnet, a lobby for radical Serb nationalists, to propound his views.

44. The incident is described in detail in David Rieff's *Slaughterhouse: Bosnia and the Failure of the West* (New York: Simon & Schuster, 1995), 150–51. Rieff dedicates the book to Dr. Turajlić.

45. soc.culture.bosna-herzgvna, 21 February 1995.

46. *New York Times* (16 July 1992), A8; S. Burg, "The International Community and the Yugoslav Crisis," in *International Organizations and Ethnic Conflict*, ed. Milton Eshman and Shibley Telhami (Ithaca: Cornell University Press, 1995), 254. For the role of Douglas Hurd, see Carol Hodge in Sullivan, *Accomplices to Genocide*, 18–19.

47. The Bosnian army authorized the rebuilding of the Franciscan church in Fojnica damaged by an attack in which two Franciscans were killed. No such gesture has been made by the authorities of the Republika Srpska in connection with any of hundreds of mosques they destroyed.

In addition to the crackdown on the Caco and Ćelo gangs (see above, n. 2), the Bosnian government alone of all the parties in the

Bosnian conflict has fully cooperated with the International Criminal Tribunal and other war crimes investigations.

In late March 1996, the International Criminal Tribunal charged three Muslims with war crimes committed against Serbs in 1992 at the Čelebići camp near Konjic: Zejnil Delalić, Hazim Delić, and Esad Landžo. Ironically, according to officials from the tribunal, the indictments were delayed not by the Bosnian government but by the authorities of the Republika Srpska who have refused to allow investigators for the tribunal to interview witnesses in territory controlled by the Serb army. See "In a First, Tribunal Cites Serb Victims," Associated Press, *Philadelphia Inquirer*, 23 March 1996.

Even when moral distinctions were made among different parties, there were suggestions, without evidence, that had Bosnian Muslims been in a position of power, they would have carried out the same atrocities. See Paul Mojzes, "The Reign of 'Ethnos': Who's to Blame in Yugoslavia," *The Christian Century*, 4 November 1992, 996: "If they [Croatians or Muslims] had been more powerful, they would have been the ones carrying out 'ethnic cleansing.'" No evidence is offered that Bosnian Muslims had any notion of committing genocide or ethnic expulsions that would have left them living in a non-Christian ghetto in Europe. The accusation that a victimized people would have been committing the same crime committed against them is a deeply serious accusation; yet this charge against Bosnian Muslims, easily made, has never been demonstrated or even shown to be plausible. The charge was made into a special boldface display quote in the Mojzes article by the editors of *The Christian Century*. Cf. Paul Mojzes, *Yugoslav Inferno* (New York: Continuum, 1994), 171–72. For another unargued claim that the atrocities by Serb nationalists would have been matched by Bosnians had they had the opportunity, see Dimitri K. Simes, "There's No Oil in Bosnia," *New York Times*, 10 March 1993, opinion page.

48. The term "warring factions," which negates the official recognition of Bosnia and equalizes the recognized Bosnian government with ethnoreligious extremist militias, was immediately adopted by the major news media in the U.S., particularly television commentators.

49. Noel Malcolm, "The Whole Lot of Them Are Serbs," *The Spectator* (London), 10 June 1995.

50. Ibid. Malcolm cites the Norwegian historian of the Balkans Professor Monnesland of Oslo University, who characterizes Stoltenberg's ethnoreligious theory as "monstrous" and "absurd." For the claims by Serbian religious nationalists that "In Bosnia the Muslims are really Serbs" and have betrayed their ancestral religion, see Florence Levinsohn, *Belgrade: Among the Serbs* (Chicago: Ivan Dee, 1994), 151, 162; and Branko Grujić, the Serb religious nationalist mayor of Zvornik who celebrated the expulsion and killing of the town's Muslims (see Chapter 1 above) and who stated: "Serbs believe that other Serbs who change their religion are actually worse than Turks," quoted in *Toronto Star*, 28 April 1993.

51. See Susan Woodward, *Balkan Tragedy: Chaos and Dissolution After the Cold War* (Washington, D.C.: The Brookings Institution, 1995), 243. In Woodward's account, the use of passive voice and intransitive verbs strips the discourse of an agent: thus "methods of population transfers varied"; "Muslim elites were murdered or brutally expelled" from some areas, while elsewhere "local rivalries were encouraged to play out."

52. Peter Brock, "Dateline Yugoslavia: The Partisan Press," *Foreign Policy* (Winter 1993–94), 152–72.

53. See Charles Lane, "Brock Crock," *New Republic* 15 September 1994, 19–21. For the use of Brock by Serb church leaders to deny systematic war crimes of the Serb military, see the letter by the Rev. Rade Merich, a Serb Orthodox priest in Ohio and editor of *Path of Orthodoxy*, "Letter to the Editor," 1 December 1994, *Religion in Eastern Europe* 15.3 (June 1995): 41–44.

See also retired General Charles Boyd, "Making Peace with the Guilty: The Truth about Bosnia," *Foreign Affairs* 74.5 (September–October 1994). When criticized by scholars on Bosnia for moral equalizing, Boyd stated (*Foreign Affairs* 74.6, November–December 1994) that he wasn't trying to deny "Serb crimes" and had called them "reprehensible." The term "reprehensible" is hardly adequate; stealing a hubcap is reprehensible—what better example of the extremes to which moral equalizing leads. Boyd also denies the genocide in Bosnia by citing the number killed in Sarajevo, despite the fact that the International Criminal Tribunal indictments for genocide concern crimes committed in northern and eastern Bosnia, as well as in Sarajevo.

54. "We are doing all we can in Bosnia, consistent with our national interests," said Secretary of State Warren Christopher at a news conference July 21, 1994. See Drew, *On the Edge*, 276. Political scientist Michael Mandelbaum suggested that the post-Dayton NATO mission in Bosnia was a form of "social work" rather than protecting the nation's role as a superpower (CNN News, 1 January 1995).

55. The refrain "What about Somalia?" was also used to criticize calls for stopping genocide in Bosnia. The implication was that those who favored stopping genocide in Bosnia were racists who only cared about European victims. Yet some who had used the "what about Somalia" argument against stopping genocide in Bosnia protested the loudest when U.S. troops were sent to Somalia. The intervention saved an estimated 500,000 people from starvation before the operation became politicized and fell apart. In both Somalia and Bosnia, the Western governments were complicit in the original problem, in Bosnia through the arms embargo that in effect armed Serb radicals, in Somalia through massive weapons sales. Activists against the Bosnia genocide were instrumental in getting the genocide in Rwanda added to the agenda of the International Criminal Tribunal and in protecting the tribunal from efforts to sabotage its deliberations and cut off its funding.

56. Thomas L. Friedman, "Allies," *New York Times*, 7 June 1995, opinion page. Friedman goes on: "The Bosnias will come and go, but good friends whom we can count on for solving problems that really do involve our national interest are hard to find." Friedman's comment is especially unintentionally ironic in view of the duplicity of British General Sir Michael Rose and the British SAS in feeding false information to NATO pilots during the Bihać debacle (see above, n. 41).

57. Živica Tucić quoted in *Los Angeles Times*, 12 August 1995, cited above, chapter 4, n. 45. The statement originally appeared in the official

Serb Church journal *Pravoslavlje* and was presented as a paraphrase of the position of Serb Patriarch Pavle, the highest-ranking Serbian Orthodox leader.

58. Albert Speer, *Erinnerungen* (Inside the Third Reich: Memoirs), trans. R. and C. Winston (New York: Macmillan, 1970).

59. For the child whose hand was blown off, see Kurt Schork, Reuters, August 29, 1995. The young boy's words were spoken during the attack on the suburb of Otes, 5 December 1992. The story of the girl of Srebrenica was related by UN relief worker Larry Hollingsworth. See John Burns, *New York Times*, 20 March 1993, A4. A spokesperson for General Mladić claimed that the Serb army had fired in self-defense at a Bosnian tank and hit the refugees by mistake. Belgrade TV has maintained that there was no 1993 Srebrenica massacre of Muslims; the victims were Serbs tortured to death by Bosnian soldiers, dressed up as Muslims and placed around the site of the alleged shelling, a story the refugee workers who witnessed the massacre called preposterous (for the Belgrade TV story, see *New York Times*, 14 April 1993).

60. For Senator Feinstein's remarks, see the *Congressional Record*, 19 July 1995, S 10276–10278.

CHAPTER SEVEN

1. To this tradition was added the influence of both European sonnets and Middle East love poetry. For centuries, Bosnian poets composed in south Slavic as well as in languages of the Ottoman empire. There was a school of Bosnian Persian poetry and a school of Bosnian literary criticism of the international Persian poetic tradition. See Hamid Algar, "Persian Literature in Bosnia-Herzegovina," *Journal of Islamic Studies* 5.2 (1994): 254–67.

2. Amila Buturovic, "Multivocality in the Lyric of Ottoman Bosnia," unpublished paper.

3. Paul Paulikawski, *Serbian Epics* (BBC, 1992), videocassette.

4. Henry Kissinger, Interview with Mortimer Zuckerman, on *The Charlie Rose Show*, September 14, 1995. Among the others who have

proposed forcing Bosnian Muslims into a religiously homogeneous enclave are John J. Mearsheimer, "Shrink Bosnia to Save It," *New York Times*, 31 March 1993; George Kenney, "Bosnia Deadline," *San Diego Union-Tribune*, 20 February 1994; and Ronald Steel, "A Realistic Entity, Greater Sarajevo," *New York Times*, 26 July 1995. Steel, a professor of international relations at the University of Southern California, begins his opinion-page essay with the statement that the turning over of the safe areas of Žepa and Srebrenica to the Serb army—during which thousands of unarmed Bosnians were raped, brutalized, tortured, killed in groups of hundreds, and put into mass graves—"may be a blessing in disguise." None of these proposals acknowledges the history of non-Christian ghettoes within Europe or proposes a viable defense for such a ghetto.

On 12 December 1995, the Croatian daily *Večernji list* ran a piece by commentator Nenad Ivanković on Kissinger's plan in what is believed by some commentators to be a trial balloon, to test a renewed effort at the partition of Bosnia that President Tudjman has always favored.

5. Ivan Lovrenović, "The Hatred of Memory," *New York Times*, 28 May 1994, A15.

6. These brief remarks cannot do justice to the exhibit. They are meant only to illustrate the intersection of artistic creation and a multireligious culture. The other works exhibited are: Josip Alebić, "Aggression"; Seid Hasanefendić, "Destruction"; Dževad Hozo, "12"; Radmila Jovandić, "Les Gens"; Mladen Kolobarić, "Wave of the Devil"; Mirsad Konstantinović, "The Message"; Esad Muftić, "Trace of the Crime"; Aida Mušanović, "Year of All Dangers"; Salim Obralić, "Eclipse of the Spirit"; Mihailo Prica, "Papa, I Don't Want to Be a Refugee"; Petar Waldegg, "Homage to the People of Sarajevo, 1992"; Mehmed Zaimović, "Pain"; and Avdo Žiga, "The Black Sun." See *Expo/Sarajevo 92* (Catalogue for the Exhibit of 2–16 March 1994) (Brussels: Musée Charlier/Charliermuseum, 1994).

7. There are many such stories. Cf. Marian Wenzel, "Obituary: Dr. Rizo Sijarić, Director of the Zemaljski Muzej, Sarajevo. Killed in Sarajevo, 10 December, 1993," *Museum Management and Curatorship* 13

(1994): 79–80. For refutations of the notion that Bosnia is artificial as a culture or a nation, see Noel Malcolm, *Bosnia: A Short History* (New York: New York University Press, 1994) and Robert Donia and John Fine, *Bosnia and Herzegovina: A Tradition Betrayed* (New York: Columbia University Press, 1994).

8. Laurie Kain Hart, Response, 1995 Annual Gest Symposium on the Cross-Cultural Study of Religions, "Art, Religion, and Cultural Survival," Haverford College, October 29, 1995.

RECOMMENDED READINGS

The events in Bosnia from 1992 to 1995 have generated a vast literature. The list below is meant to help orient the nonspecialist reader to different aspects of the story. For details on human rights and war crimes sources, see the Note on Sources, above. Sources on specialist issues are listed in the endnotes with full bibliographic information and also can be found in the bibliographies of the works listed below.

For the nonspecialist reader wishing to pursue aspects of the story told here, I would point out the following as particularly useful: Malcolm's *Bosnia: A Short History* for a very readable historical and geographical introduction and a rigorous refutation of standard stereotypes; Gutman's *Witness to Genocide* and Vulliamy's *Seasons in Hell* for works that recorded history in the making and, through the impact of the original articles and stories from which these works were composed, helped change the course of history; Emmert's *Serbian Golgotha* for the Serbian tradition of Kosovo; Filipović's *Art Treasures* and Riedlmayer's *Killing Memory* for the beauty and variety of Bosnia's cultural heritage; Buturovic's articles for Bosnian literature; *Yugoslavia: Death of a Nation* for the intrigue and power plays behind the destruction of Yugoslavia; Ali and Lifschultz's *Why Bosnia?* for selections from Bosnian writers and scholars; Cigar's *Genocide in Bosnia* for the role of Serbian clergy and intellectuals in motivating the violence; Almond's *Europe's Backyard War* and Rubenstein's "Silent Partners" for the complicity of the NATO powers; West's *Tito* for Yugoslavia during and after World War II; Fine's *The Bos-*

nian Church for pre-Ottoman religion in Bosnia and the controversy over the Bogomils; and finally, the journals *Vreme News Digest* and *Balkan War Report* for the most comprehensive ongoing coverage of the events in Bosnia-Herzegovina.

BOOKS, FILMS, ARTICLES, AND SPECIAL ISSUES OF JOURNALS

Ali, Rabia, and Lawrence Lifschulz, eds. *Why Bosnia? Writings on the Bosnian War.* Stony Creek, Conn.: Pamphleteer's Press, 1993.

Allen, Beverly. *Rape Warfare: The Hidden Genocide in Bosnia-Herzegovina and Croatia.* Minneapolis: University of Minnesota Press, 1996.

Almond, Mark. *Europe's Backyard War: The War in the Balkans.* London: Mandarin, 1994.

Andrić, Ivo. *The Bridge on the Drina.* New York: Macmillan, 1959.

———. *The Development of Spiritual Life in Bosnia under the Influence of Turkish Rule.* Trans. Z. Juricic and J. Loud. Durham: Duke University Press, 1990.

Anonymous. "Kosova, the Quiet Siege." *Cultural Survival* 19, no. 2 (1995): 35–42.

Banac, Ivo. *The National Question in Yugoslavia: Origins, History, Politics.* Ithaca, N.Y.: Cornell University Press, 1984.

Bennett, Christopher. *Yugoslavia's Bloody Collapse: Causes, Course and Consequences.* New York: New York University Press, 1995.

Buturovic, Amila. "Producing and Annihilating the Ethnos of Bosnian Islam." *Cultural Survival* 19, no. 2 (1995): 29–33.

———. "National Quest of the Anguish of Salvation: Bosnian Muslim Identity in Meša Selimović's *Dervish and Death*." *Edebiyat* 7, n. 1 (1996).

———, trans. "Neither a Church Nor a Mosque," by Ćamil Sijarić. *Edebiyat* 7, n. 1 (1996).

Christopher, Metropolitan. "The Historical Background of the Contemporary Situation of the Orthodox Church in Yugoslavia." Belleville, Mich.: Firebird Video, 1992. Videocassette.

Cigar, Norman. *Genocide in Bosnia: The Policy of "Ethnic Cleansing" in Eastern Europe*. College Station: Texas A & M University Press, 1995.

Cohen, Ben, and George Stamkoski, eds. *With No Peace to Keep: United Nations Peacekeeping and the War in the Former Yugoslavia*. London: Grainpress, 1995.

Djilas, Milovan. *Njegoš: Poet, Prince, Bishop*. New York: Harcourt Brace Jovanovich, 1966.

———. *Wartime*. New York: Harcourt Brace Jovanovich, 1977.

Donia, Robert J. *Islam under the Double Eagle: The Muslims of Bosnia and Hercegovina, 1878–1914*. Boulder: East European Quarterly, 1981; distributed by Columbia University Press.

Donia, Robert J., and John Fine, *Bosnia and Hercegovina: A Tradition Betrayed*. New York: Columbia University Press, 1994.

Dorich, William, comp. and Basil W. R. Jenkins and Anita Dorich, eds. *Kosovo*. Alhambra, Calif.: Kosovo Charity Fund, 1992.

Emmert, Thomas A. *Serbian Golgotha: Kosovo, 1389*. New York: East European Monographs, 1990.

Expo/Sarajevo 92. Catalogue for the Exhibit of 2–16 March 1994. Brussels: Museé Charlier/Charliermuseum, 1994.

Filipović, Gordana. *Kosovo: Past and Present*. Belgrade: Review of International Affairs, 1989.

Filipović, Mirza, ed. *The Art in Bosnia-Herzegovina (The Art Treasures of Bosnia and Herzegovina)*. Sarajevo: Svjetlost, 1987.

———. *Yugoslavia*. Sarajevo: Svjetlost, 1990.

Fine, John. *The Bosnian Church: A New Interpretation*. Boulder: East European Quarterly, 1975; distributed by Columbia University Press.

Garde, Paul. *Vie et mort de la Yougoslavie*. Paris: Librairie Artheme Fayard, 1992.

Greenawalt, Alexander K. A. "The Nationalization of Memory: Identity and Ideology in Nineteenth Century Serbia" (Bachelor's thesis, Princeton University, 1994).

Gutman, Roy. *Witness to Genocide*. New York: Macmillan, 1993.

Izetbegović, Alija Ali. *Islam Between East and West*. Indianapolis: American Trust Publications, 1984, 1989.

Langmuir, Gavin. *History, Religion, and Antisemitism*. Berkeley: University of California Press, 1990.

Levy, Bernard-Henry, and Gilles Hertzog. "Bosna!" Bosnia-Herzegovina/France: Zeitgeist Films, 1994.

Maass, Peter. *Love Thy Neighbor: A Story of War*. New York: Knopf, 1996.

Magaš, Branka. *The Destruction of Yugoslavia: Tracking the Break-up 1980–92*. London: Verso, 1993.

Malcolm, Noel. *Bosnia: A Short History*. New York: New York University Press, 1994.

Matthias, John, and Vladeta Vuckovic, trans. *The Battle of Kosovo*. Athens, Ohio: Swallow Press, 1987.

Njegoš, Petar II Petrović. *The Mountain Wreath (Gorski vijenac)*. Trans. and ed., Vasa D. Mihailovich. Irvine, Calif.: Charles Schlacks, Jr., 1986.

Norris, H. T. *Islam in the Balkans: Religion and Society between Europe and the Arab World*. Columbia: University of South Carolina Press, 1993.

Owen, David. *Balkan Odyssey*. New York: Harcourt Brace Jovanovich, 1995.

Pašić, Amir. *Islamic Architecture in Bosnia and Hercegovina*. Istanbul: Research Centre for Islamic History, Art, and Culture, 1994.

Paulikawski, Paul. *Serbian Epics*. BBC, 1984.

Pinson, Mark, ed. *The Muslims of Bosnia-Herzegovina: Their Historic Development from the Middle Ages to the Dissolution of Yugoslavia*. Cambridge: Harvard University Center for Middle East Studies, 1993.

Ramet, Sabrina Petra. *Balkan Babel: Politics, Culture, and Religion in Yugoslavia*. Boulder and Oxford: Westview Press, 1992.

Riedlmayer, András. *Killing Memory: Bosnia's Cultural Heritage and Its Destruction*. Haverford: Community of Bosnia Foundation, 1994. Videocassette.

Rubenstein, Richard. "Silent Partners in Ethnic Cleansing: The UN, the EC, and NATO." *In Depth: A Journal for Value* 3, no. 2 (1994), 35–57.

Silber, Laura, and Allan Little, eds. *Yugoslavia: Death of a Nation*. New York: TV Books, 1995.

Sullivan, Andrew, ed. *Accomplices to Genocide* (Entire August 7, 1995 issue of *The New Republic*). Washington, D.C.: The New Republic, 1995.

Udovicki, Jasminka, and James Ridgeway. *Yugoslavia's Ethnic Nightmare: The Inside Story of Europe's Unfolding Ordeal.* New York: Lawrence Hill Books, 1995.

Williams, Ian, ed. *The Yugoslav Wars,* special issue of the *The New Combat,* Autumn 1994.

Vucinich, Wayne S., and Thomas A. Emmert, eds. *Kosovo: Legacy of a Medieval Battle.* Minneapolis: University of Minnesota Press, 1991.

Vukadinović, Alek, ed. *Kosovo 1389–1989: Special Edition of the Serbian Literary Quarterly on the Occasion of 600 Years since the Battle of Kosovo.* Belgrade: Serbian Literary Quarterly, 1989.

Vulliamy, Edward. *Seasons in Hell.* New York: St. Martin's Press, 1994.

Warchitecture. Sarajevo: OKO, 1994.

West, Richard. *Tito and the Rise and Fall of Yugoslavia.* New York: Carroll and Graf, 1995.

Yugoslavia: Death of a Nation, four-part video. BBC/Discovery, 1995.

PERIODICALS

American Srbobran. Serbian-American publication, includes issues of *Pravoslavlje (The Path of Orthodoxy),* an official publication of the Serbian Orthodox Church in the United States.

Balkan War Report: Bulletin of the Institute for War and Peace Reporting.

Vreme News Digest. English language version. Published by Serbian writers committed to a democratic, civil society.

Zajedničar. Official organ of the Croatian Fraternal Union of America.

ELECTRONIC SOURCES

Internet Bulletin Board Newsgroups:

alt.current-events.bosnia

soc.culture.bosna-herzgvna

soc.culture.croatia

soc.culture.yugoslavia

Subscription Newsgroups:

SII (Serbian Information Initiative), Bosnet, Cronet (Subscription information is posted periodically on the Internet newsgroups).

World Wide Web:

See the sites listed in Note on Sources; new sites are being added and are usually announced in the bulletin board newsgroups or the subscription newsgroups.

INDEX

Abdić, Fikret, 101, 111, 138, 139
Academics, propagandizing of Serbian, 121–22
Adie, Kate, 3
Adrianople, Treaty of, 38
Adžamijski (lang.), 2, 147
"Aggression" (engraving), 214n.6
Ahmići, Bos., 110
Akashi, Yasushi, 135, 207n.41
Albania, 6, 54–60. *See also* Kosovo
Albanians, 6, 14, 54, 179–80n.2; of Kosovo, 54–60, 63, 69 (*see also* Kosovo, Serbo-Albanian conflict in); Serbs vs. (*see* Kosovo, Serbo-Albanian conflict in); in Yugoslavia, 6
Alcohol, Bosnian Muslims and, 123. *See also* Drunkenness
Alebić, Josip, 214n.6
Allah, 173n.37
Alphabets, Bosnian, 147
Amnesty International, 17, 57
Anatolia, 33
Anderson, Benedict, 176n.12
Andjelković, Petar, 105
Andrić, Ivo, 45–51, 59, 106, 178n.22; as nationalist hero, 179n.31
Anglican Church, 130
Anti-Semitism, 91, 94–95. *See also* Jews: persecution of

Apartheid, 150–52
Arab-Israeli war, first, 136
Arabs, Middle Eastern. *See* Palestinians
Arkan (Serb militia leader), 73, 75, 78, 82, 167n.11, 171n.28, 185n.5, 195n.18; marriage of, 82
Artists, Bosnian: engravings of, 152–53, 214n.6; persecution of, 20
Asia, as Serbo-Croatian homeland, 168–69n.16
Association of Serbian Writers, 65
Atanasije (Orthodox bishop), 80, 83, 84, 189n.35
Atheism, in Bosnia, 14, 121
Atrocities: apologists for Serb, 135, 211–12n.53; in Bosnia, xiii-xiv, 10, 11, 66, 73–77, 79–86, 96, 102, 105, 110, 111, 115, 117, 131, 134, 136, 138, 139, 142, 151, 157–59, 171n.27, 185n.4, 188n.24, 189n.35, 190n.38, 199n.40, 211n.51, 213n.59, 214n.4; Chetnik, 6; denial of, 160; Kosovo Albanians accused of, 56; Nazi, 62 (*see also* Holocaust); "sport," 19; State Department reports on, 166–67n.6, 169–70n.22, 173n.38; Western world indifference to Bosnian,

223

Nasser, Jamal Abdul, 120

National Library (Sarajevo), destruction of, 1–4, 69, 137, 146, 149, 153

National Museum (Sarajevo), destruction of, 2–3, 149, 165n.2

Native Americans, marginalization of, 91, 151

NATO (North Atlantic Treaty Organization): anti-Serb air strikes by, 182n.18; and Bosnian crisis, 11, 91, 116, 126, 128, 129, 131, 134, 136–40, 151, 182n.18, 199n.3, 201n.9, 203n.18, 204–205n.24, 206n.31, 208n.42, 212nn.54, 56; British Special Forces (SAS) betrayal of, 208n.42, 212n.56; genocide condemned by, 24, 25; and Srebrenica, 26, 27; thrust of, 139

Nazism, 121; as Medjugorje souvenir theme, 107; Waldheim service for, 190–91n.42. *See also* Holocaust; Speer, Albert; SS (Schutzstaffel)

Nemanja, Stefan, 48

Neretva River, 93, 114

Netherlands, UN troops from, 27, 207–208n.41

Neuwirth, Edwin, 188n.32

New York, N.Y.: Islamic violence in, 140

New Zealand, Serb Orthodox Church in, 58

Nikolaj (Serb Orthodox prelate), 81, 83, 84, 189n.37

Nikolić, Dragan, 21, 23, 174n.42

Njegoš (pseud. Petar II Petrović), 41, 44–46, 48, 51–52, 59, 65, 79, 106, 179n.31; Andrić on,

45–46. See also *Mountain Wreath, The*

North America: as Christian, 201; Yugoslav refugees in, 154–55. *See also* Canada; Native Americans; United States

Novi Travnik, Bos., 96, 110

Nuclear power, in Middle East, 136

Obilić, Miloš, 39–40, 44, 68, 79, 89–90, 187n.20

Obralić, Salim, 214n.6

Obrenović, Miloš, 38, 48

O'Brien, Conor Cruise, 202–203n.17

Oklahoma City, Okla.: bombing in, 71, 123–24, 140, 185n.1

Olympics, Winter: in Sarajevo, 7, 148

Omarska (camp), 11–13, 15, 19, 105, 168n.13, 170n.24, 173n.42, 196n.26; on television, 137; Western reactions to, 125, 129, 204n.22

Operation Desert Storm, 129

Oriental Institute (Sarajevo), destruction of, 2, 137, 146, 149

Orientalism, 118–24, 200n.7

Orientalism (Said), 200n.7

Orthodox Church: in Bosnia, 33, 146, 178n.25; vs. Bosnian Church, 33; Croats vs., 3; and Great Schism, 32; in Serbia (*see* Serbian Orthodox Church); Vlach congregants of, 179n.29. *See also* Greek Orthodox Church; Serbian Orthodox Church

Orthodox Peace Fellowship, 191n.44

Orthodox priests: atrocities ap-

Stadiums, as atrocity centers, 21–22, 170n.26, 174n.44
Stambolić, Ivan, 72
Stanišić, Mićo, 173n.42
Starvation, as Serb military weapon, 75
State, U.S. Department of: and Vance-Owen plan, 194n.15; war-crime reports of, 166–67n.6, 169–70n.22, 173n.38
Stećaks (monuments), 32, 97
Steel, Ronald, 214n.4
"Stefan, Abbot" (*The Mountain Wreath*), 43
Stefanović, Adam, 176n.13
Stepinac (Croat bishop), 60–61, 99, 182n.20, 193n.12
Stolac, Herz., 94, 97–98, 103, 110
Stoltenberg, Thorwald, 100, 134, 194n.15, 211n.50. *See also* Vance-Owen plan: Owen-Stoltenberg revision of
Students, rebellious Albanian, 55
Stupni Do, Bos., 199n.40
Sudan, 197, 201n.9
Suicide, over captivity, 144
Suleiman the Magnificent, 35, 49, 53–54
Šušak, Gojko, 103, 108, 111, 118, 119, 197–98n.39
Sušica (camp), 19, 21, 78
Synagogues, 148, 149

Tadić, Radoslav, 152
Talbot, Strobe, 128
Tanasković, Darko, 121–22
Tanjug (news service), 120, 200n.8
Ta'ziyya (commemorations), 175n.3
Teachers, Serb army focus on Bosnian, 20

Television: Belgrade, 213n.59; Bosnia on U.S., 210n.48; Milošević on Serbian, 67–68; Serb atrocities on, 137, 184n.29
Temperance, as Muslim "short-coming," 103
Thomas (Bib.), 145
Tickell, Crispin, 128
Tiger Militia, 75
Tito, Josip Broz, 5–7, 51, 54, 58, 63, 68, 87, 99; repression under, 69; and Stepinac trial, 182n.20. *See also* Partisans
Topalović, Mušan ("Caco"), 199n.2, 209n.47
Torture, 19, 77, 89, 158, 185n.4, 214n.4; in concentration camps, 74, 105–6; as genocide element, 24; as technique of Serb mili-tants, 13, 16, 171n.27; Serb re-cruits forced to participate in, 75
Tourism, 93, 113
"Trace of the Crime" (engraving), 214n.6
Travnik, Bos., 35, 101, 195n.17
Trebević, Mount, 147
Trebinje, Herz., 80, 83, 94, 189n.35
Trnopolje (camp), 11, 19, 20, 137; as rape center, 172n.32
T-shirts, "Serbian Pride," 191n.48
Tucić, Živica, 212n.57
Tudjman, Franjo, 7–8, 61, 94–97, 99, 103, 106, 108, 110–13, 195n.19, 214n.4; and Milošević, 95, 100, 122, 138, 194n.15
Tudjman, Miroslav, 198n.39
Turajlić, Hakija, 133, 209n.44
Turkey, 124. *See also* Ottoman Empire